Representing Latina/x Reproductive Decision-Making

Representing Latina/x Reproductive Decision-Making

Melissa Huerta

LEXINGTON BOOKS
Lanham • Boulder • New York • London

Published by Lexington Books
An imprint of The Rowman & Littlefield Publishing Group, Inc.
4501 Forbes Boulevard, Suite 200, Lanham, Maryland 20706
www.rowman.com

86-90 Paul Street, London EC2A 4NE

British Library Cataloguing in Publication Information Available

Library of Congress Cataloging-in-Publication Data

Names: Huerta, Melissa, author.
Title: Representing Latina/x reproductive decision making / Melissa Huerta.
Description: Lanham : Lexington Books, [2022] | Includes bibliographical references and index.
Identifiers: LCCN 2022024582 (print) | LCCN 2022024583 (ebook) | ISBN 9781793626974 (cloth) | ISBN 9781793626998 (paper) | ISBN 9781793626981 (ebook)
Subjects: LCSH: Hispanic Americans in popular culture. | Family planning in popular culture. | Family planning—United States. | Reproductive rights—United States.
Classification: LCC E184.S75 H84 2022 (print) | LCC E184.S75 (ebook) | DDC 973.0468—dc23/eng/20221003
LC record available at https://lccn.loc.gov/2022024582
LC ebook record available at https://lccn.loc.gov/2022024583

Para todas las mujeres de la familia Huerta Mancinas. Este libro es para ustedes.

Contents

Acknowledgments

I began to write parts of this book several years ago not knowing it would become a book. Meanwhile it became apparent I needed to write about representations of reproductive decisions at a time when attacks on access to legal and safe abortions are moving swiftly through state legislatures. Finishing this project became more important as I started to navigate my own reproductive decisions as a Latina in my late thirties, along with COVID, and the turbulent political climate that enveloped our world. Of course, I am indebted and deeply grateful to my family, friends, and colleagues.

At Lexington Books (imprint of Rowman & Littlefield), I cannot thank Judith Lakamper enough for believing in the project and helping me make it a reality. Thank you for the anonymous reviewer for your careful reading, selection of insightful comments and feedback that helped strengthen the manuscript.

A semester sabbatical allowed me to finish the manuscript. I am thankful for having the opportunity to spend several months immersed in my project. The material in this project has been presented at conferences and talks. Some of it was submitted for publication and rejected (with valuable feedback), and portions of Chapter 2 appeared in *Representing Abortion* (Rachel Alpha Johnston Hurst, ed. 2020). I have presented excerpts of this project at American Society of Theatre Research (ASTR), Northeast Modern Languages Association conference (NeMLA), Modern Languages Research Presentation (Denison), George Washington University Women's, Gender, and Sexuality Studies Program (virtual), and Monomoy Research Presentation (Denison).

I know this book could not have been produced without dialogues with colleagues and friends in the field and beyond. At Denison, my colleagues have been gracious with their time and provided space for long conversations about my work since my arrival. My circle of friends from here and there have provided generous support and our friendships endure despite time and space. I could not have done it without Bibiana Fuentes, Jennifer Rudolph,

María Isabel Ochoa, and Martín Ponti. Thank you for providing me with constant support, feedback, and conversations (including post-performances!).

Many moons ago I attended a Teatro Luna performance and that planted the seed for what would become part of this book. Thank you to Teatro Luna, all of the generations of teatristas, for your work, continued support, and for allowing me to participate in this journey with you. Warmest thanks to Alex Meda and Liza Ann Acosta, and Teatro Luna West for your continued support. A special mention for my teaching and research assistant, Maria Mayer who shared her thoughts and helped in gathering information about *Jane the Virgin* during her last year at Denison. I am also thankful to Denison students who have shared their thoughts and ideas about telenovelas, theatre, and performance.

And finally, but not least, my family in Milwaukee, Wisconsin, Chicago, Illinois, and in Durango, México, mil gracias! Living away from my family has been difficult, but even with the distance, I am grateful for their continued support, love, and inspiration. Mom, you're my super mujer, and I will be forever grateful for your love and support, always being there for me, coming to conferences, plays, and for being understanding of my never-ending work. Thank you Aaron for your constant support, love, and patience, always inspiring me to keep going. ¡Los quiero, familia!

Introduction

The nomination of conservative Judge Amy Coney Barrett to the United States Supreme Court in the fall of 2020, following the untimely death of Justice Ruth Bader Ginsburg, set in motion fervent conversations, debates, and protests surrounding the fate of *Roe v. Wade*. More importantly, a slew of states mobilized legislation to restrict reproductive rights now that Justice Barrett sits on a mostly conservative court. In early 2021, Ohio's Republican governor, Mike DeWine, signed into law a bill requiring the burial or cremation of fetal remains. This bill would require a woman who has an abortion to designate on a form how she would dispose of the remains.[1] What this recent law highlights is the skewed perceptions of what it means for women to have bodily autonomy over their reproductive decision-making.[2] Public, political, legal, or religious perceptions and discourses are distinct from the way women experience reproductive decisions. Most recently, the Texas legislature passed SB 8, one of the most restrictive abortion laws in the books, banning abortion after the sixth week of pregnancy even in cases of rape or incest.[3] As such, these new laws and potential legislation begin to chip away at *Roe v. Wade*. Although the focus of this project is not to debate current political or legal opinions regarding reproductive rights, *Representing Latina/x Reproductive Decision-Making* examines representations of Latina/x reproductive decisions in cultural texts as crucial to the study of Latina/x popular culture.

A question I have asked myself throughout this project when thinking not only of the cultural texts, but also my own relationship to my reproductive decisions is: What impact do cultural texts have on everyday Latina/x women and their reproductive decision-making? While this is a difficult question to measure, other questions interrogate the importance of Latina/x popular culture and are key to this book: How can popular culture contribute to the de-stigmatization of reproductive decisions like abortion? How can popular culture correct misinformation and misunderstanding about Latina/x stories surrounding reproductive decisions? What do these representations in theater and in the small screen mean for Latina/x popular culture? The texts I discuss examine the representation of Latina reproductive decision-making in

Latina theater, television, film, and visual art.[4] This project documents how Latinas in theater, on the small screen, and through visual art build narratives and worlds that reaffirm or defy what Latina reproductive decision-making looks or sounds like. These cultural products present varying perspectives of reproductive decision-making such as desiring motherhood or choosing abortion. For this project, reproductive decision making involves any decision about a woman's sexuality, fertility, or reproductive system (Redshaw & Martin, 2011). The nature of reproductive decision-making instances in these cultural texts brings with it related social and biological constraints such as class, gender, and sex.

What is important for this project is the transgressive quality of these representations since all of these mediums require an active audience. Latinx Media and cultural studies scholars such as Angharad Valdivia, Isabel Molina-Guzmán, Jillian Báez, Frederick Aldama, among others, have consistently argued and shown that Latinx consumers are not passive viewers, but they also "talk back" and resist what mainstream (read=white) media outlets deem representative of *latinidad.* In television, theater and film, the characters or artistic rendition of reproductive decision making ultimately emphasizes the woman's agency in acting upon their reproductive decisions. As these case studies will show, the work done by and about Latina/x reproductive decision-making demonstrates how race, class, gender, and sexuality in popular culture provide viewers and readers ways to confront certain topics, such as pregnancy and abortion.

A NOTE ON TERMINOLOGY

In order to critically understand the complexity of Latina/x representation one must begin with the question of what or who represents Latina/x? The term has been historically, socially, and politically constructed, internalized and challenged at the same time. The term Hispanic, as coined by the Richard Nixon administration for census purposes, later led to the creation of "Hispanic Market," can be "understood as an 'imagined community' in which social and political alliances are formed based on 'lived experience and historical memory'" (Báez, 2007, 110). The term was coined to also encompass a large swath of the population in the US that identified with speaking Spanish for demographic purposes, also originating from Latin America and including people from Europe. The term Latino/a began to take precedence over Hispanic in the 1990s, in higher education and in the music industry, with the popularity of Latino artists such as Ricky Martín and Jennifer López. Latino/a represents people of Latin American origin or descent within the United States. Within the US cultural context, *Latinidad* emerges as a way to collectively define Latinos/as within the United States.[5] Scholars agree that this latter umbrella term can also be divisive and suspect for its homogenizing potential (Aparicio 114). Aparicio (2017) also pushes scholars to reclaim the term and "deploy it in ways that allow our communities and others to exert agency and more control over the public definitions of who we are" (113). For scholars and community organizations alike, the terms Latino/a and Latinidad can signify empowerment and agency. The term Latinx fits Aparicio's call to reclaim the term Latino/a. This a more recent term, espousing the "x" instead of the oft-used "a/o" to signify inclusivity, the term becomes more fluid and mobile.

These terms, especially Latina/o/x can serve as a visual reminder that these categories tend to make all Latinos uniform, but for the purpose of this project, I prefer to use the term "Latina" or "Latina/x." It seems fitting to use the term "Latina" for the work of Teatro Luna and in *Jane the Virgin* because both move away from familiar representations of Mexican and Mexican American experiences. For Teatro Luna, their impetus is demonstrating the varied and diverse Latina experiences on stage, while the producers of *Jane the Virgin* opted to present a narrative about a Venezuelan American family, exposing audiences to a nationally specific culture not typically presented on American television. Thus, by relying on the term Latina, I will identify whenever possible national-origin specificity to add complexity to the analysis. Furthermore, since I am also addressing ways in which non-heteronormative couples or individuals choose to pursue reproductive decision-making, I want to emphasize the use of Latinx to remain fluid and nonbinary whenever possible, unless the characters or writers are specific about their national origin or the label they use. Certainly, reproductive decision-making is not exclusive to people born as females. However, the texts analyzed here focus specifically on people who identify as women or are presented as cis-gendered people.

The selected works of Teatro Luna, Favianna Rodriguez, several seasons and episodes of *Jane the Virgin* (2014–2019), season three of *Vida* (2018–2020), and the independent film, *Quinceañera* (Dir. Richard Glatzer and Wash Westmoreland, 2006) enable us to also examine how feminism and women of color theories are made evident in Latina and womanhood representation. This project has particular resonance with women of color feminism, in particular. Certainly, all women across different categories of difference and historical epochs have a conflicted history with reproductive rights as well as violent connections to ideas about female empowerment and bodily autonomy. However, in the context of women of color experiences and feminism, such as Gloria Anzaldúa, Cherríe Moraga, and Audre Lorde's writings about their experiences as women of color in the US Women of color theorists and artists have long called for their experiences to be included and represented across mediums, especially theater, television, film, and visual arts. Many of these women's voices, including Moraga and Ana Castillo, for example, used their lived experiences through an autobiographical voice, placing front and center women's experiences allowing for what Tiffany Ana López (2009) calls the "personal as a springboard for critical engagement" ("Reading Violence" 205). Women of color, especially Latinas, write their characters because they recognize that heteropatriarchal constructs rely on certain bodies remaining invisible and silent.

I have found Anzaldúa and Moraga's discussion about lived experiences constructive as it relates to reproductive decision making. But what interests me most is looking at the work of these women of color theorists as literary and cultural foremothers, for future women of color artists, including future Teatro Luna members and artists like Favianna Rodriguez. Furthermore, as a reflection of the theorists themselves, the work of Teatro Luna, Rodriguez, and the protagonists in *Jane the Virgin*, *Vida*, and *Quinceañera* share a bond with past women of color theorists and activists. Building on theories in the flesh, as coined by Anzaldúa and Moraga, this project seeks to explore Latina reproductive decision-making linking generations of women before and after them that write, stage, and perform intimate stories in cultural texts and mediums. These 21st century artists and television programs insert reproductive decisions into a cultural studies arena most often skewed by misrepresentation of Latinas in media and mainstream culture.

Teatro Luna's early work in *Dejame contarte*, (2001), *S-e-x-oh!* (2006) and *Solo tú* (2008) gives voice to Latina stories that echo varying degrees of Latina/x reproductive decision-making.[6] These theatrical vignettes offer perspectives ranging from a lesbian woman yearning to have a child to one that decides to terminate her pregnancy. In addition, *Jane the Virgin* (2014–2019) offers viewers another look at the ways in which Latina womanhood and mother figures such as the Virgin Mary or the whore influence views on motherhood and maternity.[7] In the Starz show, *Vida* (2018–2020) and the 2006 movie, *Quinceañera* (dir. Richard Glatzer and Wash Westmoreland) challenge representations of Latinx reproductive decision-making on the small screen. These two cultural texts build on and contrast with the varying degrees of reproductive decision-making in *Jane the Virgin* and Teatro Luna's work, all exploring boundaries and challenging historical, political, and social limitations of Latinidad. As I demonstrate in my analysis of the television series as a hybrid form (telenovela and serial narrative), the young Latina protagonist's views on maternity and motherhood stem from her strong relationships to her mother-grandmother; however, certain decisions and conversations between the Villanueva women rebuke patriarchal notions of these expectations.[8] Social justice Latinx artist Favianna Rodriguez is committed to representing and giving voice to women of color and fighting for reproductive justice. The powerful images in Rodriguez's posters, accompanied by her powerful words rewrite and reimagine women of color exploring the liberating possibilities of reproductive decision-making. Rodriguez's posters serve to raise awareness about agency and empowerment, specifically giving voice to carrying the burden of abortion as shameful.

The aim of *Representing Latina/x Reproductive Decision-Making* is to investigate Latina representations of reproductive decisions in contemporary Latina/x cultural productions. A central premise of these case studies is to encourage readings of these representations as crucial to the study of contemporary Latina/x popular culture. All the cases analyzed, save *Quinceañera,* offer what Jeannie Ludlow (2020) calls "abortion positive" representations. These representations "support abortion decisions and access without conforming to the narrow, politicized expectations of prochoice discourse" (49). I employ reproductive decision positive narratives following Ludlow's definition to analyze these diverse Latina/x case studies highlighting the significance of the role(s) of reproductive decision making in the lives of women of color and demonstrating how those decisions reinforce or upend socio-cultural understandings and relationships that go beyond religion or culture but emerge from the Latina/x bodies making meaning and complicating notions of womanhood in the 21st century. Furthermore, these reproductive decisions, especially those abortion positive representations, seek to inspire viewers to think differently about reproductive decision-making and to reshape one's vocabulary about these Latinx stories.

Mainstream feminists of the 1970s did not always include the experiences of women of color in their writings and activist organizations. Women of color writers and artists, such as bell hooks, Gloria Anzaldúa, and Patricia Hill Collins, were doubly excluded, since their needs were understated or ignored by both mainstream feminism and civil rights movements of their time, like the Black Panther Party and Chicano Movement. In *Feminist Theory: From Margin to Center* (2000), bell hooks argues for a feminist theory that includes the perspectives of the "lives of women and men who live on the margin" providing a nuanced understanding of the human experience; suggesting that such theory "will emerge from individuals who have knowledge of both margin and center" (xvii). Gloria Anzaldúa and Cherríe Moraga in *This Bridge Called My Back* (2002) bring together a variety of women of color theorists and artists to explore a counter-genealogy demonstrating the difference between Third World and Anglo-American women. In *This Bridge* (2002), the writers and artists deconstruct the space of dominant white women by constructing a productive site for rewriting a women of color feminism that considers their cultural backgrounds and experiences. Women of color creative texts challenge white and heteropatriarchal constructions of the body, specifically through storytelling and the characters they highlight.[9]

To discuss reproductive decision making such as pregnancy and abortion in 21st century women of color creative texts like theater, the visual arts, television, and film, is important because these concepts remain locked within a reductive definition of attitudes that are either pro-life or pro-choice in the public arena. Staging and representing the realities of 21st century Latina's experiences around reproductive decisions continues the transformative and transgressive lineage of women of color artists and theorists. In *Representations of Latina/x Reproductive Decision-Making*, I argue that Teatro Luna *teatristas*[10] and artist-activist Favianna Rodriguez are actively engaged in representing Latina reproductive decision making, contesting the static stereotypes of the (hyper) fertile virgin or sultry Latina. At the same time, *Jane the Virgin* and *Quinceañera*'s female protagonists reaffirm and contest the same stereotypes that permeate in the 21st century. Furthermore, these Latina artists and Latina representations signal to readers and viewers that multifaceted representations matter and that they can be a source of power and agency. While these dramatic and visual texts present multifaceted representations of Latinas that are beyond the stereotypes of virgin/mother/whore, these case studies actively foreground a resistance to limited Latina representations based on preconceived notions of Latinidad. Furthermore it is important to also acknowledge that these narratives also represent people who choose the path to parenthood, in the case of *Jane the Virgin* and *Quinceañera*, for example, and are agents of their decisions as they navigate that path. By presenting and framing Latina/x lives around reproductive decisions, including maternity, these works demonstrate an empowered revisioning of notions of Latina identity beyond and including parenthood. Rewriting and reclaiming Latina/x reproductive decision-making signals a departure from viewing reproductive decisions based external and dominant notions of Latina/x identity and envisions a distinctive and empowered voice.

In *Radical Reproductive Justice* (2017), the editors define reproductive justice as "a theoretical paradigm and model for activist organizing centering on three interconnected human rights: the right not to have children using safe birth control, abortion, or abstinence; the right to have children under the conditions we choose; and the right to parent the children we have in safe and healthy environments" (14). By aligning the work of women of color theorists and artists like Teatro Luna, Favianna Rodriguez, the protagonists in *Jane the Virgin, Vida,* and *Quinceañera,* I am drawn to conclude that these cultural texts are centered on reproductive justice. I invite a closer examination of the material, be it a dramatic text, an audio-visual text or a visual representation concerning pregnancy and parenthood, especially with an eye toward underrepresented women's voices and experiences. *Representing Latina/x Reproductive Decision-Making* examines Latina/x cultural productions that represent Latina reproductive decisions in content, including narrative choices and characters, and artistic approaches to interrogate how these creative elements redefine what reproductive decisions looks, and sound like for Latina characters and Latina artists. For example, how do artists represent infertility or decisions to remain child-free? How do Latinas understand and express their sexuality, gender identity, and the body in terms of reproductive decisions? Indeed, more traditional representations of Latina womanhood may posit restrictive and sexist notions of reproductive decisions, like *telenovelas*.[11] Given the predominance of Christian (mainly Catholic) values and norms in both the US and in Latin America, more traditional cultural contexts present a pro-life rhetoric, emphasizing the sanctity of the unborn life, shaping what it means to become a mother or have offspring.[12] Furthermore framing reproductive decision-making narratives as always pro-life or antichoice fails to provide viewers and consumers with any meaningful information about the structural causes affecting full access to reproductive healthcare for women of color.

Writers like Gloria Anzaldúa and Cherríe Moraga consciously critiqued the mainstream feminist movement and the Chicano Movement for excluding women of color. In *This Bridge*, Moraga asserts, "My disillusionment in those movements marked my own coming of age politically, for it required of me, as it did for so many women of color, the creation of a critical consciousness that had not been reflected in the mass social movements" (xvi). The work of women of color as theorists and artists thus serves as a bridge between mainstream feminist movements and national movements of the period. Their work is still relevant and significant in the 21st century, since their perspectives on the female body as a site where heteropatriarchal and racial constraints manifest informs the work of women of color artists such as Teatro Luna and Favianna Rodriguez.

Research on Latina/x reproductive decision-making has become more common since the emergence of the work by Cherríe Moraga, Gloria Anzaldúa, and Norma Alarcón. For example, Moraga negotiates her maternal identity in her memoir, and theatricalizes present, past, and future Chicana maternity in her plays. Scholarship on this topic in cultural productions such as literature and media remain rare. For example, Benigno Trigo's *Remembering Maternal Bodies: Melancholy in Latina and Latin American Women's Writing* (2006). In theater studies L. Bailey McDaniel's *(Re) Constructing Maternal Performance in Twentieth-Century American Drama* (2013) (includes a chapter on Cherríe Moraga). In Chicana/Latina studies, Susan Bost's *Encarnación: Illness and Body in Chicana Feminist Literature* (2010), and Dorsía Smith Silva's (ed.) *Latina/Chicana Mothering* (2011), Clara Román-Odio's *Sacred Iconographies in Chicana Cultural Production* (2013), Cristina Herrera's *Contemporary Chicana Literature: (Re)Writing the*

Maternal Script (2014), Gisela Norat's work on Latin American and Latina writers, and Kristi Ulibarrí's 2017 article on *Lunar Braceros 2125–2148* provide significant contributions to discussions on Latin American and Latina/ Chicana (future) maternity and motherhood. All of these scholars are invested in a goal similar to mine, to help view and outline the significance of Latina writers and artists, as well as protagonists, rebuking and rewriting their own narratives about reproductive decision-making.

Women writers of color, such as Audre Lorde, Ntozake Shange, and Migdalia Cruz, for example, have produced creative work representing reproductive decisions characterized by the intersections of race, class, and gender. Latina/x writers, like Moraga, also shape this type of work within the intersections of race, class, and sexuality. At the core of this project is a look at the work of a Pan-Latina theater ensemble, a Latinx visual artist and the Latina protagonists of *Jane the Virgin*, Jane (Gina Rodriguez), her mother Xiomara (Andrea Navedo), *Vida's* Emma Hernández (Mishel Prada), and *Quinceañera's* Magdalena (Emily Ríos). A comprehensive study devoted to Latina/x reproductive decision-making in cultural texts has yet to be written; thus, *Representing Latina/x Reproductive Decision-Making* serves as a necessary contribution in the field of Latina/o/x Cultural Studies.

The scarcity of scholarship on Latina/x reproductive decision-making narratives about infertility or abortion in cultural texts is evident in studies solely focusing on sociological or media studies tend to exclude Latina/x artists and topics. Writers such as Kia Corthorn, Shange, and Suzan-Lori Parks, for example, are included in anthologies and studies analyzing women of color and the role of reproductive decision-making and social justice in their creative work.[13] For example, Heather Latimer's *Reproductive Acts: Sexual Politics in North American Fiction and Film* (2013) analyzes film and fiction through a hemispheric lens, focusing on writers such as Margaret Atwood and Toni Morrison. Most recently, Anne Carruther's book, *Fertile Visions* (2021) analyzes cinema from the Americas, like *Ixcanul* (2015), and interrogates the uterus as a narrative space where we can possibly come to understand the female reproductive body beyond confined notions of a gendered analysis. The erasure of diversity in scholarship about Latina cultural texts that place reproductive decisions front and center is evident in my own research since I also had a difficult time locating previous scholarship on this subject matter. I build on the work done by Norat and Bost to further add more critical analysis of Latina reproductive decision-making in cultural texts to Latino and Latin American Studies. There are a series of important social science studies invested in researching and Chicana/Latina reproductive decision-making and reproductive justice grassroots organizations. The influential work of historian Alexandra Mina Stern, *Eugenic*

Nation: Faults and Frontiers of Better Breeding in Modern America (2005), focuses on the intersections of race, class, and gender and the US conducting eugenics programs that impacted communities of color, such as Mexican Americans in the Southwest. Building on Stern's work, sociologist Elena R. Gutiérrez's, *Fertile Matters*: T*he Politics of Mexican-origin Women's Reproduction* (2008) focuses on the so-called problem of the "hyper-fertile" Mexican-origin woman has been constructed leading to social policies and medical interventions, like coercive sterilization. Gutiérrez and Loretta Ross, et al., have also published *Undivided Rights: Women of Color Organize for Reproductive Justice* (2016), which draws on historical research and case studies to illuminate how women of color have led the fight for reproductive justice. Sociologist Lorena García's book, *Respect Yourself, Protect Yourself: Latina Girls and Sexuality* (2012) extends the work done by Gutiérrez insofar as García uses transdisciplinary approaches to gauge the ways Latinas gain sexual literacy in contexts that shape Latina youth sexuality. More recently the work of Patricia Zavella, *The Movement for Reproductive Justice* (2020) draws on ethnographic research on women of color organizations that are engaged in reproductive justice work, such as the National Latina Institute for Reproductive Health (NLIRH). In 2018, two anthologies came out and focused on Latina lives and reproductive freedom and choice. Iris Morales' *Latinas: An Anthology of Struggles and Protests in 21st Century USA* (2018) brings together scholars, artists, and activists to reveal a range of Latina perspectives on issues such as (im)migration, afro and indigenous identities, LGBTQ+ struggles, and reproductive justice. Cindy Cooper and Stacey Linnartz curated plays for *Short Plays on Reproductive Freedom* from the Reproductive Freedom Festival and Words as Choice, Inc. (2016). In this anthology, Cooper and Linnartz offer thirty-four short plays or performance pieces by artists/authors from all walks of life, exploring reproductive rights, health, freedom, and justice. In 2019 a group of Latina/Chicana academics published *The Chicana M(other)work Anthology*, bringing together emerging scholarship and testimonies centered on mothering as transformative labor. From migration and mothering to loss and reproductive justice, this anthology draws attention to the lived experiences of Chicana/Latina mother-scholars-activists in the 21st century, addressing racism, classism, and heteropatriarchy (4). Despite the steady published scholarly work on the topic of mothering, motherwork and reproductive freedom and justice, much of the work focuses on social science approaches, such as ethnographies or humanities research, focused on historical documentation, with the work of Chicana motherwork and Cooper and Linnartz combining both scholarship and artistic work. Well-known and new scholars are actively studying these topics, yet

Latina maternity and reproductive decision-making themes in popular culture (theater, small screen, and visual arts) have not been investigated fully.

Methodology and Organization

What accounts for the complexity of Latina reproductive decision-making, including pregnancy and abortion? How do theater-makers, visual artists, and Latina protagonists represent reproductive decisions beyond notions of the overjoyed mother? In light of social and cultural discourses that have limited Latina/x reproductive decision-making representations, how do these cultural texts reaffirm, challenge, and resist traditional notions of reproductive decisions? If we accept that Latinas in cultural texts are always either overjoyed expectant mothers or sexy and hyper-fertile women that reject motherhood, then it is a strictly limited view of Latinas and womanhood. Can these stereotypical views present in cultural texts serve as starting points for a refreshed and empowered identity and affirmation of Latina reproductive decisions? As I explore specific case studies, it is not my intent to read and analyze the work of Teatro Luna, *Jane the Virgin, Vida, Quinceañera* or Favianna Rodriguez through an idealized lens nor do I intend to argue these cultural texts only address issues of reproductive decisions. Some of these narratives, visual and written, illustrate the power of holding the tension of ambivalence surrounding reproductive decision-making, especially as it relates to abortion stories. Further, even if Teatro Luna or *Jane the Virgin,* for example, present the common image of the sacrificial mother or hyper-sexualized Latina, the artists (Teatro Luna and Favianna Rodriguez), have not constructed these images to signal acceptance or truth; instead, these cultural texts critique and upend Latinx and mainstream culture's demand for certain Latina/x and womanhood ideals and expectations. In their critique, these artists and protagonists can reclaim the multifaceted Latina figure and affirm their commitment to upending stereotypes and shifting the reproductive rights debate away from a purely religious, ideological, or political perspective. The representations analyzed range from written texts to visual texts, which require a multidimensional approach, that includes literary, media (visual) and performance methods. The women in these cultural texts, including those represented by posters in Favianna Rodriguez's series, do not reject womanhood or Latinidad, but they do reject and contest heteropatriarchal and cultural roles that expect them to adhere to rigid expectations, such as becoming a mother. Although at first some protagonists and characters may appear to outrightly reject their future mothering roles, the same women show more ambivalence than rejection, fear, or anger about their future. These reproductive decision-positive narratives present empowered characters through strength and ambivalence in their reproductive decisions.

The multiple theoretical frameworks of Chicana/Latina theories and scholars can also inform an analysis of the Chicana/Latina reproductive decision-making experience means that we can consider how history, myths and folklore, gender norms, sexual orientation, race, and class impact reproductive decisions. Chicana theorist Gloria Anzaldúa asserts that Chicana culture holds three expectations when it comes to women and their identity: "For a woman of my [Chicanx] culture there used to be only three directions she could turn: to the Church as a nun, to the streets as a prostitute, or to the home as a mother" (Anzaldúa, *Borderlands* 39). Chicana scholar Alicia Gaspar de Alba builds on this and theorizes the "Three Marías Syndrome," in *[Un]framing the "Bad Women"* (2014). She defines this syndrome as "the patriarchal social discourse of Chicano/Mexicano culture that constructs women's gender and sexuality according to three Biblical archetypes-virgins, mothers, and whores" (159). These figures represent the three "Marías" present at Jesus Christ's crucifixion: his mother, the virgin Mary; the "other Mary," who is the mother of James and Joseph; and Mary Magdalene (the reformed prostitute). These three women serve as prototypes for behaviors and ways of being/acting for Chicana/Latina women. Following Gaspar de Alba's work, I borrow her categories of the three *Marías* to further interrogate those figures through the lens of reproductive decision making. Gaspar de Alba defines the three figures the following way: "*La madre*-María: sacrifices herself for her children; always forgiving; nurturer; protector; does it all; gives birth to the future heirs; sex only to procreate; abnegated; *La virgen*-María: obedient, virgin until marriage; decent woman; doesn't call attention to herself; knows nothing about sex or sexuality; innocent; and *La prostituta*-María: sex for pleasure; sells sex; uses contraception; corrupts men; shames her family; loose and easy; gets what she deserves" (2014, 158–59). These categories implore competition between women, noting that the bad woman repudiates being a mother or virgin, and serves as a cautionary tale for those women who move beyond notions of virginity and motherhood.

As part of the larger genealogy of Chicana theorists like Gloria Anzaldúa, Cherríe Moraga have mutually influenced the work of women of color artists and scholars, like Gaspar de Alba. These writers explored the physical and emotional experiences of women whose voices and bodies were largely absent from US feminism and other social movements in the 1970s. Ana Castillo's work also challenges the set of binaries that have shaped Latina sexuality of the everyday. In her critical work, *Massacre of Dreamers* (1995), her essay "The Mother-Bond Principle" critiques narrow conceptions of the nuclear family and the self-sacrificing mother, while calling on all to be responsible for children: "As Xicanistas, female and male alike, whether we are biological mothers or not, we can learn to incorporate qualities customarily seen as inherent in mothering and apply them to how we treat ourselves, our relationships, and, of course, our children" (204). Castillo also incorporates this critique of mothering in her creative work, *The Guardians* (2007) and her poem, *Since the Creation of My Son and My First Book* (1993). Along with Castillo, Moraga has also explored these topics in her critical and creative work. In Moraga's memoir, *Waiting in the Wings: Portrait of a Queer Motherhood* (1997), she chronicles coming into motherhood through raw emotion and directly related to her queer identity: "I cry for this life, this miracle, this sexuality that is happening to me unlike any I have experienced. The slightest contact evokes a response. Touching myself, remembering Ella touching me" (76). For Moraga, her experience reflects Latina/Chicana representations often tied to heterosexual notions of reproductive decisions and making queer couples invisible. By acknowledging the influence "Maria and Joseph" figures have on Chicana/Latina culture, these writers name their experience as women and daughters through an empowered woman of color feminism. As Suzanne Bost (2010) argues in her work on these authors, Castillo, and Moraga's work "opens up a different set of questions about the relationship between the body and identity, between one body and others, as well as between an individual body and itself" (*Encarnación* 3). For these Chicana/Latina artists and scholars, the relationship between the body and identity remains paramount to being Chicana/Latina and empowered in their reproductive decisions. Anzaldúa and Moraga call this theory in the flesh, "where the physical reality of our lives—our skin color, the land or concrete we grew up on, our sexual longings—all fuse together to create a politic born out of necessity" (*This Bridge* 19). Through this theorization, Chicana/Latina writers like Moraga and Castillo, echo what Anzaldúa theorized in *Borderlands* about identity and representation: "Seek new images of identity . . . [break] down the unitary aspect of each new paradigm . . . [surrender] all notions of safety, of the familiar . . . to [deconstruct], construct identity" (80, 82, 87). As Anzaldúa notes, "culture forms our beliefs. We perceive the version of reality that it communicates" (38). As such, these Chicana/Latinas' approach to theorizing lived experiences further helps us understand the importance of discussing reproductive decision-making in Latina cultural texts such as theater, media, and art.

Latina playwrights like Migdalia Cruz and Moraga represent women of color discussing reproductive decisions in dramatic texts. Their work brings to the surface some of the most difficult and taboo issues for women, including their experiences of racism and sexism as it relates to reproductive decisions. Feminist theaters created by women of color that emerged from the feminist movement and Chicano movement, like Teatro de la Chicana (Teatro Raíces) also serve as important moments of the lineage, since these groups served as alternatives to male-dominated theatrical institutions, like Teatro Campesino, and functioned as places of resistance and change.[14] Article VI of Teatro Chicana's bylaws encapsulates this directly: "Our ideals and goals have grown from our personal experiences in this society, our studies, and our hope to build a better society in which we and our children can live decently" (García, Gutiérrez and Nuñez 2008, 266). Their work is still relevant and significant in the twenty-first century since their perspectives on the female body to inform the work of Teatro Luna and Favianna Rodriguez.

Early works by women of color such as Audre Lorde's poem "Bloodbirth" (1977) describes violence and powerlessness in the act of birth. Laura Major (2007) notes that "Lorde locates her lived experience of the body as the source of her texts" (210). It is interesting to further extend this observation about playwrights that have taken up the experience of pregnancy and motherhood where the woman's voice locates ambivalence in reproductive decision-making. Ana Castillo also references her experience giving birth to her son in her poem, *Since the Creation of My Son and My First Book* (1991), recounting his premature delivery: "They took blood from us, stuck tubes in every orifice, put us in isolation and watched us for five days" (91). In the case of other women of color authors, ambivalence surfaces in reproductive decisions as early as 1916, with the work of African American playwright Angelina Grimké's play, *Rachel*. Rachel, the protagonist yearns to become a mother, but she realizes the implications of racism for her children as well as her own powerlessness as a mother. As Joyce Meier (2000) asserts in her study on early African American women's theater, "Grimke's intent was not just to challenge the stereotypes of black people by presenting learned blacks who adhered to middle-class ideals, but also to show the tremendous incongruities between such ideals and the realities of black existence" (123). These ambivalent yet explicit narratives were often silenced because of the stigma placed on rejecting motherhood and contributed to the lack of understanding of women of color's reproductive experiences in the early 20th century. Lorde, Castillo, and Grimké demonstrate the vital importance of representing reproductive decision-making in creative texts in a world that continues to undervalue or silence these types of narratives.

According to Adrienne Rich, confirming to heteropatriarchal motherhood prevents women as mothers from creating a women-oriented model of mothering further noting that conforming to such notions then creates a legacy that ultimately gets passed down to daughters (qtd. in O'Reilly and Abbey 7). Gisela Norat (2010) asserts in her work on Latina and Latin American playwrights that "In order for any social institution to change, its most invested and affected members must work toward new possibilities that will bring about long-term, permanent transformation" (24). As such, an institution like motherhood needs to change from those that understand the institution, women themselves, regardless of choosing motherhood or not. Undoubtedly, the work of Teatro Luna, Favianna Rodriguez, and the Latina characters in

Jane the Virgin, Vida, and *Quinceañera* seek to upend and rewrite reproductive decisions like becoming mothers or being childfree. Some of the characters in Teatro Luna's plays do define their identity as expectant mothers, while other characters seek to define their own relationship with(out) children beyond notions of heteropatriarchal motherhood. In the case of some of the characters in *Jane the Virgin*, especially, Jane, seeks to understand her identity as a Latina and as an expectant mother and not as two mutually exclusive categories. Throughout the first season and the series, there are moments that Jane looks to her grandmother and mother for advice on becoming a mother. Even in this example, the series does not call for a perpetuation of traditional motherhood or those qualities as the essential elements to a Latina experience, but rather, the nuances might further empower audiences and readers to question preconceived notions of Latina and womanhood.

Other scholars such as Evelyn Nakano Glenn (1994) have argued that the act of mothering is one that "is socially constructed, not biologically rooted" (3). As a result of socialization, mothering is constructed as a heteropatriarchal practice: "motherhood functions as an institution that serves to expand patriarchal power, emphasizing empowerment through heteropatriarchal notions of motherhood" (O'Reilly and Abbey 7). Notions of fathering then have different meanings since mothering within a heteropatriarchal culture denotes acceptance and sacrifice as mothers or future mothers. Ana Castillo (1995) also agrees that the act of mothering exclusive to women's expectations is socially and culturally constructed: "Even the woman, who, for any number of reasons, chooses not to involve herself in an ongoing relationship with a man, is made to believe that motherhood is not an option but rather her duty as a female member of her family, community, and society. She cannot reach maturity, truly become a woman, or earn good standing if she refuses to procreate" (*Massacre of Dreamers* 128). As Cristina Herrera (2014) argues in her book, *Contemporary Chicana Literature*, writers like Castillo, Moraga, and Sandra Cisneros, use resistance imagery to rewrite and challenge mother-daughter representation, rejecting traditional notions of motherhood in their memoirs and novels. Building on the work of Herrera and Bost, *Representing Latina/x Reproductive Decision-Making* seeks to expand our understanding of reproductive decisions in Latina/x cultural texts such as theatre, television, and visual art. As Bost (2010) indicates, Anzaldúa and Moraga shaped Chicanx theorizations of the body, in terms of pain and women's health. For Bost, Anzaldúa emphasizes how women of color are made to feel inappropriate and impure given the histories of violation and pathologizing of women of color's bodies (89). Even though pregnancy is not considered an "illness" per se, Moraga's account of pregnancy and queer motherhood, according to Bost, addresses how Moraga's representation of pregnancy opens up both bodies (woman and fetus) and clinics beyond institutionalized boundaries (118). These bodily experiences are imperative to include in studies like Bost and Herrera's work. Furthermore, Moraga and Anzaldúa set some of the steppingstones for the work of other Chicana/Latina writers such as Irene Vilar, Migdalia Cruz, and the work of Teatro Luna. By addressing reproductive decisions beyond pregnancy and motherhood, these writers/artists call into question preconceived notions of what it means to be Latina. Rather than emphasizing and exalting joyful, sacrificial, and traditional notions of reproductive decisions that emphasize metaphors such as the virginal or sexy woman.

Storytelling and Reproductive Decisions

Narratives like memoirs tackling reproductive decision-making, be it to have children (biological, artificial reproductive technologies, adoption, etc.) or not to (childfree, abortion, adoption) offer important insights into tensions emerging from the foundation underlying mainstream claims for and against motherhood and reproductive rights, specifically for women of color. Speaking honestly and openly about reproductive decision-making is an act of resistance and agency. As this project will attest, fiction narratives about Latina/x reproductive decision-making such as theater, television, as well as material culture such as social justice posters are particularly important within the context of our current social and political climate. As noted before, discussing reproductive decision-making through these different mediums is imperative given the uptick in legislation in the United States against access to reproductive health care, including contraceptives and abortion.

The tensions between abortion positive narratives and those that tend to castigate or view abortion as morally wrong require audiences and readers of these cultural texts see and read differently. As such, these texts in the case studies that follow we must read and view them in way that enables us to break away from traditional expectations of what reproductive decisions look like and to image how these texts can give new meaning to reproductive decision-making. As Caroline Lundquist argues in her work on Iris Young's work, *Pregnant Embodiment: Subjectivity and Alienation*:

> There is no lived experience comparable to pregnancy. In most cases, pregnancy, labor, delivery, and the postpartum period entail a wide range of new sensations and cryptic emotions for the pregnant subject. Pregnancy also entails disrupted perceptions of subjectivity, and shifts in perceived spatiality and temporality. Yet, although all women may experience similar phenomena during their time as pregnant subjects, something is lost in the assumption that their lived experiences are qualitatively similar. (140, 2008)

As such, we can argue, following Lundquist, that all pregnant people or people who aspire to be pregnant or choose to remain childfree, will all have different experiences, regardless of the similarities in their experiences. While first-person Latina/x and women of color narratives about reproductive decisions are not the focus of this project, memoirs consider how speaking from the autobiographical "I" is an apolitical act that forms the bedrock for bringing awareness and mobilizing change. By briefly examining reproductive decision-making narratives such as memoirs in contexts ranging from pregnancy, abortion to childbirth, it will demonstrate a deeper understanding about individual narratives based on experiences, furthermore, this guides our understanding about reproductive decisions as reaffirming or disrupting such conversations.

Cherríe Moraga's memoir, *Waiting in the Wings* (1997), and Irene Vilar's *Impossible Motherhood* (2009) highlight two important examples of how the personal narrative about reproductive decision-making sheds light on the realities of women of color. While memoirs are not the focus of this project, I find it imperative to take a quick detour to discuss these storytelling projects as a way to broaden the reader's idea of Latina/x womanhood and reproductive decision-making beyond notions of choice. These first-person narratives bring notions of womanhood, through pregnancy, loss, and maternity into conflict with the act of writing.

In Cherríe Moraga's memoir, the writer takes readers through her journey to become a mother, specifically a queer Chicana mother. Moraga's memoir is structured with real journal entries and the subsequent addition of factual data and passages of reflection recounting that period in her life where she wants to have a child, detailing the many people in her LGBTQ community that died from AIDS, her conception, pregnancy and the premature birth of her son, Rafael, and his extended stay in the NICU. Moraga's own words exemplify the importance of the representation of her experience as a queer soon-to-be mother: "We cannot make babies with one another" (15). For Chicanx and Moraga scholar, Yvonne Yarbro-Bejarano, Moraga's memoir brings identity and writing into conflict. For Chicanx scholar Suzanne Bost, Moraga's memoir brings into play the notion of illness and pain. Bost asserts that traditional narratives of birth serve to assert to the readers that even in the process of pregnancy and birth, regardless of how gory or gruesome it may be or sound, the end result will be a beautiful child thanks to medical practices and the will of the parents to bring a lovely child into this world. In Yarbro-Bejarano's analysis, Moraga's writing and her pregnancy are presented as two forms of creativity that enter into a kind of alignment, at times paralleling and competing with each other (134). Moraga's memoir does present a conundrum in regard to definitions of motherhood, pregnancy, and birth as well as dominant understandings of queer motherhood as seen in the previous quotes.

For Moraga, her partner, as well as other queer women who want to have children, the act of conceiving and being a mother forced them to navigate the uncertain terrain of traditional, heterosexual reproductive decision-making within the context of also a traditional medical industrial complex.

As Moraga attests, "Nothing has been given to me, not even my womanhood" (17). There is no doubt that Moraga's intimacies of conception, pregnancy and birth transgressed and redefined what it meant for a queer Chicanx to document her coming into motherhood as a reproductive decision, filled with uncertainty and at times fear. This personal narrative marks the self in two different and at times opposing positions, just as Yarbro-Bejarano attests. Furthermore as cultural studies scholar Gisela Norat (2009) argues, Moraga's details of the birthing process, for example, counters the typical romanticization of pregnancy and motherhood. Norat adds "Moraga records the psychic and physical interiority of pregnancy from a lived experience, a reality that cannot be topped by even modern technologies that . . . into the uterus" (10). As such, Moraga's memoir about reproductive decision-making intersects with creative writing through connections to her plays and how they are connected to her lived experiences, such as *Giving up the Ghost, Heroes and Saints and A Hungry Woman*, to name a few, redefine the representation of Chicanx/Latinx identity diverging from a heteronormative understanding of womanhood and motherhood.

Similarly, Irene Vilar's memoir, *Impossible Motherhood* (2009) about her abortions and coming into motherhood forces readers to confront abortion through the lens of a personal narrative. Vilar's memoir about her relationship with her mother, grandmother, and her husband and former professor constitutes a compelling first-person narrative that testifies about her process of becoming who she is through her reproductive decision-making and generational trauma related to the women in her life, her mother and grandmother. Her grandmother is Lolita Lebrón, one of Puerto Rico's nationalist fighters, convicted of attempted murder and other crimes after carrying out an armed attack on the US Capitol in 1954.[15] Vilar's mother suffered depression and committed suicide with a young Vilar in the car. Her mother was part of the US backed program that sterilized women in Puerto Rico during the 1970s as a technique for population control.[16] It is through the intertext of these generational traumas and experiences that Vilar's personal narrative about her abortions and coming into motherhood bring to the forefront the challenges of reducing our understanding of what it means to make reproductive decisions and understand the legacy of long-term generational gynecological trauma. Vilar's personal narrative reconciles history and synthesizes her identity as a Puerto Rican-American writer.

Similar to Moraga's memoir, *Impossible Motherhood* also presents a compelling narrative to testify that writing as well as being a woman is a perpetual process of becoming. Vilar's narrative positions the "I" as she reflects her time married to her former professor and during her unplanned pregnancies and abortions, motivated by both a lack of self-care and a desire to defy her former husband's push to remain childless. The use of a prologue homes in on Vilar's need to want to tell the readers that this narrative seeks to not be didactic or partisan when it comes to abortion, but what it does want to do is tell her personal struggle as well as the interconnectedness with her mother and grandmother's stories.

The lineage Vilar discusses makes it evident to the reader that she chooses to interlace her personal and familial experiences with the ways in which heteropatriarchal discourses surrounding womanhood and motherhood are imposed upon reproductive decision-making. "Everything can be explained, justified, our last century tells us. Everything except for the burden of life interrupted that shall die with me" (5). Like Moraga's memoir, Vilar's narrative does politicize women's right to bodily autonomy and the varying degrees it has affected the debates surrounding access to women's health care and the right to bodily autonomy. In *Intersections of Harm* (2015), Laura Halperin argues that Vilar's memoirs emphasize the interconnectedness of the individual and the collective in relation to issues of choice and coercion and how these ideas actually seize freedom and not allow for it. Halperin also makes connections between Vilar's memoirs and Moraga's in that there's an ardent critique of US policy and history, constantly linking the geographical, political, and physical (30). For Vilar, her struggles with mental illness and with control are things she inherited form her mother and grandmother. Throughout the memoir, Vilar oscillates between allowing herself to take control of her life and leave her abusive relationship or feel ambivalent about her being who she is throughout the fifteen abortions and becoming the woman she is today. Furthermore, Halperin's analysis elucidates Vilar's constant search for something, a "belonging . . . a home" (46). As Vilar's memoir shows, it is evident through her contextualization of her reproductive decisions, her relationship to the women in her family, the history of Puerto Rico, and her personal experiences as a woman, coming into motherhood, that storytelling is powerful. Much like Moraga's memoir, Vilar's also describes and highlights intersectional experiences as they relate to reproductive decision-making and larger socio-cultural discourses around womanhood and motherhood. In Vilar's case, she admits that she abused the right to seek and have an abortion, and while that could lead to antichoice advocates justifying further defunding access to reproductive health care or overturning *Roe v. Wade*, she advocates for the importance of a woman's right to choose. As Halperin argues, as Vilar's memoir illustrates, "choice goes hand in hand with control and power, and these are not readily abundant or available to all, despite claims to the contrary [. . .]" (49). While I agree with

Halperin's analysis of Vilar's perspective on choice, it is imperative that we question what it means to even talk about choice when access to abortion or contraception was readily available or if we take into consideration the relationship Vilar had with her then partner.

Cherríe Moraga's memoir about coming into motherhood not only influenced the work of Irene Vilar, but also the contributions of other women of color artists, activists, and scholars as they navigate the public and private aspects of their lives as women of color at the intersection of pregnancy and motherhood. In Gloria Anzaldúa's anthology, *Making Face, Making Soul* (1990), she wants to make a mark, stating: "The world knows us by our faces, the most naked, most vulnerable, exposed and significant topography of the body. When our caras do not live up to the 'image' that the family or community wants us to wear and when we rebel against the engraving of our bodies, we experience ostracism, alienation, isolation and shame" (xv). As such, Moraga and Vilar's memoirs shed light on these "images" that others expect these women to wear while at the same time bringing compelling stories about embodying reproductive decision-making. Like Moraga and Vilar, *Revolutionary Mothering* (2017) and *The Chicana M(other)work Anthology* (2019) demonstrate other ways in which exposing and upending expectations around pregnancy and motherhood for women of color can mobilize and bring forth other ways of coalition-building around womanhood beyond becoming biological mothers.

In the edited volume by Alexis Pauline Gumbs, China Martens and Mai'a Williams, *Revolutionary Mothering* (2016), the editors, and contributors provide a multiplicity of mothering voices, including mothers of color, queer mothers, young, poor, etc. These personal narratives, although not something groundbreaking given the history of first-person narratives about mothering from anthologies such as *This bridge called my back*, *The Black Woman*, among others. *Revolutionary Mothering* offers the roles of productive rage and love in mothering as strategic ways of being a "mother," regardless of biological connections. The anthology includes different approaches to motherhood, including Gumbs' essay "m/other ourselves: a Black queer feminist genealogy for radical mothering," that can be seen as a manifesto for queer mothering following in the footsteps of Audre Lorde and Patricia Hill Collins. Within the context of this essay, Gumbs calls for the potential of radical mothering based on the notion of how-to mother and not what is a mother. In her essay, Gumbs calls for us to look at the word "mother" less as a gendered identity and more as a possible action (23). This essay drives the rest of the personal narratives included in the anthology, focused on identity and mothering beyond heteropatriarchal and biological notions of "mother." Like the work of Moraga, *Revolutionary Mothering* sheds light on queer motherhood as well as other ways of understanding what it means to be a mother, along the lines of collective/community notions of the term. The important narratives in this anthology are the voices of strong mothers of color, queer mothers, young mothers, poor mothers, mothers who will not be pushed to feel shame or be ostracized, but thrive, and fight for social justice, including reproductive decision-making.

Another example that sheds light on reproductive decision-making beyond becoming a parent is Esteli Juarez's narrative, "Choice." Like the generational and historical impact of coerced sterilization on Irene Vilar's family, Juarez learned about why one family member could not have children since she was sterilized because of a disability. Similarly, she learns about the US-backed sterilization program in Puerto Rico and in the efforts to sterilize indigenous women in the US. As the narrator states, "the older I get the more passionate I become about retaining control over my body and allowing other women the same opportunity to do so" (161). She became more involved in social justice organizations and inspired her to work with victims of domestic violence. As a college senior she got pregnant and decided to have an abortion but while the clinic, she decided she would keep her child. Juarez's testimony reveals that reproductive decision-making is something that challenges how we perceive notions of choice, especially for women. For Juarez, choosing to have her child brought on the task of making sure her children understand what it means to have the privilege of choice as men, but also for her "choice . . . is not just about abortion. It's about all the other choices. It's about the choice to conceive children at all . . . a woman's right to choose goes both ways" (162). As an advocate for victims of abuse she understands the difficult history of marginalized bodies and reproductive decisions, especially when governments practiced involuntary hysterectomies or served as guinea pigs for experimental contraceptives. As such, the narrator makes a commitment to fight for women to choose, following a reproductive justice practice, "to continue a pregnancy but it is also the right to choose to get pregnant in the first place" (162). In the case of these two examples from *Revolutionary Mothering*, the writers bear witness to heal, resist and make their *movidas*, shifting our preconceived notions of what it means to become a parent or not, including choosing an abortion.

Likewise, *The Chicana M(other)work* (2019), edited by Chicanx and women of color mother-scholars, activists, and allies, also centers on personal narratives about mothering as a transformational experience. Like *Revolutionary Mothering*, The *Chicana M(other)work*, edited by Cecilia Caballero, Yvette Martínez-Vu, Judith Pérez-Torres, Michelle Téllez, and Christine Vega, uses a reproductive justice framework that seeks to define m(other)work, borrowing the term from Patricia Hill Collins, as layered labor, and the term as multiple and fluid. Through these personal narratives, writers actively challenge what it means to do *motherwork*, both as concept and praxis. There are narratives focused on teenage motherhood and systemic violence, another essay focuses on motherhood and formerly incarcerated women, as well as testimonios about being a mother-scholar of color in academic spaces. Of particular importance to this project is part IV, focusing on loss, reproductive justice, and holistic pregnancy. While the other parts reflect equally important narratives about what it means to be a mother, in all its iterations, part IV collectively centers on conversations seldomly had, until recently, such as miscarriages, abortions, adoption, or choosing to be childfree. By centering on women of color experiences and issues related to reproductive decision-making, this anthology seeks to provide narratives that have been silenced or not made evident in spaces such as academic circles and on media platforms. These contributors are either raising kids or not and sharing their experiences critically and calling attention to terms such as mother/other, boys, men, girls, as to grapple with what it means to raise children or not through a critical lens.

For example, Corina Benavides López's essay on adoption, following years of reproductive losses, such as miscarriages, reveals a candid narrative about her decision to exit the roller-coaster ride of pursuing motherhood via medical appointments, exams, etc. to find answers to her losses. From being asked about having children to navigating the traditional adoption process in the US, which for many is difficult and costly, to having another pregnancy loss during the process of adoption, López's personal narrative demonstrates why the act of mothering is not a race or social class neutral act. López recounts their experience with the birthmother of their son and the bond they now share, knowing that "she consciously chose us as his parents, enduring the mental, spiritual and emotional aguish of handing over her baby and entrusting us with his life, her m(other)work" (208). Unfortunately, for López and her partner, having adopted brought on criticism from family and friends, about why? Or emphasizing the importance of a biological child with statements like "Keep trying!" Such sentiments, while well-intentioned, demonstrate a level of misunderstanding about what people are dealing with as they navigate infertility or loss, for example, because it focuses on a person's worth based on the productivity of their womb. Furthermore, this narrative also speaks about the silence surrounding reproductive loss and gains, and as adoptive parents. Following in the small acts of *rebeldía* that Anzaldúa calls *movidas*, these testimonies and this anthology about reproductive decision-making contribute to the "shifting grounds upon which women of color stage their strategies for social change . . . " (2).

In *The Chicana M(other)work* anthology, other essays in this part touch on healing after a miscarriage and stillbirth. This section on loss, reproductive choices and adoption highlights the privileges and the challenges of mothers who can and cannot physically have children, while also recognizing that not all women choose to have children.

For the editors and the contributors, by focusing on mothering as a collective notion, the conversation breaks away from heteropatriarchal norms that teach us to place mothering as an individual notion. For example, in the testimonio by Mara Chavez-Diaz, "Birthing Healing Justice," the narrator takes the reader through her experience with an undiagnosed ectopic pregnancy, as she experienced shame and racial/linguistic profiling while at an OBGYN's office. She was asked if she spoke English, whether she was sleeping with more than one person, etc., while the doctors failing to perform a thorough exam to see why she was bleeding for over a month despite having an IUD (272). For the narrator, going through a miscarriage because of the ectopic pregnancy in silence is fraught with questions about reproductive health care for women of color as well as about the common collective experiences about miscarriages in a woman's reproductive life. As such, the narrator's experience, and common story by a lot of women makes her push for an understanding and linking between " . . . reproductive freedom, white supremacy, and the rape of mother earth as critical to reproductive justice" (274).

The narrator's testimony of her miscarriages focuses on the importance and centrality of generational trauma, especially as it relates to reproductive health care: "the spiritual ritual of doing an inventory with my womb of all she had been through since birth provided me the opportunity to heal my own wounded spirit and that of past generations of muxeres in my family" (278). Furthermore, what stands out from this narrative is the importance of reclaiming one's narrative through embodied praxis as a way to begin to heal from generational and individual trauma. The last testimonio by Rose G. Salseda, "My Forever Sleeping Baby" further discusses pregnancy loss through her narrative about her stillborn child, Sebastián. For the narrator the difficulty lies in how as a society we rarely discuss pregnancy loss even though it is not uncommon. This narrative draws upon grief, like the previous ones and Moraga's memoir to navigate the silence around loss and death, pregnancy, and birth, as well as sorrow. As the narrator comments, it was due to her experience as an academic that she was able to navigate the uncertainty of knowing what happens when you find out your unborn child may not survive because of a chromosomal disorder. As she and her partner navigated the pregnancy, they find out that the baby had trisomy 21 (Down syndrome), but they felt confident because of their background that they could raise a child with the syndrome. After further testing, the diagnosis was different, it pointed to trisomy 18, which is life threatening and only a few babies survive the first month of birth. For the narrator and her family, relying on their research skills as academics she was able to navigate the different options, such as seeking an abortion, which for them was limited given the restrictions in their home state. As such, the couple decided to continue the pregnancy, knowing that the experience may lead to the death of her unborn child in utero or early in his life. Relying on their circumstances and privileges, deepened their commitment to access to better healthcare for reproductive-aged women, including the right to have an abortion. The narrator's story reminds us about the difficult reproductive decisions that people must make and it highlights the importance of dialoguing and being informed about one's options or treatment. By bearing witness to such a difficult and painful experience, the narrator and her family shed light on the importance of bringing awareness to pregnancy loss and the importance of reproductive justice for all, especially women of color.

By challenging cultural expectations of what it means to do motherwork this anthology also extends the conversation to past generations of women that endured abuse and trauma as mothers. Along with the written book, this anthology started hosting a podcast on their website, adding another space where women can share stories and dialogue about the act of "mothering" as a scholar and beyond. Throughout their archived three seasons, the podcasters hosted different women, including an interview with the editors of *Revolutionary Mothering.* Some of the stories vary in content beyond mothering experiences. For example, a few from Season 2 focus on the aftermath of the 2017 presidential election, while some from Season 3 address how COVID-19 has affected women of color mothers or what it's like to raise trans kids. While the written anthology seeks to break traditional notions of mothering for Chicanx/Latinx communities, other narratives remain absent from this anthology, especially those individuals who choose to remain childfree, who choose abortion, undergo alternative forms of conception such as insemination or IVF, same-sex parents, or partake in other roles such as caregiver. The podcast complements the written narrative by expanding on stories that often remain unspoken or seldomly presented in academic and personal spaces.

More importantly, these personal testimonios challenge and upend coercive and damaging discourses that silence m(other)work. *Revolutionary Mothering* and *The Chicana M(other)work*, along with the trailblazing memoirs, *Waiting in the Wings* by Cherríe Moraga, and *Impossible Motherhood* by Irene Vilar refuse to stay silent and they bear witness to what traditional narratives about motherhood and womanhood obscure, the silences of reproductive loss, difficult pregnancies, the stigma around abortion, among other reproductive decisions.

What Moraga, Vilar, and these women of color anthologies demonstrate is the power of storytelling, especially about experiences like abortion. In 2013, scholar and activist Melissa Madera created "The Abortion Diary." Madera spoke to and recorded people's experiences with abortion throughout the country and the world. These narratives are quite diverse across geographic location (thirty-six US states and twenty-one countries), socioeconomic background, age, ethnicity, race, religion, and gender, and span of experiences from the late 1950s to 2019. Madera's own abortion story compelled her to start collecting stories to remove the stigma around abortion and the silence surrounding reproductive decision-making. The abortion stories on Madera's website are part of a larger community of digital storytellers, like the accompanying podcast by the creators of *The M(other)work Anthology.*

Through these digital stories, Madera's storytellers create a digital community and a shared space for people to tell their abortion story without placing shame or blame on their experience. As Madera says in a short MSNBC video about her work, "by collecting oral histories, people are not trying to fit into or be put into a category, rather it shifts the paradigm to allow for someone to tell a story and for someone to listen" (2015). As such, polarizing and moralizing experiences like abortion are heard and these narratives create a space for people to listen and to hear similar experiences as well. "The abortion diary" categorizes the stories based on type of abortion, "Pre-Roe" or "medicated," by region (Asia, Europe, Middle East, North America, South America), or in Spanish. Madera's podcast and body of work was built on solidarity, compassion, and on social justice. All facets of the personal experience of an abortion are equalized in this collection since Madera's approach offers a holistic model of storytelling, reminiscent of the women of color anthologies and predecessors such as Cherríe Moraga's memoir, *Waiting in the Wings* or Gloria Anzaldúa's groundbreaking text, *Borderlands/La Frontera.* Madera's collection of abortion stories from those underrepresented by dominant systems, such as women of color, queer women, enact critical transformative-justice outcomes. These abortion stories write and rights *herstories* so that participants contextualize stories and make voices and perspectives of those who have been historically marginalized heard and listened to. As such, the power in meeting and collecting these narratives lies in the way in which opening up conversation and spaces to fill the silence and stigma surrounding abortion experiences. Given the importance of sharing one's story about reproductive decision-making, especially difficult and stigmatized decisions such as an abortion, "The Abortion Diary" seeks to abide by the mission: "We are healing each other by sharing our stories" (Madera 2015). The dissemination of first-person narratives about abortion is necessary in fighting the stigma and shame that still impacts people who have abortions. Furthermore, this collection of stories transgresses the indefinable aspects of abortion for people who have experienced them, reaching beyond the moralizing, and politicizing of the medical procedure. For example, one of the stories from North America, focuses on Robin, from the state of Georgia. Robin is disabled, a quadriplegic, already with one child, but after a debilitating first pregnancy, she knew she could not keep her second child because of a number of circumstances, especially her health: "As I am talking about my experience, it's raising a lot of not so much questions, but it's kind of though, it's a bit of a relief, and also that I also see it, I hope that maybe somebody else learns from my story. I regret the choices that led me to the point to where I needed to make that choice, but I do not regret making that choice. It was completely, 100%, the right thing for me to do" (Madera 2015). The collection of stories from South America, specifically Maritsa's story, addresses having a clandestine abortion in Peru, where abortion is illegal (2014). For Maritsa it was a difficult decision given her broken relationship, leading to a divorce, and her faith in God. She reveals to Madera that she was alone, had to find the money for it, and because it is an illegal act, it was challenging for her to go through with it. Throughout the story, Maritsa reveals that in her experience, although difficult, she relied on her faith despite the lack of support she encountered in her home country. In this narrative, Maritsa reveals that she has not shouted her experience, but would like to know that through her experience she wants others to mobilize and support women that choose to have abortions.

Platforms like "The Abortion Diary" and recent social media movements like #YouKnowMe, and #Shoutyourabortion can counter stigma around reproductive decision-making, reaching a varying degree of listeners/viewers/users. The emerging research and feminist and reproductive justice work that Madera is doing will help dismantle the entrenched moralizing and polarizing view about abortion and the silence around speaking about abortion and Madera's work also more accurately presents a more diverse abortion experience beyond the confines of the United States.

In their work on reproductive justice, scholars Jael Silliman, Marlene Gerber Fried, Loretta Ross, and Elena R. Gutiérrez (2016), advocate for understanding and acknowledging the work of women of color and their struggle for reproductive justice. According to the authors, the work of those organizations led by women of color have been undocumented, unanalyzed, and unacknowledged (7). Many of these organizations understand reproductive rights beyond notions of choice. These organizations along with the reproductive justice movement frames their approach to reproductive rights based on an understanding that these rights encompass race, class, gender, sexuality, and immigration experiences (12). Many stereotypes and lack of understanding about communities of color from healthcare providers to mainstream media only create more barriers for women of color who need information about and for their health care needs. One of the tenets of reproductive justice is to fight for the right to have or not to have children, recognizing the history of eugenics in this country and the population control programs established throughout our history as rooted in racism and heteropatriarchal power.[17] By moving beyond seeing reproductive rights as solely contraception or choice, a reproductive justice framework is inclusive of understanding how women of color view their reproductive decisions as everyday lived experiences.

So, what does a reproductive justice framework have to do with Latina cultural texts? How do these cultural texts work in light of a reproductive justice framework? While these texts are not stemming from organizations or individuals organizing reproductive justice organizations such as National Latina Institute of Reproductive Health (NLIRH), these cultural texts challenge traditional notions of reproductive decision-making and point to more inclusive understandings of women of color's reproductive rights. Reproductive justice organizations and activists address multiple forms of reproductive injustice, ranging from women in underserved communities not receiving adequate health care to high maternal mortality rates. In this respect, following the call from activists and organizations, *Representing Latina/x Reproductive Decision-Making* looks at the ways in which cultural texts like theater and television also address some of these issues for women of color, especially Latinas. The work of Teatro Luna and Favianna Rodriguez are born out of social movements such as the Chicano Movement and the women of color feminist movement, as such, these creators use their platforms to challenge traditional conventions of Latina reproductive decisions. Through their creative work, Teatro Luna and Rodríguez focus on engaging issues of Latina representation and advocate for more inclusive understandings of reproductive decision-making, moving beyond discourses of pro-life or pro-choice. Like their predecessors before them, Cherríe Moraga, Migdalia Cruz, Amalia Mesa-Bains, and Alma López, artists like Teatro Luna and Favianna Rodriguez use their art to advocate for new ways of being and seeing Latina.

Latina/o cultural studies scholars have questioned and problematized heteropatriarchal constructions of the body in representation, especially the Latina maternal body. According to Chicana feminist writer Ana Castillo (1995) and other feminist scholars, the cult of the virgin mother Mary has been perpetuated by institutionalized religions in an attempt to further impose patriarchal authority over women (Castillo 119). In Dorsía Smith Silva's edited volume, *Latina/Chicana Mothering* (2011), the authors argue for revisiting the role of mothering in cultural texts such as telenovelas and literature as well as through first-person narratives. Its significance is fundamental in mapping out the connections between Latina/Chicana fictional narratives and lived experiences over time, space, and medium.

In the case of Chicana/Latina narratives, Cristina Herrera has laid similar groundwork in *Contemporary Chicana Literature: (Re)Writing the Maternal Script* (2014) and Bailey L. McDaniel has done similar work in documenting the trajectory of the maternal performance in American Drama, including the work of Cherríe Moraga, in *(Re)Constructing Maternal Performance in*

Twentieth-Century American Drama (2013). The work of these scholars has been crucial in organizing a frame of reference for more in-depth inquiries into maternal narratives that until very recently has been ignored, such as queer motherhood. Gisela Norat and Susanne Bost's work has been influential in conversations about illness, pregnancy and reproductive decisions in fictional narratives and their implications for interrogating masculinist values, such as compulsory procreation. Bost, Herrera and Norat's work examine contemporary Latina/Chicana narratives in the 20th and 21st centuries, centering on novels or dramatic texts. While I am also interested in fictional narratives and the representation of maternity, my approach to them emphasizes the role of reproductive decision-making like negotiating infertility or choosing abortion as sources of empowerment and agency. As such, when addressing reproductive decisions in fictional texts, be it theater or television, there might be a tendency to frame them as "reproductive rights" narratives, which can be limiting in their representations. Increasingly when narratives about reproductive decisions are presented, they can become over-politicized, on the prolife/prochoice binary.

ORGANIZATION

Teatro Luna and Reproductive Decisions in Theater and Performance

The first chapter examines Teatro Luna's various dramatic and performance texts from the 20th century, specifically three of their early plays. Early playwrights like Migdalia Cruz, for example, represent women of color making reproductive decisions in her dramatic texts. Her work brings to the surface some of the most difficult and taboo issues for women, including teenage pregnancy. As such, women of color literary texts and performances have never lacked discussions of first-hand experiences and the female body, such as pregnancy and motherhood. The work of Migdalia Cruz in *The Have-Little* (1991) focuses on a young Latina protagonist, who finds strength in her unplanned pregnancy despite her impoverished and violent upbringing. In Teatro Chicana's work "So Ruff, So Tuff" (1974), the ensemble depicts strength in reproductive decision-making in this dramatic text. It is in the earlier Chicana/Latina work that Teatro Luna finds its inspiration as an artivist group, working toward upending negative representations of women of color. Teatro Luna's work, specifically *Déjame contarte* (2001), *S-e-x-oh!* (2006), and *Sólo tú* (2008), give a collective voice to experiences at times unattended and explains thematic issues such ambivalence in reproductive decision making.

Jane the Virgin: Reproductive Decision-Making in a 21st century *Telenovela*

It is widely acknowledged that issues related to women and reproduction, particularly with respect to reproductive decision-making have historically been controversial on and off the media.[18] Building on the previous chapter, this next case study shifts to a different kind of representation, television. *Jane the Virgin* (2014–2019) upends and reimagines a more nuanced understanding of Latina reproductive decision-making through mediated representation. This chapter contextualizes *Jane the Virgin's* engagement with Latina identity and reproductive decisions, specifically drawing upon the discussion of the cultural adaptation of the telenovela genre and implementation of open-ended serial narrative. The series destabilizes traditional Latina narratives of reproductive decision-making, on the small screen. As such, *Jane the Virgin* complicates notions of the virgin/whore dichotomy through the female protagonists, Jane (Gina Rodriguez), her mother, Xiomara (Andrea Navedo), and her grandmother Alba (Yvonne Coll). The various constructions of Latinx womanhood inform audiences about complicated notions of reproductive decision-making through telenovela excess. That is through framing of genre excess, the two women conform to and also resist to conventional notions of Latina motherhood, giving viewers perspectives that support or disavow opinions related to reproductive decision-making. Like Teatro Luna's work, through the complicated representation of Latina maternity in *Jane the Virgin*, this case study makes an argument for the ways in which the show challenges the gendered norms of society and creates dialogue around Latina television representation.

Navigating Reproductive Decisions and Transgressions in *Vida* and *Quinceañera*

This chapter considers the importance of two dramatic visual texts, one television series and the other a film. In Starz's *Vida* (2018–2020), Emma Hernandez (Mishel Prada) and her sister Lyn Hernandez (Melissa Barrera) return to their childhood home to deal with the untimely death of their mother. Both women are estranged from their mother and each other. The reproductive decision-making narrative in *Vida*, specifically season 3 (episodes 4 and 5), illustrate the power of abortion positive narratives. While the entire show reflects a productive relationship between the power of representation and agency in the characters striving to be during a confusing and challenging time in their lives, the series also demonstrates the ambivalence surrounding Latina reproductive decision-making. Emma's abortion as an abortion positive representation highlights the ambivalent nature of women's reproductive decisions, providing a realistic view of the process of a medicated abortion without shame or fear attached to such decisions. In the independent film *Quinceañera* (dir. Richard Glatzer and Wash Westmoreland, 2006), Magdalena's (Emily Ríos) 15th birthday celebration is around the corner and as the preparations are underway, Magdalena learns she is pregnant. Magdalena's parents are a very traditional, religious, and working-class Mexican family, as such, her father, a pastor, forces her to leave home. Magdalena maintains her innocence-stating that she did not have intercourse with her boyfriend, Hernán (J. R. Cruz), and even though her mother is sympathetic, Magdalena finds solace in her great-uncle Tomás's (Chalo González) home. While this film is completely different from the other case studies here, however, it demonstrates the ways in which the expectations and life of a young woman revolve around notions of purity and virginity and how shame is represented as a way to ostracize her. Even though Magdalena maintains her innocence while she transgresses the traditional expectations, the film maintains a positive representation of a young pregnant Latina. The film attempts to recast the negative representations of teen pregnancy, focused on the mother not caring for her child or overall, the negative consequences of teen pregnancy. Instead of framing Magdalena's pregnancy as problematic and deviant, the film is careful to consider how, even though it is a difficult situation, Magdalena finds solace in her innocence and support from her extended family. While it is not clear by the conclusion of the film if Magdalena will have her child's father present, it is important to note that her parents and friends support her and demonstrate that by throwing her a quinceañera. Although the film shows some of the challenges Magdalena may face, such as lack of financial stability to support herself and her child, Magdalena and her family are portrayed as sympathetic towards the end of the film while at the same time, Magdalena's portrayal presents a positive tone for representing a young Latina facing an unplanned pregnancy.

Mi cuerpo. Yo decido: Reproductive Decision-Making and Social Justice

Favianna Rodriguez's work as an interdisciplinary artist, cultural strategist, and social justice activist signals another approach to reproductive decision-making through cultural production. In this last case study, I discuss and analyze Rodriguez's approach to reproductive justice through her artistic work, specifically two of her poster series that focus on reproductive decision-making. In her artistic work, Rodriguez uses poster making as one way to challenge and critique negative representations of women of color. In addition to her artistic work, Rodriguez has collaborated with reproductive justice organizations to offer workshops, for example, to further educate the public about reproductive injustices. In this chapter, my analysis of Rodriguez's prints and artivist work is contextualized within an exploration of the larger social, political, and historical relationship between Chicana/ Latina art and activism, as noted in the chapter on Teatro Luna.

CONCLUSION

All these cultural texts share the creator's shared intent in portraying a multifaceted Latina/x identity and reproductive decision making. These cultural texts look to shift audience and viewer perceptions as it related to heteropatriarchal notions of Latina reproductive decision-making. Though reproductive decision-making has been part of the literature in nearly every discipline, it has not been included as a stand-alone project that includes these specific case studies. The work analyzed in this study continues records experiences about Latina reproductive decisions such as infertility and abortion seldom represented. For example, now more than ever attacks from conservative organizations and politicians look to ban or limit reproductive rights, which disproportionately affect people of color and low-income communities. Understanding the nuances as it relates to reproductive decision-making beyond notions of pro-life or pro-choice are imperative to our discussion of access to reproductive rights, including the right to information and affordable healthcare Investigating reproductive decision-making in theater, television, and visual art adds a new dimension to the discussion of Latina reproductive decision-making.

NOTES

1. The bill, SB27, updates an existing law that requires fetal remains to be disposed of in a "humane" manner. The bill was under consideration for about two years by the Ohio legislature. WOSU.org. Accessed 12/29/2020. https://radio.wosu.org/post /gov-mike-dewine-signs-law-requiring-burial-or-cremation-fetal-remains#stream/0.

2. By reproductive decision making, I understand the term to mean the agency women have to make reproductive decisions, such as access to contraception, prenatal care or abortion. This term focuses on the ability for women, be it individually or collectively (with their doctor, partner, etc.) to come to identify what goals, actions to take. See Redshaw and Martin, 2011).

3. The Texas state bill also gives private citizens, including those who live outside of Texas, the right to sue a person they "reasonably believed" provided an illegal abortion in Texas.

4. I chose to focus on these three mediums because of the limited scholarship on Latina reproductive decision making in cultural texts.

5. See Suzanne Oboler (1995) and Marta Caminero-Santangelo (2007).

6. For this project, I am relying on direct quotations from Teatro Luna's unpublished scripts and descriptions from a 2009 DVD reboot of *S-e-x-oh!* at the 16th Street Theater in Berwyn, IL.

7. For an excellent discussion on the virgin-whore binary see Alicia Gaspar de Alba's (2014).

8. For this analysis, I rely on Season 1 of the series using Netflix. The series was first released in the fall of 2014.

9. The term heteropatriarchy is a social system that relies on the oppression of women and non-heterosexuals, since it derives its power through racist, sexist, and classist ideologies, which are perpetuated by normative beliefs and values (Butler, *Gender Trouble* 46). For the purposes of this project, the term will be implemented to define heteronormative representations of Latinas and womanhood as bound by binaries such as virginal mother/bad mother, or good woman/bad woman.

10. I will use the term *teatristas* (theater-makers) to describe Teatro Luna since their work is multifaceted and based on grassroots, and it includes not only devising, but set design, costume design, and sound editing for their plays.

11. See the work of Ana López (1993), Aída Hurtado (1998), Carolina Acosta-Alzuru (2017), Julee Tate (2007, 2018), Petra Guerra, Diana Ríos, and Stokes (2011).

12. More recently (2021, 2022), Argentina, México City and Colombia have decriminalized abortion.

13. See the work of Lisa M. Anderson (2008) and Kathy Perkins and Roberta Uno (1996).

14. Teatro Campesino emerged in the late 1960s as a grassroots ensemble focused on bringing theater to the people, specifically the farmworkers in California. Founded by Luis Valdez, Teatro Campesino served as a cultural arm of the Chicano Movement and relied on commedia dell'arte, Mexican carpa (tent/vaudeville) traditions to engage with topics such as racism and labor issues. See the work of Yolanda Broyles-Gonzalez (1999), Jorge Huerta (2000), and Luis Valdez (1990).

15. Parrish, Erin. *Lebrón, Lolita*. Vol. 2 2020.

16. Stern, Alexandra Minna, "Sterilization" *Keywords for Latino/a Studies*, eds. Deborah R. Vargas, Nancy Raquel Mirabal, and Lawrence La Fountain-Stokes. New York: New York University Press, 2017.

17. See the work of Alexandra Minna Stern (2015) and Elena Guitérrez (2008).

18. See Jude Davies and Carol R. Smith (1998), Elizabeth Arveda Kissling (2017).

Chapter 1

Teatro Luna and Reproductive Decisions in Theater and Performance

CHICANA/LATINA THEATER AND PERFORMANCE

In her groundbreaking work on Latina theater, *Latina Performance: Traversing the Stage*, Alicia Arrizón (1999) offers a reading of the Latina body in constant movement from the late 1920s to the contemporary period, focusing on Latina theatrical and performative accomplishments by artists such as Dolores del Río, Josefina Niggli and Milcha Sánchez-Scott, among others. She traces a genealogy of Latina performance to locate the multiple movements the Latina subject must embark-from Latin American aesthetics to Chicano movement to Chicana identity and performance art, Latinidad and queer representations.[1] Chicana/Latina theater and performance scholars such as Denise Chávez and Linda Feyder (1992), have spoken of the role of Chicana/Latina theater as a source of resistance and power as women of color artists. In the introduction to *Latinas on Stage* (2002), Arrizón and Lillian Manzor note that Latina theater replicates the intersectionality of Latinas as women of color in United States society.[2] It is in the tracing of Latina performance in between ethnic and Anglo women's performances that Arrizón and Manzor create a lineage of performances deeply rooted in social activism. The recovery work that Arrizón and Manzor undertook led to more scholarship on Chicana/Latina theater and performance, such as the work of Elizabeth C. Ramírez, Alberto Sandoval-Sánchez and Nancy Saporta-Sternbach, Linda Saborío, and Anne García-Romero.

More recently, the work of Anne García-Romero (2016) looks to the legacy of María Irene Fornes as a framework, and inspiration in the work of Latina

playwrights at the onset of the 21st century, including the work of Cherríe
Moraga, Karen Zacarías, and Quiara Alegría Hudes. García-Romero's work
also uses a genealogical approach by tracing Fornes' influence in the work
of Latina playwrights. In this light, reading women of color theorists and
Latina theater and performance offers an invaluable experience of understanding Latina representation. Like García-Romero and other scholars, this
case study seeks to elucidate the work of *teatristas*, specifically, Teatro Luna
(Chicago and L.A.). Teatro Luna's performances stage how Latina theater and
performance more broadly challenges heteropatriarchal constructions of the
body, specifically through representations of Latina reproductive decision-
making. Joanna Mitchell (2011) argues that Teatro Luna's work, specifically,
S-e-x-oh! (a section of it subject of this chapter) where the life-sized nude/
barely dressed photographs of the actress included in the 2006 staging, par-
tially decorated with words and drawings, added verbal and symbolic layers,
making the private thoughts of the women visible and legible (*Gestos* 124).
More recently, Maria Soyla Enriquez's 2019 dissertation on Latinx theater in
Chicago argues that Teatro Luna's work, along with other Chicago companies
like Teatro Vista, offer theater-makers and audiences alike social ties that
reinforce and trouble the demarcation of cultural boundaries and identity-
forming transactions for Latinx practitioners in the 21st century (iv). As such,
Teatro Luna's work seeks to not only challenge Latina narratives through the
scripts, but rather, their emphasis on the Latina body on stage makes their
approach to storytelling even more rich.[3] For this chapter, instead of relying
strictly on textual analysis, I will analyze performative elements of space,
movement, design, costume, and spectator gaze. Furthermore, I also rely on
my experience as a spectator for some of Teatro Luna's performances, specifically as an outsider/insider, offering a vantage point sometimes taken for
granted. While this is not an ethnography, I do rely on my observations and
to certain degree, my participation in some of Teatro Luna's workshops.[4] This
project examines live (recorded performances) of one of the texts and a close
reading of three vignettes. Teatro Luna "recreates" Latina identity through
their scripts and performances by unfixing reproductive decision-making,
unsettling oft-used stereotypes, like the overjoyed mother-to-be, the sultry
Latina, or the sacrificial mother.

Teatro Luna: Background and History

Teatro Luna, the only all-Latina theater collective still in existence in the US,
was founded in Chicago, Illinois in 2000 by Coya Paz and Tanya Saracho
as a grassroots ensemble focused on bringing Latina stories and experiences
onto Chicago stages. At the time of Teatro Luna's inception, and to this day,
ensemble members create and perform their and other Pan-Latinas' stories

through collective work. Teatro Luna was created as feminist theater collective with the aim of stewarding Latina stories and placing them on local and global stages. Seeing that their stories were not being told or they were told through oft-used stereotypes such as the domestic, the sexy Latinas or as pregnant teenagers, Paz and Saracho focused their work on original ensemble work. As Emily Klein (2011) argues, given the use of the semi-improvisational comic *carpa* form, there is an obvious link between Teatro Luna's brand of politicized Latina sketch theater and the groundbreaking work of El Teatro Campesino, as further made evident in their 2015 manifesto (114). During the first ten years of work, Teatro Luna created several original ensemble-based works focused on autobiographical experiences and community stories. Some of their early work (2000–2010) like *Generic Latina* (Phoenix Ascending Theater & Pilsen 2001), *Déjame contarte* (INTAR/ Storefront Theater, Chicago 2001), and *S-e-x-Oh!* (Chicago Dramatists 2006), focuses on multitude of Latina stories at the onset of the 21st century. Other original early works include *The Maria Chronicles* (Goodman theater, 2003), *MACHOS* (Chicago Dramatists, 2007), *Solo tú (*Chicago Dramatists, 2008) and *Lunáticas* (Chicago Dramatists, 2009).

In 2010, Teatro Luna was faced with a change in leadership and ensemble make-up. Paz and Saracho decided to move on to different projects, like directing and screenwriting. One of Tanya Saracho's first solo play after leaving Teatro Luna was *El Nogalar* (Goodman 2010), a commissioned adaptation of Anton Chekov's *The Cherry Orchard*. Saracho has gone to write and produce for HBO's *Looking* (2014–2016), and most recently, created and produced *Vida* (2018–2020) on Starz. Coya Paz is currently Associate Dean of Curriculum and Instruction at DePaul University Theater School, where is also the chair of the Theatre Studies Department. In 2010 and 2011 she adapted two plays, one by María Irene Fornés and the other by Anna Cara Mowatt, for the Alcyone Festival at Halcyon theater (Chicago). She is currently working as Free Street Theater's (Chicago) artistic director and has published, *Ensemble-Made Chicago: A Guide to Devised Theater* (with Chloe Johnston) (2020).

Some twenty years and several ensembles later, Teatro Luna expanded and redefined what is means to be a Latina theater collective. Under the leadership of Alexandra Meda and LizaAnn Acosta, Teatro Luna has expanded to include more women who identify as Pan-Latina and women of color in their ensemble. Furthermore, the ensemble collaborated with Chicana playwright and actress Diane Rodríguez by producing and directing her play, *Living Large in a Mini Kind of Way* (2012) and extending their circle to include Emilio Williams with *Your Problem with Men* (2013). After 2010, Teatro Luna created and workshopped several plays such as *Crossed* (2012) (which addressed immigration and immigrant experiences), *Generation Sex* (2015), and most recently, *Lovesick* (2017) and *The Times* (2018). Teatro Luna has also grown in location, expanding to the west coast as Teatro Luna West/ Teatro Luna Collaboration. During these last years, Teatro Luna has launched a robust travel component, focusing on universities and community centers and theater festivals abroad. Teatro Luna sought offers new and old ensemble members opportunities for development and leadership. Teatro Luna's approach to create a space out of necessity for Latinas and all women of color artists to tell their stories, create and play characters that are relevant and nuanced continues to evolve. As Klein, Joanna Mitchell, and Chloe Johnson and Coya Paz Brownrigg have argued, Teatro Luna's work gives voice to a desire for archetypal revisioning, by emphasizing semiautobiographical stories and placing diverse Latina bodies on stage "as a mode of refusing political erasure and representational homogenization" (Klein 115). As such, by expanding to Los Angeles, working collaboratively with other theater-makers like Diane Rodríguez and Emilio Williams, and collaborating with Audible to make *Talking While Female and Other Dangerous Acts* (2019), Teatro Luna in the 21st century aims to challenge preconceived notions of Latinidad in theater, performance, and beyond.

Teatro Luna's approach to storytelling relies on collaborative work in their writing process for their scripts. As they workshop their stories in groups, the ensemble members experiment with movement, sound, additional characters, or stylistic changes. Teatro Luna explores Latina issues with *teatropoesía*, a theatrical form scholar Yvonne Yarbro-Bejarano (1983) describes as "a collage of poetry, prose, music, dance and pantomime" (397). Once the stories are altered or seen differently, the group decides on the preferred approach. Each member then "try on" the same role to expand and explore more character possibilities ("History," teatroluna.org). As Johnson and Brownrigg argue in their text, ensemble-created work is largely a "repertoire event" . . . it is the result of a particular group of people coming together, making something together, and adjusting as they go" (xi). As such, a major component of Teatro Luna's approach is the use of their bodies during rehearsals/workshops and in performance. In 2015, Alexandra Meda and LizaAnn Acosta published the very first Teatro Luna Manifesto in *Gestos*. In the manifesto, Teatro Luna articulates and shares core beliefs of their ensemble practice and co-creative work as a Latina and women of color ensemble. In the manifesto, Teatro Luna articulates that they stand for intersectionality, embrace sisterhood and honor their feminist and social justice approach to theater-making (157–158). In line with other feminist theaters, Teatro Luna places their bodies and stories on the line through the act of writing and performing.[5] These vignettes interrogate Latina women, their bodies, and their sexuality, as a means of problematizing stereotypes. As Meda and Acosta argue in their 2015 manifesto about their process, "Teatro Luna started with the written word, and we will always launch projects with written story as a touchstone. However, we include the expression of story in the body, movement, gesture, image and sound as part of our aesthetic" (156). By insisting on placing a wide array of bodies on stage, be it brown, white, mixed race, large and small, Teatro Luna's work reconfigures notions of Latina performance practices in the 21st century and deploys theatrical strategies for Latina artists by challenging essentialized suppositions of Latina identity.

How does Teatro Luna's work, specifically three of their early plays, represent more nuanced Latina reproductive decision-making stories? Johnson and Brownrigg note in their book, "the practice of basing its [Teatro Luna's] work on real-life stories stems from the desire to present a fuller, more complicated vision for Latina lives, to disrupt stereotypical inventions and monolithic narratives that frame Latinidad and womanhood within narrow confines" (151). As such, by starting their stories with real-life experiences, Teatro Luna focuses on narratives that upend simplistic and stereotyped Latina images, like the sacrificial mother or the sexy Latina. Like reproductive justice organizations such as the National Institute for Latina Reproductive Health (NILRH), Teatro Luna's work frames stories and issues from the perspective of women of color. Stereotypes about women of color such as "teenage mothers," "welfare queens," or most recently, "immigrant mothers having anchor babies," in media have continued to circulate despite the fact that we have more Latinos behind the cameras and in writer's rooms. Critical to reproductive justice organizations is to disavow these negative discourses that blame and shame women of color by reframing and flipping the script, as Patricia Zavella (2020) notes in her work on reproductive justice organizations, like NILRH "deploy framing that incorporates strength-based narratives to motivate collective action, to define appropriate strategies of action, and to shape dominant discourses about women of color" (Zavella 39). Furthermore, as noted by activist-scholar Loretta Ross, reproductive justice is "the complete physical, mental, spiritual, political, social, and economic well-being of women and girls, based on the full achievement and protection of women's human rights" (2006, 14). As such, groups like NILRH seek to redefine the need for women of color to access the resources and services needed to control their reproductive decision-making. While Teatro Luna is not a reproductive justice organization by definition, their work considers their commitment to feminist theater and "a process that allows members to share the kinds of stories that might not be heard or acknowledged elsewhere" (Johnson and Brownrigg 152). Furthermore, by acknowledging lived details of Latina experiences in reproductive decisions, Teatro Luna's work as a culturally relevant vehicle highlights the importance of reproductive rights in Latina stories. Indeed, Teatro Luna's work raises awareness and conversations about the multiplicity of Latina lives beyond conventional notions of Latinidad and give voice and agency to women of color reproductive decision-making stories.

My intention in this chapter is not to analyze Teatro Luna's entire body of work since its inception, but to trace themes of reproductive decision-making in their early dramatic work, through a close reading of their texts, analysis of available videotaped performances, and my participation as a spectator.[6] Teatro Luna's plays, specifically *Déjame contarte* (2001), *S-e-x-Oh!* (2006, 2009), and *Sólo tú* (2008), give voice to experiences or silences at times unexplored, and explain thematic issues such as pregnancy and motherhood that still resonate with other women of color artists and 21st century audiences.[7] These specific plays fit within their larger body of work in that they were created collectively and are samples from the first ten years of their work that specifically focused on Latina experiences at the onset of the 21st century. For the purposes of this case study, these selected plays also include various vignettes that speak to larger conversations about Latina reproductive decision-making. Teatro Luna's work rewrites and challenges the glorification of oft-used images of the sacrificial mother or the overjoyed expectant mother by asserting the importance of reproductive decision-making in Latina lives.

Déjame contarte (*Let me tell you*) (2001) was the second devised play by Teatro Luna. The play confronts the results of the 2000 Census and what it means to be Latina/Hispana at the onset of the 21st century, beyond the limited information gathered by Census data or media portrayals of Latinidad such as the immigrant or domestic worker. *Déjame Contarte* premiered at INTAR in June 2001 and was remounted for a Chicago premiere at the Storefront Theater (dir. Alexandra Lopez) in February 2002 (http://www .teatroluna.org/hist.html). In this play, the vignette "Trapped" by Maria Vega, explicates the theme of reproductive decisions in abortion. *S-e-x-Oh!* (2006, 2009) premiered in 2006 at the Chicago Dramatists (dir. Coya Paz and Tanya Saracho). In *S-e-x-Oh!* (2006), the ensemble offered a humorous yet unapologetic view of Latina sexuality from a Latina/x perspective. "What I want to tell" tells the story of two women and their experience with maternity, one desires it while the other woman feels ambivalent. In "Cama-Camaleon," a woman recalls her experience at an abortion clinic. *Sólo tú* (2008) started as "Solo Latinas" readings in 2004, which evolved into a full-length play by Miranda González, Diane Herrera, Tanya Saracho, and Marisabel Suarez. It premiered in 2008 at the Chicago Dramatists (dir. Tanya Saracho). This play delves into Latina maternity and motherhood, specifically the vignette "It's never the right time" by Desiree T. Castro. This vignette talks about the protagonist, Chelly's unplanned pregnancy, and how she navigates that uncertainty. Given the specificity of these vignettes for this case study, I focus on closely reading the scripts, videotaped performances as made available, and my experience as a spectator for *S-e-x-Oh!* (2009). To discuss reproductive decisions in these examples challenges reductive notions of Latina identity in theater and performance. Furthermore, these texts offer an opportunity to examine debates surrounding reproductive decision-making, such as abortion, by framing them beyond ideological perspective as an individual choice or right. There are some questions to consider for this chapter: What have Teatro Luna's plays documented about reproductive decisions? In this way, ambivalence in reproductive decision-making illuminates the ways we create and recreate narratives to come to a fuller understanding of pregnancy and parenthood in works by underrepresented women.

Scenes of Ambivalence in Teatro Luna's Work

Chicana Feminist playwright Cherríe Moraga has explored narratives and metaphors concerning ambivalence in reproductive decision-making and its influence over our understanding of those experiences. Moraga further expresses a need for a queer *familia* by desiring motherhood and challenging biological kinship. Her memoir *Waiting in the Wings* (1997) demonstrates how fraught pregnancy is for queer women of color and that her early pregnancy triggered a sense of strangeness felt in her body: "Today I feel my hormones acting up, blowing me up. . . . I wonder if I am pregnant. I feel my body a stranger. I am without desire" (26). Moraga's texts illustrate the complexity women of color experience through pregnancy and motherhood. Contemporary feminist theater collectives like Teatro Luna further explore ambivalence and desire in pregnancy and parenthood.

Ambivalence can be defined as the coexistence, in one person of opposing emotions or attitudes. For the purposes of this case study, ambivalence can be defined as the character's possible opposing feelings or emotions related to reproductive decision-making, but also the tone and sense explicated through staging or use of certain movements in the actors. For example, in literary and media representations, pregnancy was seen as the most defining of female activities, causing women of all walks of life to feel obligated, to marry because they are pregnant, to keep an unwanted child because of socioeconomic reasons, or to feel conflicted as working mothers.[8] For most, ambivalence in reproductive decision-making is inevitable since it is a time in a woman's life that prompt changes in the body, mind, and life in general.

Ambivalence in pregnancy and motherhood as a painful is expressed by Miranda in the vignette "What I want to tell." *S-e-x-oh!* (2006, 2009) is a devised performance piece, organized in vignettes addressing the complicated connections between sex, gender, and the Latina body through monologues, dialogues, and songs. In "What I want to tell," Miranda and

Coya (two characters) address the audience and one another to express their contrasting views of pregnancy and motherhood. In the script it is clear that Miranda experiences pregnancy as an anxiety-filled period, like the emotion expressed in Audre Lorde's poetic voice. This is further made explicit by the actress' body on stage in the 2009 live performance at the 16th St. Theater in Berwyn, IL. Miranda exhibits anxiety knowing that pregnancy for her leads her to feel powerless over her body and her life, thus ambivalence is made evident through her vivid descriptions and explicit emotions. In the opening during the 2009 performance, the two characters are side-by-side, Miranda sitting, holding a tray with a bag of chips and dip, while Coya is standing. They are separated by a wooden frame meant to serve as a mirror, and stage lighting focused on each woman throughout the performance (2009).

Miranda subverts society's idealized view of becoming a mother through a frank description of her bodily experience. She says, "Why would anyone do this on purpose. . . . I hate being pregnant. There I've said it. I hate it from the pit of my gut and I am not exaggerating."[9] In the live performance video, Miranda accompanies these strong feelings with similar facial and bodily gestures. In the video, the actress that plays Miranda sits and fidgets with the bag of chips until she is able to open it, signaling frustration over her situation while the tone she uses is imbued with a tinge of sarcasm meant to elicit laughter from the audience.[10] Her descriptions and feelings are in opposition to *marianismo*, as Evelyn P. Stevens defines it, "the cult of feminine superiority . . . an infinite capacity of humility and sacrifice."[11] This cult attributes to women a moral and spiritual strength manifested as silent suffering and abnegation, two qualities absent from Miranda's experience of pregnancy.[12] Furthermore, this vignette also stresses the physical and psychological effects that pregnancy has on the characters. While neither actor is visibly pregnant on stage, Miranda gives voice to feelings of vulnerability and ambivalence, refusing to suffer physically and emotionally in silence.

Like Moraga, Miranda describes her ambivalence about her pregnancy in physical terms: "I can't eat anything because this fetus is picky and every time I put something in my mouth I get hot and then I start to burp and the next thing you know I'm puking out the window. . . . I'm being held captive by this fetus. . . . "[13] During this scene in the live video performance, Miranda starts to rip open the bag of chips and starts eating while visibly looking ill. Miranda's complaints vividly echo Shulamith Firestone's assertion that "pregnancy is barbaric. [. . .] Pregnancy is the temporary deformation of the body of the individual for the sake of the species."[14] Miranda's ambivalence, anxiety, and physical discomfort demonstrates physical powerlessness of subverting romanticized versions of pregnancy. As Kelly Oliver has noted in her work on pregnancy, choice, and film, *Knock me up, Knock me down* (2012), in some Hollywood or international films, "the focus is either the fetus and potential abortion or the maternal body, but not both" (90). In the live performance of "What I want to tell," Miranda's nonverbal expressions, such as disgust, demonstrate the physical effects of pregnancy in a way that sometimes gets seldomly expressed. By representing the potential pregnant body and the fetus in this vignette, the character represents ambivalence surrounding impending parenthood beyond focusing only on the fetus or an overjoyed pregnant person. Miranda's experience in this vignette, then, not only reveals changing attitudes toward pregnancy (being honest about how she feels) but calls attention to the persistent need for a public conversation that acknowledges women's differing experiences with pregnancy and challenges the shame felt or imposed of not wanting to be pregnant.

Implicit in this vignette is a rewriting of the glorification of social media motherhood. This trend is seen in today's renewed attention to celebrity pregnancies, social media's obsession with fit pregnancies, chic maternity clothes, and career women who can do it all, even as single parents. Miranda's pregnancy in the vignette effectively goes against the two-parent household, the father, mother, and child. Miranda presents an alternate view of pregnancy and single parenthood: "How about this? When I get up to walk my hips hurt, I'm always tired, I pee constantly, and to top it all off I'm single . . . "[15] Miranda makes sure that the social and economic tolls of the pregnancy on her psyche are not overlooked. Miranda is fearful of what a future without a partner would look like: "I lie awake at night trying to think of ways to explain to my daughter why Mami is not with Daddy. I lie awake at night wondering how I am going to pay for everything. How I'm going to manage working full time, paying the bills. . . . " ("What I want to tell" n.p.). The uncertainty in Miranda's words gestures towards her possible lack of choices in the matter. It is important to highlight, as literary critic Heather Latimer (2015) argues about notions of choice when defining reproductive "choices," "[choices] are always constrained by circumstances" (11). Miranda transmits to the readers and audience the anger, fear, and uncertainty of bringing a child into the world in the 21st century, despite her decision to keep the child. Emily Klein (2011) notes that the 2006 staging allows the bodies to be visually represented as contested sites, written and rewritten by society and Latina women themselves ("Spectacular Citizenships" 110). In this respect, the bodies on stage are represented by Latina women and they too transmit to the audience stories fraught with contradictions. Although Miranda never speaks about having an abortion or giving up the child for adoption, her words directly address the uncertainty of having a child and the ambivalence Miranda feels during this time of her life.

The vignette further develops the theme of ambivalence as something Miranda's daughter may experience, a "bridge between generations."[16] Miranda admits: "'She's [her daughter] gonna think that's ok [her father going out], she's going to find a man who goes out all the damn time and say, 'well my father did it.' That's jut [sic] how men are.'"[17] Echoing other women of color writers like Moraga, Teatro Luna's work, specifically through Miranda's story, creates a space in the line of women of color authors who have experienced ambivalence in motherhood as they confront/experience bringing their daughters into a patriarchal world.

In her memoir about pregnancy and childbirth *Waiting in the Wings*, Moraga finds strength in pregnancy and motherhood as something that she could create "beyond the confines of heterosexual family ties."[18] As noted earlier, Moraga creates a queer *familia* through her desire to become a mother and in that way she challenges biological kinship as it related to heteropatriarchal notions of a nuclear, heteronormative family. Cristina Herrera argues that Moraga's motherhood "affirms her commitment not only to Chicana women but to one woman in particular: her own Chicana mother, Elvira."[19] By helping to address strength and power in the experiences of lesbian pregnancy and motherhood, not only did Moraga's writing help bring her mother's voice into focus, but also shape other women of color theorists and playwrights to write and perform their experiences as women.[20] The alliance between Moraga, her mother and Teatro Luna's work lies at the core of the line of women of color who find strength and ambivalence in desiring pregnancy and motherhood.

Choosing to create a family on her own terms can be a site of empowerment and frustration for the other character, Coya, in "What I want to tell" of *S-e-x-Oh!* Heteropatriarchal discourses reinforce the belief that becoming a mother is a natural and desired choice while simultaneously assuming that all women have free will outside social processes to decide to become mothers or be childfree.[21] Undoubtedly, ambivalence in pregnancy and motherhood stems from women's experiences in navigating their experiences as daughters, caregivers, granddaughters and as women in patriarchal cultures. In the vignette, juxtaposed to Miranda's perspective, Coya's empowerment goes against traditional images of heterosexual women-centered images of the process of conception that are still prevalent in the 21st century, such as procreating with a male partner. In the live performance from 2009's staging, Coya spends the entire time standing next to Miranda, while the wooden frame separates them. Coya is also dressed in black with pink, wearing a headband. At times, she faces the wooden frame, using it as a mirror.

At the onset of the vignette, Coya emphasizes she wants a baby and that she loves babies. In the video performance, the actress sounds and seems upbeat while she describes how she and her partner have been trying to get pregnant with the help of their friend providing the sperm for conception. Part of Emily Klein's observation of Teatro Luna's 2006 performance rests on spectacularly performative inversions of the disruptive, raucous spirit that Yolanda Broyles-Gonzalez identifies as *relajo* when she describes the work of Teatro Campesino (103). Even when performing stories of pain and anger Teatro Luna employs the resistant, mocking mood of *relajo*, defined by Mexican philosopher Jorge Portilla as a "negation of required conduct" that "constitutes a subjective positioning of dissent vis-à-vis the dominant values of the social whole" (qtd. in Klein 103). Coya's decision to use alternative means to conceive challenges biological and essentialist assumptions about pregnancy and motherhood. In the video performance, Coya moves around and constantly looks at herself through the wooden frame separating both women on stage. There is joy in her voice while she describes how she and her partner are trying to get pregnant, but at the same time, the expressions on her face indicate a sense of fear and excitement for what's to come. Throughout the vignette, Coya touches her stomach while she describes her and her partner's experience getting pregnant. In juxtaposition to Coya's perspective, on the other side of the frame, the audience sees Miranda, sitting and progressively sounding more and more unhappy with her pregnancy.

Compared to Miranda, Coya reflects on not being able to get pregnant: "And if one more person (Miranda) tells me maybe I should relax and it would just happen, I am going to lose my mind. And If one more person (Miranda) asks me if I'm sure I really want to be pregnant, I am going to lose my mind" (n.p.). In the video performance, Coya visibly angry, reacts to past conversations perhaps with Miranda, while describing her experiences. As noted in the script, Miranda's name appears in parentheses, as a stage direction, to indicate a glance at Miranda on stage. Furthermore, once Coya is done telling us this, she turns around and starts doing yoga moves and the tone of her voice begins to settle down.

By seeing Coya and Miranda's monologues overlap in terms of pregnancy and maternity narratives, Coya's story reflects a more nuanced understanding of how women make sense of reproductive decision-making especially as it relates to larger conversations about what constitutes a family. During the climax of the video performance, both actresses begin to talk over each other, and their voices become more elevated as they try to express their emotions regarding their experiences. Coya defines her experience: "Thirteen months we've been trying. That's over a year I've been putting myself through this. . . . I'm trying so hard to be perfect. . . . I'm not used to this. My whole life, I've been really good at getting what I want. . . . No matter how hard I try I can't get pregnant. . . . "[22] In this example, the vignette offers an opportunity to examine queer reproductive decision-making in Latina cultural production. As the vignette ends, the tone changes, sounding less hopeful for Coya and for Miranda. At this point, both women stand up and shout in unison to the audience "I hope this kid is worth it," looking somber and with tears in their eyes as the lights fade. In this moment, both actresses interpret the last line in a similar manner even though throughout the vignette they experience different desires in motherhood and pregnancy. While the written dialogue did not indicate the two actresses should stand up, their simultaneous actions project strength and self-confidence in their approach to motherhood. These Latina narratives make it clear that focusing on individual experience is not enough to understand the complex ways in which women's experiences are structured by gender, race, sex, and class. On stage, Coya and Miranda use their physicality to shift and negotiate what it means to want motherhood or feel constrained by it, respectively, their bodily movement and perhaps directorial choices intended to give these characters space to express their frustrations and desires beyond feeling upbeat, cheery, or just frustrated.

Other women of color artists and playwrights have created characters who find ambivalence in pregnancy and motherhood. Migdalia Cruz's play, *The Have-Little* (1991) presents a similar understanding of pregnancy and motherhood as ambivalent. Lillian, the young Latina protagonist, lives with her abusive parents and gets pregnant by her drug-addicted boyfriend, Ricky. As the narrative develops, Ricky dies from an overdose and Lilian is left alone to navigate her pregnancy and ultimately her future motherhood. In contrast, Lillian's mom, Carmen, finds pregnancy and motherhood a disappointment, filled with pain because her husband left her, and she was unable to fulfill life goals. Carmen also indicates finding strength in relying on religious thoughts because she views a proper woman's role that of the virgin/martyr or saint. In the second half of the play, Lillian insists on keeping and raising the baby as a single mother, revealing that she has made a choice to change the mother-child relationship given her complicated experience as Carmen's daughter (118). The script demonstrates the gendered and racialized social structures that restrict women's life choices. Lillian and her mother are confined to their apartment in the Bronx and their lack of social mobility and marginalization that leads the young protagonist to feel ambivalent in certain aspects of her life throughout the play. As Marci McMahon (2013) discusses Diane Rodríguez directing Cruz's play in 2002, "The play's focus on Lillian's marginalization to domesticity, and the narrative's suggestion that young Latinas have few possibilities for transcending racial and gendered ideologies, led to Rodríguez's difficulty with directing Cruz's play" (176). McMahon further argues that despite the tragic narrative that leaves Lillian at the end of the play with a sense of hopelessness, Rodríguez sought to use stage lighting at the end of the play to signal a sense of optimism and not to perpetuate certain aspects of womanhood (178). Lillian does not only view or sense pregnancy as ambivalent in the script, but her pregnancy is also her response to her mother's and society's cultural expectations. Through her pregnancy, and ultimately in light of Rodríguez's direction and artistic liberties, the play does critique heteropatriarchal views of women's proper gendered and cultural roles. First, the play makes it clear that that Lillian and her mom have limited economic and social options in society and sets up Lillian's pregnancy as both a response to her co-dependent relationship with her mother and the abusive relationship with her father. Secondly, as McMahon argues, Rodriguez's approach to the play further illustrates the power of staging to navigate the narratives about Latina domesticity (173). Even though the play emphasizes Lillian's socio-cultural confinement in terms of expectations and her ultimate powerlessness, what McMahon highlights is the way Rodríguez sought to give Lillian's character and ultimately, Cruz's play, a glimmer of hope and "create ambiguity regarding whether or not Lillian's baby actually dies at the end" (178). Even though this play considers a Latina teen, pregnant and alone, the framing of Rodriguez's direction provides spectators with meaningful cues about Lillian's situation while at the same time, illustrating through staging that there is a sense of hope for Lillian or other young women like her. While the script points to a tragic narrative of confinement, it is important to highlight how audiences can interpret a script through directorial choices without completely glossing over gendered and social structures that restrict agency.

Challenging patriarchal authority and traditions in reproductive decision-making, Teatro de la Chicana, an early feminist theater ensemble born out of the Chicano Movement, depicts strength and ambivalence in pregnancy and choice in one of their plays, "So Ruff, So Tuff." The use of personal narrative in their theatre provides socio-historical contexts while at the same time it might have spurred more mobilization from spectators. Rudy and Rosie, two high school graduates and their Mexican mother, who wants them to pursue traditional professions: a low-wage, blue-collar job, and a stay-at-home wife, respectively. In an exchange between the three, Rudy discloses that he knows that Rosie got an abortion at fifteen. Their mother could not believe it and shames her for not being a virgin and "taking a life."[23] Rosie candidly and powerfully admits: "Abortion was my choice because I am not ready to give up my life to raise a child [. . .]."[24] Rosie's perspective demonstrates strength in deciding about her future, regardless of what her mother or brother brought to the table. By showing the readers that she is a young woman with conviction and with a different future than her mother's, Rosie's choice to terminate her pregnancy shows transgression in reclaiming her body and her future, evident in Moraga's memoir and the early of work of Teatro Luna. Rosie joins Lillian and other powerful protagonists in the lineage of women of color works to openly challenge traditional Chicano/Latino culture and traditions to find strength in their choices over their bodies.

Similarly, one of Teatro Luna's vignettes from *Solo tú* reflects ambivalence coming into pregnancy and parenthood despite hardship and pain. "It's never the right time" by Desiree T. Castro focuses on Chelly, who tells us about her experience with reproductive decision-making. The stage directions indicate that Chelly is in her room, folding baby clothes. Chelly's seemingly normal day-to-day activities play with domestic tropes. The stage directions indicate a restrictive representation of a woman's work in the home, but as the vignette progresses, the readers come to find out that Chelly felt confused and in disbelief about her pregnancy, because "it wasn't the right time,"[25] having ended her relationship, prompting her to further question her future. It is no surprise that her disbelief permeates her point of view, even though doubt sets the tone for the vignette. As the vignette progresses, Chelly's words emanate strength in her choice and in describing her experience as a mother: bluntly and vividly.

Chelly fears that she will not accomplish her future, goals like traveling and finishing school. After she takes an at-home pregnancy test, resulting in a positive result, Chelly goes to a clinic to confirm or deny, since as she says, "I want to make sure I'm not pregnant" (17). In indicating her disbelief even after several tests and going to a clinic, Chelly tells us that the smiling lady at the clinic told her that "the baby was a blessing and that God knows best" (18). As Chelly narrates her experience at the clinic she highlights the invasive and manipulating approach some real-life clinics take to convince women to rethink an abortion. Some states require abortion providers to provide ultrasound imaging for all women thinking about or seeking abortions.[26] Chelly goes on to describe the ultrasound and how the doctor pressured her to view the image and listen to the heartbeat: "She turned the screen toward me and said, 'look'" (18). After undergoing an ultrasound, confirming her pregnancy, she admits: "I did not want her [doctor] to see that I knew, that I now knew-that I was pregnant" (18).[27] Ultimately, based on her experience, Chelly finds strength in her process of coming into motherhood after revealing to her mom that she was pregnant. She admits that her mother was overjoyed though she expected quite the opposite reaction: "'I told you not to have sex . . . but now you have a beautiful baby growing inside you.'"[28] On the one hand her mother reprimanded her for having sex but on the other she agreed and "accepted the reason for [our] having sex; which is to become mothers. . . . "[29] In this example, Chelly's words speak to the wide-ranging dissonance that is made explicit in the ways in which Latinidad, and parenthood are presented as intertwined, as made explicit by her mother's comments. Chelly's mother scolding for having sex is in line with attempting to keep young women virgins until marriage per the virgin/whore dichotomy, while at the same time her mother revels in her future grandchild. This dissonance removes any agency from Chelly in potentially deciding whether she will keep the child. We can read this vignette as an indication of some of the naturalized concepts of femininity and maternity. As indicated, Chelly's mom's response is in line with stereotypes women fall into, mother/whore, in Latina/o popular culture. Furthermore, her reaction to the unborn child brings into the forefront Lee

Edelman's notion of futurity. Edelman argues that the child who does not yet exist represents the one figure that is always worth fighting for . . . because as a symbol of the future it is part of the logic of futurity (qtd. Latimer 148). Considering this, it is imperative for Chelly's mom to see her unborn grandchild as "beautiful" regardless of her initial reaction and Chelly's ambivalence toward her pregnancy.

Like Lillian and Miranda, Chelly also questions her identity as a single mother, but she uses those doubts and fights back against her child's father, and his abusive behavior: "It was the baby crawling over to Benito and hitting his leg that made him snap out of his rage and get off me."[30] In recounting this incident, Chelly expressed her humiliation and her strength in taking control of the situation by not allowing Benito to come near their son or her. Chelly tells us that after falling victim to her partner, he served her with a protection order and ultimately, she ends up as a single parent. Chelly also reveals to the readers that she thought about having an abortion but never told Benito or her mom. Thus, at the end of the vignette, Chelly gains strength from knowing that she needed to defend her child and herself, especially when she too lived a similar situation with her mother. Chelly's perspective changes toward the end of the vignette when she admits that she read a pamphlet the clinic gave her and it quoted a bible verse, persuading the reader to think about keeping the unborn child. It is clear in her story that the clinic's influence coupled with the role of religion as factor in influencing her decision to keep her child. Ultimately, it was her decision to keep her child but at the same time, her narrative demonstrates adherence to a religious experience that shapes perceptions of heteropatriarchal rhetoric anchored in the assumption that women have two options: mother/saint. At times Chelly shows ambivalence toward pregnancy and motherhood, but she becomes emboldened by her commitment to her son. Different from Lillian, Miranda, and Coya, Chelly's draws attention to women's reproductive decisions and takes into consideration varying degrees of circumstances, influences, and socio-cultural elements. These decisions, to have a child, not to or to consider other options like termination or adoption are not made in a vacuum.

Recently, Rachel Alpha Johnston Hurst published an edited anthology, *Representing Abortion* (2020). In this anthology scholars from across disciplines interrogated how abortion is visualized, heard, and felt. How we see and feel abortion in cultural representation such as film and theater speak volumes about how artists challenge heteropatriarchal dominance of images and descriptions about pregnancy loss or abortion. This anthology seeks to upend oft-used images outside of abortion clinics that continue to pervade everyday conversations about fetus-as-person and against reproductive freedoms. For example, Jeannie Ludlow's chapter on "abortion positive" representations in graphic narratives argues that examples such as an episode from *BoJack Horseman*, destabilize and exceed prochoice discourses when representing abortion experiences. Melissa Huerta's chapter on Teatro Luna's play, *Déjame contarte* elucidates this point because the vignette, "Trapped" complicates how we understand abortion and resist totalizing or universalizing these experiences within the pro-life versus pro-choice. Huerta argues that the protagonist in "Trapped," "draws on ambivalence in her decision and finds power and agency in her choice" (221). By drawing on Chicana theorists like Anzaldúa and her theorization of the *Coatlicue* state (a state of ambiguity for the mestiza, looking to empower herself and emerge more powerful), Huerta's analysis places Teatro Luna's work as part of a larger movement that uses art as a form of critique as it relates to reproductive decisions. As a polarizing issue across popular culture, politics, and in individual households, abortion as a subject can be relegated to the silences between couples, ignored or placing blame and shame on the woman having the abortion. Like Huerta argues, "Teatro Luna's work sheds light on the potential of ambiguity to create stories from lived experiences as Latinas, like pregnancy and motherhood. In both theatrical practice and in their creative work, Teatro Luna employs a reproductive justice framework" (226). Building on Huerta's approach to include how "Trapped" subverts the expectation of keeping a child after a rape.

"Trapped" from *Déjame contarte* is the first vignette that tackles reproductive decision-making with abortion in Teatro Luna's early work. The unnamed character in this vignette describes her experience dealing with pregnancy and abortion after being raped. The shame surrounding her rape and fear that the protagonist exudes in the script is made evident in the opening where female figures, as "Shadows," repeating "una senorita [*sic*] que no es virgencita, no sirve pa nada" (a young woman who is not a virgin is worthless),[31] circling a woman covered in a sheet. The unnamed woman sits up and embarks on a journey fraught with shame and silences as well, leading up to her finding access to an abortion provider.

The character subverts, just like Miranda and Chelly, the most traditional role for women: the overjoyed pregnant woman by feeling like her body will explode (n.p.). As Mary Lou Babineu notes in her chapter on Latin American women novelists in *Latina/Chicana Mothering*, nontraditional and controversial representations "represent significant transgressions of traditional conceptions of motherhood."[32] Chicana/Latina writers use the theme of the virgin/whore dichotomy to illustrate how it constrains women's selfhood.[33] For the character in "Trapped," the words of the "Shadows" resonate in her mother's words, as indicated in the stage directions overlapping the character's own words: "(*At the word mother's SHADOWS start chanting their corresponding lines in staccato: Una senorita/los hombres nomas quieren*

una cosita, etc.) [a young woman/men only want one thing]/My mother/
My mother whose words were like razor blades/My mother's nightmare had
become my reality/I had wanted so much for myself]" (n.p.). The character
hears and relives her mother's words attempting to navigate the painful experience of her rape and her decision to pursue an abortion. By expressing varying degrees of shame and anger throughout the vignette, the script makes it
clear that those conflicting narratives are in line with what Anzaldúa, Moraga
and Castillo have argued as it relates to the *marianista* cult of virginity so
prevalent in heteropatriarchal discourses, as well as the issue of going through
an abortion. The work of Teatro Luna, specifically these representations of
reproductive decision-making challenge gender stereotypes and give these
Latina characters agency.

As the unnamed woman in this vignette proceeds to secure money to have
an abortion, she continues to express her ambivalence toward everything that
has happened. While it might seem as though it is a bleak and stigmatized
representation of abortion narratives, it is important to note that it represents
reproductive decision-making outside of the scope of heteropatriarchal values. Through an abortion positive narrative, fear and shame that resounds
in the character's words mark this representation, it is presented as discrete,
yet public. It is meant to be staged and in public (entering the political and
religious realm) and it is also a private (relational) matter. Throughout the
vignette there are interjections from several segments of society, including
doctors who refuse to perform the abortion because she was too far along
or the police who tell her that she cannot report the rape because too much
time has lapsed. These interjections do not provide the unnamed woman with
any solutions or alternatives because at the end of the day, these segments
of society (systemic barriers) want the unnamed woman to give up and not
have an abortion. In the interactions with the members of institutions such as
the doctors and police, the unnamed woman is confronted with shame and
rejection, reinscribing the way in which public spaces continue to frame a
person's reproductive decisions within the contexts of political or religious
perspectives.

The vignette not only represents a woman's path toward abortion but it
also defies the image of the distraught woman, feeling regret or shame for
having an abortion. The private and relational debate happens between the
unnamed woman and her sister and in ruminations with herself. In this space,
she maneuvers through the ambivalence of her situation and at the end of
the vignette she declares, "My life had been given back to me. This is how
I was born on the operating table of an abortion clinic."[34] Coming to her
voice and declaring her sense of hope for a new future is an act of resistance.
Through voice, these characters express their context, conditions, and identity

as it relates to reproductive decision-making. As Gisela Norat argues in her work on Hispanic playwrights and maternal representations: "plays that raise awareness about life-transforming issues related to pregnancy and abortion . . . reposition female experiences from the private realm where silence, abuse and isolation continue to prevail and insert them in the public sphere in order to spur social change" (54). To underscore this in Teatro Luna's play, both the public and private come together in the script and eventual staging of the play challenging secrecy, shame, and fear surrounding abortion narratives. As such, by removing the compulsory pregnancy and birth from "Trapped," this vignette gives voice to women to tell their abortion positive stories by overcoming shame and silence.

Tanya's character in "Cama-Camaleon" from *S-e-x-Oh!* builds on "Trapped" by addressing a second experience of abortion in Teatro Luna's early work. "Cama-Camaleon" is a monologue that oscillates between self-reflection and stream of consciousness in the script. Tanya recounts her experience at an abortion clinic on the day of her procedure. The 2009 video performance features Tanya sitting in a pink chair, talking to the audience with a spotlight on her face. Ambivalence shows up in this vignette through Tanya's stream of consciousness, feeling that her choice to terminate the pregnancy is both positive and negative at the same time. Similar to the experience in "Trapped," ambivalence in "Cama-Camaleon" appears in the form of a first-person narrative, describing not only her presence at the clinic but also her feelings throughout the process, like Moraga's pregnancy and birthing account, making women's lived experiences even more visible. Tanya's description of the space expresses an ambivalent point of view: "I look around this little dressing room. [. . .] There is a bench-a locker. [. . .] What kind of stuff do people put in here? Lots of backpacks I'm sure. But maybe some briefcases too. Maybe. I mean, what am I doing here?"[35] In the 2009 video, the actress uses a lot of hand gestures while she describes her surroundings, including what the other people around her are doing. The descriptions and emotions in the script, although not directly referencing pregnancy or motherhood, make it clear that she feels conflicted, recognizing the physical and emotional toll. In a brief metatheatrical moment, she says, "This is going really fast . . . the woman walking ahead of me says . . . 'Were you in Generic Latina?' [a Teatro Luna show] . . . a sudden air goes up my robe and through my ass. . . . My spine freezes over. Now I get that glazed on look. [. . .] Asking me questions about the plays and acting. [. . .] I felt like I was being dismembered."[36] Tanya's expressions of ambivalence clearly bring dual feelings to the stage, symbolized by her descriptions and what is exactly happening. While she acknowledges her feelings, she is scrutinized, by those around her at the clinic, echoing what Norat argues about Hispanic playwrights such as Ana Istarú and Sara Joffré whose work "make headway toward raising consciousness about issues related to a primal experience shared by a significant number of the world's population" (43). By bringing these narratives into public spaces like a theater, Teatro Luna and other Latina playwrights unravel and upend traditional notions of Latinaness and womanhood directly related to compulsory reproduction.

In the 2009 video performance, Tanya stands up and goes in and out of her character to give voice the people around her, like the nurse or her partner. The actress not only switches her voice into another character, but she also accompanies this with distinct facial expressions, reacting to what is occurring to the character. Different from the unnamed woman's experience in "Trapped," Tanya's descriptions of her experience are tinged with humor, connected back to Miranda and Coya's experiences in *S-e-x-oh!* Humor is one of Teatro Luna's signature styles and as such, the experiences noted in these examples use it to transmit to their audiences and readers a viable way of consuming the story. Instead of staying in the realm of silence or humiliation, these difficult reproductive decisions are represented through humorous and explicit body movements on stage. In the 2009 video, once Tanya sits back down, she takes out a string that looks braided and says to the audience: "I guess we sit for a while until a girl asks me, 'what are you doing?' I look down and I've made this . . . this necklace from the laces of my robe. God, talk about defense mechanism" (n.p.). Once Tanya looks down and realizes what she's made, her face and tone of voice changes, reflecting a solemn felling, especially as she starts to look around the room and notice the other women there with her: "I look around. I must be the oldest one in here. Oh, no. There are 4 African American girls and one Latina, two with me . . . " (n.p.). By imbuing the scene with solemnity as she comes to terms with where she is and who is the room, the actress gives physicality and voice to feelings of ambivalence in terms of her decision to have an abortion. The character sounds matter of fact, but in the video performance, she appears shocked to hear what the other women around her are saying. A voice over calling her name startles her as she leans her body back in the chair and spreads her arms out as if she were on a hospital bed. Tanya's detailed ethnographic observations of the waiting and procedure room further leads the readers/audiences to see ambivalence take shape. She says, "'Ok, now it was hitting me. [. . .] They juice me up and as I'm going out of it-floating on my last few doubts-I hear 'Lucy tells me you're a performer. Do you know any songs?' [. . .] and I'm out.'"[37] The ambivalent feelings Tanya expresses throughout, leading up to the start of the procedure emerge as something real, both visible and invisible in her lived reality in conjunction with distancing the viewer/reader from the procedure. More importantly, by writing and staging reproductive decision-making, Teatro Luna seeks to insert more nuanced representations of pregnancy, motherhood, and loss beyond binary notions of pro-life and pro-choice.

As writers, performers and directors of Latina theatre, Teatro Luna has consistently negotiated dominant scripts of Latina reproductive decisions, including pregnancy and loss. Although these representations are less commonly staged, they represent Latinas questioning heteropatriarchal notions of maternity and motherhood by asserting their reproductive decision-making beyond notions of choice. In repositioning their narratives on stage, beyond the privacy of the doctor's office or just on the script, these stories openly challenge heteropatriarchal narratives about the sacrificial mother or the overjoyed expectant mother. By placing Latina reproductive decision-making stories on the page and on stage, Teatro Luna affirms their principle of storytelling beyond the written word, to include expressions of the body ("Manifesto," 156), especially from narratives surrounding reproductive decision-making. By including these vignettes in their early work, Teatro Luna suggests that to effect change, these reproductive decision-making stories must be told and staged to shed shame surrounding difficult emotions and decisions. As in the next case studies, the transformative power of giving voice to one's story allows for more nuanced representations of Latina reproductive decision-making, helping underscore the complexity of Latina identity in cultural texts.

Beyond the specific examples from Migdalia Cruz and Teatro de la Chicana (Teatro Raíces), there are other Chicanx/Latinx plays and performances that center the role of the female body in relation to womanhood and pregnancy and motherhood. Works by Evelina Fernandez, Anne García-Romero, Lisa Loomer and Virginia Grise, and Irma Mayorga, to name a few, challenges Latina representation about what it means to negotiate the embodiment of womanhood as it concerns becoming a mother. Chicana *teatrista*, Evelina Fernandez began her work with Teatro Campesino and Teatro de la Esperanza. Her first solo play, *How Else am I supposed to know I'm still alive* (2005) sheds light on reproductive taboo issues through a more comical approach. In it, Angie and Nellie are life-long Chicana friends, in their 40s-50s. Angie faces the possibility of an unwanted pregnancy while Nellie, her best friend reminisces on her past experiences with infertility. Fernandez draws on humor, working-class life and lived experiences of middle-aged Chicanas to speak to how to deal with pregnancy, specifically through a more comical and lighthearted context. Angie decides to have an abortion but as she ponders when she will have it:

> Angie: I don't know yet. I still gotta make all the arrangements. (Pause) Nellie, when you say you always wanted a baby, you mean before don't you? You don't mean you still want one now?

Nellie: [. . .] I had this hole in my heart . . . (She sees if she still feels it). Yeah, I still feel it, so I guess I still want one . . . why?

Angie: Because, I don't want this baby, it's true. And I wouldn't have it for any man . . . but you're my best friend and if you want this baby, I'll have it for you.

[. . .] And I couldn't have done it [raising her 9 kids] without you. You're like my sister. I want to do this for you. (Perkins and Uno 166)

Unsure about the proposal, Nellie agrees, and they start planning, but Angie realizes that she just may be off her menstrual cycle with flu-like symptoms; in the end Angie realizes that she was not pregnant. By representing reproductive decision-making in this context, Fernandez's play demonstrates other Chicanx characters navigating the intricacies of potential pregnancy. In the case of Angie, there is hesitation and certainty in going forward with the pregnancy, while for Nellie, she demonstrates ambivalence based on her pauses and in conflicting feelings revealed in her movements, as seen in the previous exchange. She then reacts to Angie's false pregnancy: "Here we go again! (Pause. She sits. To herself). There goes my baby . . . (to God). You shit" (Perkins and Uno 167). Furthermore, this play also represents a collective approach to also understanding Chicanidad based on these two characters' love for one another. These examples give a hint that neither Angie's nor Nellie's feelings about pregnancy and abortion are black or white, although we have very little exposure to their experiences.

In *Santa Concepción* (2008), playwright and scholar Anne García-Romero takes on the sexuality and spirituality dilemma with the two-act play about two sisters and their bed-ridden mother, one sister infertile and convinced that God will make her the next Mary and the other, complete opposite, lustful and always looking forward to some sexual satisfaction. The spiritual-sexual tensions abound in this play, focused on upending and questioning heteropatriarchal notions of womanhood, like sexuality and fertility and at the same time, shuddering tensions between the spiritual-sexual dimensions of religion. Linda Saborío's (2012) study on Latina embodiment in Latina theater argues that Garcia-Romero's play dramatizes the imposed hierarchy of genders in religious institutions and within the context of families and consequently, nations. In *Santa Concepción*, the two sisters, one representing sexual containment (good) and the other of sexual liberation (bad). Furthermore, the play examines the ways in which repression and expectations represent the oft-mentioned characteristics of females as virgins and chaste. Connie, the well-behaved sister, wants to understand why she is infertile and keeps praying to God that she will get pregnant as a "second" annunciation of a virgin pregnancy. Meanwhile, her sister, Aurora can bypass getting pregnant despite her sexual liberation because she engages in the "power of dark and magical jungle rituals" (35). Both Connie and Aurora are constantly egged on by their mother to marry, especially Connie to Reynaldo. Connie decides to marry Reynaldo and Aurora, confused by her desire for her sister's husband, decides to enter the convent. At this point, the sisters are in a conundrum and exchange places, making it especially difficult for Connie. For Saborío, Connie and Aurora seek to relocate their difference in myths and *milagros* (miracles), thereby working within the system to change it (121). As such, the two characters end up having something they had once desired, Connie, a baby (claiming it is a miracle from God) and a space in the convent and Aurora, happily married to Reynaldo. Both women, specifically Connie defy cultural norms and expectations to become a happily married woman and then a mother. Connie looks for answers in nature and in her faith, but she finds herself also struggling to navigate what is expected of her as a woman of reproductive age. For Aurora, her mother wants her to find a husband so she would calm down and accept her role as a future wife and mother. Once Aurora returns from the convent, realizing that she was unfulfilled in that space, she runs into Reynaldo and he is smitten by her new look, demure, saintly, and due to his obsession to be with a virgin. Aurora decides that she will play the role and wants to become a "proper" "good" Latina and marry Reynaldo. Something completely different than what he experiences with Connie and on discovering their relationship, Connie begins to question her beliefs in God and her spiritual connection. Much like the good woman/ mother figure, La Virgen de Guadalupe or the virgin Mary, Connie miraculously gives birth to a baby girl, defying her expectations, as an infertile woman, to a mother through a miracle, however she is further praised for actions as a mother, and at the same time she is seen with authority given her status as "Santa Concepción."

Playwright Lisa Loomer illustrates the theatricalization reproductive decision-making and motherhood. Through a comedic lens, Loomer explores infertility in *Expecting Isabel* (2005). Nick and Miranda are married, he is a sculptor and Miranda writes greeting cards. When Miranda was about to turn 40, Nick asks: "You know what I'd really love?" . . . "A child" (10). In the opening monologue, Miranda addresses how she feels about her upbringing and childhood, then she realizes that she "Hadn't done much" (10). This apparently is the first airing of this subject, for this particular couple. For months, they try to conceive. Then, the infertility specialists enter, the support groups (laden with grotesques) materialize. In Act 2, their marriage is now strained yet they explore adoption. Unfortunately, Nick's family does not offer useful advice for the couple and their marriage runs the strength test leading to more strife. As the couple navigates their reproductive choices, one of the most interesting reactions to their process of becoming parents involves Nick's mom, Yolanda: " . . . but for us this is a sin! . . . Let me tell you something, if God wanted you to have a kid, you would have had one by now" (24). As Miranda navigates the infertility roller coaster process, she is confronted Yolanda's hurtful comments, but also the expectation that she does not fit the norm in terms of who should and can become a mother. Miranda believe that she might be punished for not having children, confirming that she had an abortion in the past. In connecting these two elements as cause and effect, Miranda plays into the narrative of shame and blame surrounding abortion. For as scholar Myra Mendible (2016) argues in her edited volume on shame, "to 'feel' shame is to participate in a cultural economy of prescribed behaviors and expectations, cued responses and decodings [. . .]" (10). Drawing from Erving Goffman, one type of shame he associated with stigma was connected to immoral character.[38] In judging Miranda, Yolanda places blame on her for not having a child but judges her for having the abortion prior to her meeting Nick. As such, Miranda becomes the object that is irredeemable in Yolanda's perspective. In the shadow of shame, Miranda and Nick go through multiple tests, medications and they find out that the problem is Nick's sperm. Once the fertility specialist recommends IVF, Miranda understands the enormity of the process, be it the medications, egg retrieval and embryo transfer, and if successful, a pregnancy: " . . . I was taking a lot of different hormones, so . . . you could say it became a source of conflict with my job" (27). In a comedic manner, Loomer's play delves into the intricacies of reproductive decision-making beyond the confines of the couple or individual.

Miranda writes greeting cards and writes something blunt and not "sympathetic" according to her boss, but she is unable to justify why she wrote what she did. Unfortunately, she was fired because she also asked to leave more than six times in the past two weeks for "dentist" appointments. This scene is representative, albeit comically, of situations where a person's reproductive decision-making and the physiological and psychological consequences of that interferes with the capitalist and neoliberal notions of individual responsibility and work. The multitude of doctor appointments during fertility treatments without justifying medical leave goes against the notion of responsibility and being a dedicated worker. Now unemployed, Miranda concentrates on taking care of herself but Nick, as a full-time artist, will not be able to take care of the family since he was relying on Miranda's income. Unfortunately, the couple's relationship troubles continue, and they end up in a support group for infertile couples. As the story progresses, we find out that in the fourth round of IVF, Miranda produced nine eggs and were elated to find out that they have embryos, but they did not survive the waiting process. Throughout the play, the couple navigates different spaces, both public and private as they make sense of their reproductive decisions. As much as Nick wanted to have a child, he was not expecting the ups and downs and the cost of going through having a child beyond the confines of a couple's bedroom. Miranda, on the other hand, bore the grunt of it because she was under pressure to get pregnant and find alternative ways of doing so. After the doctor's appointment Miranda reveals to Nick that she wants to keep trying but he is not willing to continue because they already owe a lot of money for the procedures. Miranda wants to keep trying and says, "you're going to tell me what to do with my body??" (33).

In the second act, Nick picks up the story where Miranda left off, and directly tells us that he and Miranda decided to part ways for now as Miranda explored other ways of becoming pregnant. As the two explore their options and think about their future together or not, Nick gets a job and Miranda learned more about sperm donation. At the end of the day, they decided they want to have a child together but that they would adopt. As they make this decision, they are further confronted by their respective families, with judgment and questions surrounding the decision to adopt. These different snapshots that Loomer sketches about varying degrees of reproductive decision-making through the ups and downs of navigating infertility. While the play does enter these conversations through the lens of two fictional characters, the focus is a heteronormative, cisgender and white dominant narrative.

Despite this typical narrative, the play does offer moments of conversation surrounding a woman's reproductive decision-making through infertility. By addressing an innately personal subject like infertility and the roller coaster ride that that process entails, Loomer's play presents a sanitized yet candid framing of reproductive decision-making when there are other elements in place to permit the choosing a path, be it remain childfree, have a child, adopt, try IVF, or have an abortion. While these representations do matter, what is missing are stories or examples of Latinx/Chicanx stories about reproductive decision-making. In the second act, once Miranda and Nick decide to adopt, they encounter a potential adoption and come to find out that the young birth mother chose another couple and then another woman never followed up on the adoption. Both women, while not specified in the character description or through dialogue or details are women who are young or working-class. These women then while they do not stray from the heteronormative white dominant narrative, they are focused on two women that decide to give up a child for adoption because of their socioeconomic circumstances. By expanding on issues like prohibitively expensive reproductive health care, it also addresses, albeit on the surface the varying degrees of womanhood and motherhood. Loomer's play does include an example of this context but through the lens of a stereotypical, hyperfertile, and single-parent Latina, Lupe, who is pregnant but needs to give up her child for adoption because she cannot take care of another child. Miranda and Nick meet with her about adopting her newborn and she agrees that they are the right couple for adoption. Lupe admits that she is in over her head with two kids and a third on the way while attempting to go to school: "Look—I just want to do what's right, you know? . . . " (53). Unfortunately, she decides not to give up her child because her "church" convinced her baby's father that what Lupe was doing was wrong and that she should keep the child.

Within the context of the larger discourses around maternity and Latinx representation, Loomer's play stands out in that Lupe is racialized through the language coming from her television, her name, and where she lives, East Harlem. Furthermore, it is made evident that because of the ways in which religious discourses prevail in predominantly Latinx communities and households, Lupe is left without executing her decision to give up her child for adoption. As such, the notion of reproductive decisions are not available for Lupe or at least the notion of having an option to choose something to improve the life of the unborn child. By representing how discourses surrounding what is wrong and right when it comes to a mother's right to decide what to do with her child is predicated on the religious and patriarchal norms of where and to whom the child belongs (to), then we are faced with a restrictive notion of what it means to be a woman and the control one has over the decisions she makes for the betterment of her children. Moreover, this moment elucidates the problematic nature of notions of "choice" for women of color and women coming from economically struggling families. Miranda on the other hand, even though IVF and adoption are extremely expensive, she is able to access these options. Meanwhile, someone in Lupe's situation might not have had an option to decide the number of children to have or when to plan her pregnancies or her readiness for the children. This is a perfect example of the emotional and social repercussions of having to choose for someone that autonomy in reproductive decisions are not theirs to have. Here is where the reproductive justice framework redefines what it means to have a choice, linking larger systemic problems that placed a character like Lupe in this situation to larger issues such as poverty, economic justice, access to women's health care, etc., and move beyond the singular focus of abortion.

As noted, reproductive justice calls for women of color organizations and allies to redefine and broaden the scope of reproductive rights as a collective matter, away from neoliberal structures and imperatives that place the onus on individuals. That is in the case of Loomer's play, we can read Lupe's decision to not give up her child for adoption as passive because she was influenced by her religious beliefs and the institution of religion. Furthermore, within a context of reproductive decision-making, Lupe should have the right to access to reproductive health care, an abortion, to have children and to parent those children. For Miranda, access to having a choice to become a mother relied on her right to personal choice, but also because of her privilege as a white, blue-collar working woman with more cultural capital and access. At the conclusion of act 2, Miranda and Nick consider life without a child, defaulting to the narratives their parents gave them, "a sign" that they were not supposed to have children (58). Just as they were settling into new jobs, their adoption social worker, Julia, calls and lets them know that there is a baby up for adoption. Both Nick and Miranda are overjoyed to have the opportunity to adopt become parents.

In 2017, Lisa Loomer's play, *Roe* premiered at Arena Stage in Washington, DC, on the heels of Donald J. Trump's inauguration. Loomer's play drama-tizes the parallel lives of real-life plaintiff, Norma McCorvey ("Jane Roe"), Sara Weddington, and Linda Coffee, the lawyers who argued the case before the Supreme Court in 1973. The play provides a plethora of characters that provide readers and audiences with perspectives from every side of the debate. Loomer's play moves away from the legal argument and places in the public sphere, allowing for stories of women surrounding the decisive case to be told.

The play sheds light on deepening crisis over abortion access then and more so now given the various restrictions and legislation passed in certain states to restrict access to reproductive healthcare, including abortion. While the play is about the stories surrounding the Supreme Court case, Loomer's play places McCorvey, Weddington, and Coffee front and center to develop a compelling narrative about the impact of the case for these women. As Loomer describes the play to Chicago Tribune's theater critic Chris Jones in anticipation of the Goodman Theater's opening, "One of the things this play does is show how the issue has been used. People have used this issue for their own political gains, and this is why it is important and a theatrical chal-lenge to actually hear the damn case" (Jones n.p.). Like Miranda and Nick in *Expecting Isabel*, Loomer's Norma and Sarah address the audience/readers directly to discuss their perspectives and how they contradict each other.

Chicana scholars and artists Virginia Grise and Irma Mayorga's *The Panza Monologues* (2014) was originally conceived in 2004 while they worked together in San Antonio, Texas. Grise and Mayorga documented the experiences they had and overheard while working at Esperanza Peace and Justice Center. They drew on these stories and created a solo performance piece that evolved into *The Panza Monologues*. Their work draws on the monologue-driven drama and performance of other Latinx/Chicanx voices, including Coco Fusco and Nao Bustamante, among others. Such work places the female body front and center that bridges the public and private spaces. The bodies of these performers are exposed, and they become the primary sources of representation, interpretation, and intervention. For Grise and Mayorga, the panza (belly) is a physical reminder of how body image shapes experiences and perceptions for all women. In the performance and in the text, the panza represents various things, including life and the core of experiences. In the narrative, we learn about the origins of the panza through the story of a goddess, for example, to traumatic coming of age stories, relationships and experiences that focus on women's relationships to their bodies, both in private and public spaces. The varying vignettes display scenes related to body image and shoes, fitting into that pair of jeans or anxieties about being pregnant or having an abortion, all to make connections about health and body image in the Latinx/Chicanx community and beyond.

Cherríe Moraga and Gloria Anzaldúa advocate the necessity for "women to act in the everyday world . . . [and] perform visible and public acts" (217). Grise and Mayorga's collection of vignettes along with the performances, explicitly make visible the way heteropatriarchal discourses affect the female body. Rich in humor and sadness, resistance and acceptance, the monologues reveal how the panza connects to everything as situated within the context of Latinx/Chicanx experiences, thus providing readers/audiences an alternative way of seeing Latinx/Chicanx womanhood. For theater scholar Tiffany Ana López, "theatre intensifies communication and heightens one's ability to come into awareness" (xv). As such, Grise and Moyorga's work "affirms that women's experiences are worthy of sharing as the subject of art and merit documentation within the archive of public discourse" (xv). For the writers and performers, Grise and Mayorga, they articulate a "panza politics," anchored in consciousness that " . . . can materialize forms a crucial step toward resistance, enablement, and change" (xxxi). The vignette, "El vientre" (the womb), important to the present study, discusses a woman's abortion. Like many of the other vignettes in the collection, "El vientre" refers to the various markers of excess and deviation from the norm that marginal bodies experience, womanhood and latinidad. Vicki, Grise's persona, claims her identity as Tejana/Chicana, and becomes the medium through which the collective memory of her community is performed throughout the monologues. Scholar Dorinne Kondo explains in "Bad Girls: Theatre, Women of Color and the Politics of Representation": since avantgarde theater is in the margins itself, it has functioned as a space and a medium for women of color to develop performance art. "The stage is the place where we can be 'bad girls,' to invoke Donna Summers, not as 'sad girls' but as women of color daring to be outspoken and outrageous, uniting to fight the sources of our common oppression" (64). This example raises questions about standards of womanhood in the US, how they relate to race, and how Latinas' realities fit or don't fit within these constructions of womanhood. As Lynn Miller, Jacqueline Taylor, and M. Heather Carver explain in the introduction to *Voices Made Flesh: Performing Women's Autobiography*: "women's autobiography is the story of resistance to the disembodied, traditionally masculine that presents an 'universal subject,' whose implicit denial of skin color, gender, sexual orientation (other than heterosexual), and economic disparity constrained many women as 'others' with no voices or physicality" (4). Thus, autobiographical performance facilitates the gorda and woman subjectivity, living in a space that oscillates between spaces where their identities intersect. Representations of Latinas mostly fall into one of two stereotypes: respectable, sacrificing mother or sex bomb. In *The Panza Monologues*, Grise's body lends itself to the voice and memories of members of her community, and at the same time represents the multilayered, multiracial, multicultural self. As a result, these three performances expand the genre of solo autobiographical Latina performance.

In "El Vientre" ("The Womb") the words presented on the page and in the stage directions make it somber if we compare to some of the other vignettes. Vicki sits on a chair center stage with her back to the audience. She opens her legs wide, and bends back, as if she was at an appointment with her OB/GYN and had just put her legs in the stirrups. The language in the *teatro-poesía* reflects, how she tried, without success, to provoke a natural abortion and had to resort to a medical one. Like the other examples here, *The Panza Monologues* honors the voices of a silenced majority whose histories have been excluded, erased, and contorted and points to a potential to remake the world through cultural production, specifically as it relates to womanhood and embodiment. The poetic voice says "sedated. alone . . . hands on my *panza*. holding onto you . . . " (78). The poetic voice opens about her abortion after she fails to self-abort using alcohol and matter-of-factly, she indicates that she felt regret. While it may seem as if the poetic voice faced an impossible situation after self-harm, it is evident that the process of aborting, be it through self-harm or medicated ultimately was something that she wanted to do. While the context of the pregnancy or abortion are not revealed, there is an ambivalent tone surrounding her reproductive decision-making, especially as she recounts hitting herself and then proceeding to have an abortion. If we read in between the lines, it is possible that there are social pressures and requirements to become pregnant or stay pregnant regardless of the woman's perspective, but we can also infer that she might not be ready to become a parent at that moment. Much like we will see in the work of Teatro Luna, the ambivalence shared by the poetic voice with regards to reproductive decision-making reflects the divergences between expectations and the reality of motherhood. The visibility of these narratives coupled with the embodiment of teatropoesía through the actor reveals the embodied stories of reproductive decision-making divided between responsibility to the self and to others. In "El vientre," there is a divide between how the poetic voice feels about her situation and why she prevented her pregnancy from continuing while at the same time speaking to her *panza* in a loving manner. Here the body of the story is told also through movement as indicated in the stage directions revealing that the knowledge of the body in performance and beyond is legitimatized, especially as we talk about notions of reproductive decision-making for women of color. The narrative of womanhood and reproductive decision-making emerge with in the context of the language implemented in the text as well as the discussion that can exist around the performed text.

Most recently, in *Encuentro: Latinx Performance for the New American Theater*, editors Trevor Boffone, Teresa Marrero and Chantal Rodríguez historicizes and documents Encuentro 2014, one of the largest national Latinx theater festivals and convening of Latinx theater artists and scholars in over 20 years. The gathering was made possible by the Los Angeles-based Latino Theater Company (LATC) and the Latinx Theatre Commons. This edited volume presents six new works presented at the convening, including works such as *La Esquinita, U.S.A.* by Rubén C. González, *Patience, Fortitude, and Other Antidepressants* by Mariana Carreño King, and *Premeditation* by Evelina Fernández, to name a few. These works represent a variety of aesthetics, dramatic structures, themes and from distinct backgrounds. Specifically, Carreño King's play focuses on relationships, family dynamics and self-preservation. This full-length play, unpublished, sets in motion a collective of women characters trapped between their personal desires and societal expectations. According to Latin American theater scholar, Beatriz J. Rizk, who wrote the critical introduction to the play, Carreño King's work, based on Federico García Lorca's *Yerma* and harkening back to Estela Portillo-Trambley's *The Day of the Swallows*, Patience . . . "highlights and reinforces the female tradition but also denotes that, despite significant changes, progress has been slow" (171). The basic storyline centers on an infertile woman who longs for a child, like *Santa Concepción*, unable to fulfill her desire, along with other women confronting sexism, police brutality and homophobia. Isabella, Carreño King's protagonist, escapes the world she lives in, one that positions women who are in a loving marriage, procreating, to enter the world of art. Isabella cannot escape her situation since she is she is supposed to stay home, be happy and proceed to procreate. Her escape is painting, reminiscent of Frida Kahlo's life. Isabella's paintings are her creations and function like extensions of her personality-they are titled "Fortitude, patience and the unfinished, Bella." In the play, Isabella struggles to navigate the conventional marriage expectations, such as staying home and taking care of future children. She laments the things she could have done in scene 2 when she says, "I thought with him [Juan] I would have a better life. . . . I thought maybe I'd become a great painter and travel the world and drink wine from his mouth on rooftops overlooking infinity" (191). Isabella feels a void in her life and through her artwork she can have these conversations and consider the reasons why she ultimately wants a child is to not to feel alone. As the play progresses, she encounters more pushback from her husband, Juan, and his family, for Isabella to be content with her life and have children, however, Isabella becomes increasingly frustrated and begins to verbalize her desires. "I can't anymore. I haven't said anything for two years! . . . Because I want to be kissed and desired by my husband? Because I want to be touched? Does that make me a whore? You [to Juan] are the one with the problem, not me. You're the one who can't get it up!" (250). Juan proceeds to slap Isabella and Victor pushes Juan and he loses his balance and falls, causing him to not wake up and end up in the hospital. There, Isabella and her paintings, Patience, Fortitude, and Bella are there with her at the hospital, next to her husband, contemplating what to do next since he is stable but not awake, in a coma. Bella goes ahead and pulls the plug on Juan's breathing machine, to which Isabella says she killed her child, but Bella reminds her that she has yet to finish painting her. In this contemporary tragedy, Isabella's paintings are mirrors to her subconscious and through these she can break free from Juan's control on heteropatriarchal discourses around womanhood and reproduction. Even though she loses her husband, Isabella regains her freedom to continue painting and pursue other things without the pressure of marriage and future children. Her painting, *Bella*, remains unfinished and it becomes the driving force for Isabella to pursue her goals as a woman, a painter, and childfree. In this respect, Isabella is affirming her life decision to pursue her desire to continue painting and look forward to possibly having children or not in the future, without the pressure of the conventions of marriage and procreation.

Patricia Herrera's most recent book, *Nuyorican Feminist Performance: From Café to Hip Hop Theater* (2020), documents the Nuyorican movement, specifically the feminist performeras that contributed to the Nyuorican Poets Café and the aesthetic. Understanding the emergence of the movement along with the rise of hip hop, Herrera's book brings together, through archival work, interviews and critical analysis the various Nuyorican feminist practices deployed at the onset and through the post-1970s generation of performers. Herrera's book raises awareness of the work of these Nuyorican feminist icons, such as Sandra María Esteves, La Bruja, Luz Rodríguez and Nilaja Sun, to name a few. What is important in the context of this present study on reproductive decision-making in theater and performance is the work highlighted by Herrera, specifically the poems of Esteves and Rodríguez, as some of the few focuses on cultural taboos such as abortion and menstruation. Much like other women of color feminists, Esteves and Rodríguez's work raise cultural awareness about taboos and address gender issues as Nuyorican women (57). Herrera argues that Esteves' poem "I look for peace great graveyard" brings to the forefront the connection between the most taboo and denigrated part of the body, the anus, "to make palpable the physical and emotional trauma that women experienced" (57). Esteves' poem describes her insides as "rotting" and "my womb disintegrates in anal slurs." This powerful imagery brings to the forefront visceral imagery of abortion and the dire consequences of overturning *Roe v. Wade* because it mobilizes to take a stand against restrictions on access to reproductive health care, especially in underserved communities. There is consciousness-raising in her poetry, echoing the other Latinx/Chicanx feminists of her time and beyond. By taking a personal and private experiences such as abortion, Esteves highlights and places it beyond the taboo and into the public, communal sphere. As for Luz Rodriguez's poem about menstruation, Herrera argues that she transforms menstruation into a "desirable event," something that empowers the poetic voice to say "I fell the eve/of my body/flowing through . . . " (57). By underscoring menstruation as a powerful and not shameful event, Rodriguez's poem sheds light on the importance for women to reclaims the power over their bodies and it fiercely responds to the systemic debasement and patriarchal control of all that is female (58).

These past and present works reveal the importance of storytelling and embodiment as it relates to notions of womanhood and Latinidad. These theatrical works and performances shed light on the varying ways in which Latina reproductive lives, decisions, and experiences have been represented throughout the 20th century and in the present. Like the work of Migdalia Cruz, Teatro Chicana, Evelina Fernandez, and Cherríe Moraga, to name a few foundational matrilineal dramatic texts representing notions of womanhood, maternity and reproductive experiences, García-Romero, Loomer, Grise and Mayorga continue to shed light on the importance of storytelling and imagining the world through the lens of strong women and women of color. Furthermore, as the recent anthology by Herrera argues, the work of Latina/x performers, specifically Nuyorican performeras are committed to deploying feminist practices to create works that expand and problematize notions of Latinidad, Afro-Latinidad, and female-identified experiences. Reminiscent of other teatristas mentioned, Teatro Luna's work then and now also deploys feminist practices to create stories to further blur the lines between the private, collective, and political. Teatro Luna's work builds on the work of women of color playwrights, performers, activists, and scholars to write about Latina/x reproductive decision-making for theatrical and performance stages.

NOTES

1. Alicia Arrizón, *Latina Performance: Traversing the Stage* (Bloomington: Indiana Univ. Press, 1999) 166.

2. Alicia Arrizón and Lillian Manzor, eds., *Latinas on Stage* (Berkeley: Third Woman Press, 2000) 13.

3. See Melissa Huerta's 2014 dissertation (University of Illinois, Chicago) and Maria Soyla Enriquez's 2019 dissertation (University of Pittsburgh).

4. Since 2016, I have worked collaboratively with Teatro Luna as an Ensemble Member Scholar.

5. See Charlotte Canning (1996), Alicia Arrizón (1999), and Linda Saborío 2012.

6.. For more analysis on Teatro Luna's work see Joanna Mitchell (2011), Melissa Huerta (Dissertation, 2014), Sobeira Latorre and Joanna Mitchell (2006), Maria Soyla Enriquez (Dissertation, 2019).

7. All citations from *Déjame contarte, S-e-x-Oh!* and *Solo tú* come from unpublished manuscripts.

8. Several scholars have written on this topic, see Ann Kaplan (1992), Lisa Anderson (1997), and L. Bailey McDaniel (2013).

9. Teatro Luna. "What I want to tell," in *S-e-x-oh!*. Chicago: Unpublished manuscript, 2006.

10. Teatro Luna. "S-e-x-oh!" DVD, 16th St Theater (Berwyn, IL), 2009.

11. Evelyn P. Stevens, "Marianismo: The Other Face of Machismo," in *Female and Male in Latin America*, ed. Ann Pescatello (Pittsburgh: Univ. of Pittsburgh, 1973) 94.

12. Ana Castillo, *Massacre of the Dreamers: Essays On Xicanisma* (New York: Plume, 1995) 119.

13. Teatro Luna. "What I want to tell," in *S-e-x-oh!*. Chicago: Unpublished manuscript, 2006.

14. Shulamith Firestone, "The Dialectic of Sex," in *The Second Wave: A Reader in Feminist Theory*, ed. Linda J. Nicholson (New York: Routledge, 1997) 188–89.

15. Teatro Luna. "What I want to tell," in *S-e-x-oh!*. Chicago: Unpublished manuscript, 2006.

16. Naomi R. Lowinsky, *Stories from the Motherline: Every Woman's Journey to find her Female Roots* (New York: J. P. Tarcher/Perigee, 1992) 287.

17. Teatro Luna. "What I want to tell," in *S-e-x-oh!*. Chicago: Unpublished manuscript, 2006.

18. Moraga 17.

19. Cristina Herrera, *Contemporary Chicana Literature: (Re)Writing the Maternal Script* (Amherst: Cambria Press, 2014) 12.

20. Most recently, Moraga published *Native Country of Heart* (2020) focusing on her relationship to her mother, coming out as lesbian, and the experiences of caring for her mother with Alzheimer's.

21. Nancy J. Mezey, *New Choices, New Families: How Lesbians Decide About Motherhood* (Baltimore: Johns Hopkins Univ. Press, 2008) 11.

22. Teatro Luna. "What I want to tell," in *S-e-x-oh!*. Chicago: Unpublished manuscript, 2006.

23. Laura F. García, Sandra M. Gutierrez, and Felicitas Nuñez, *Teatro Chicana: A Collective Memoir and Selected Plays* (Austin: Univ. of Texas Press, 2008) 201.

24. Garcia, Gutierrez, and Nuñez 202.

25. Desiree T. Castro, "It's Never the Right Time," in *Sólo tú* by Desiree Castro, Diane Herrera, Coya Paz y Tanya Saracho. Chicago: Unpublished manuscript, 18.

26. According to Guttmacher Institute, twenty-six states currently regulate the provision of ultrasound by abortion providers (2020 www.guttmacher.org/state-policy/explore/requirements-ultrasound).

27. Castro 18.

28. Castro 18.

29. Castillo 184.

30. Castro 20.

31. Maria Vega. "Trapped," in *Déjame contarte* by Teatro Luna. Chicago: Unpublished manuscript, 2001.

32. Mary Lou Babineu, "Counternarratives in the Literary Works of Mexican Author Angeles Mastretta and Chilean Author Pía Barros," in *Latina/Chicana Mothering,* ed. Dorsía Smith Silva (Ontario, Canada: Demeter Press, 2011) 177.

33. Several Chicana/Latina writers who include the virgin/whore dichotomy as a theme in their creative and critical work are: Gloria Anzaldúa, Cherríe Moraga, Carla Trujillo, Sandra Cisneros, Ana Castillo, Denise Chávez, Angie Cruz, Josefina López, Milcha Sánchez-Scott, Alicia Gaspar de Alba, Julia Alvarez, Mónica Palacios, Helena María Viramontes, Lucha Corpi, and Anne García-Romero.

34. Vega, "Trapped."

35. Teatro Luna, "Cama-Camaleon" in *S-e-x-Oh!*. Chicago: Unpublished manuscript, 2006.

36. Teatro Luna, "Cama-Camaleon."

37. Teatro Luna, "Cama-Camaleon."

38. Mendible, Myra. "Introduction: American Shame and the Boundaries of Belonging." In *American Shame: Stigma and the Body Politic*, edited by Myra Mendible, 1–24. Indiana University Press, 2016. www.jstor.org/stable/j.ctt1bmzmdz.4.

Chapter 2

Jane the Virgin

Reproductive Decision-Making in a 21st Century Telenovela

In this chapter, I analyze representations of reproductive decisions in a television series whose protagonists are three Latina women. Building on Latino/Chicano and Latin American media scholarship that frames media such as television as an important site that reproduces and challenges Latina stereotypes, this next case study seeks to contribute to the scarce scholarship on Latina reproductive decision-making representation in media. Building on previous chapters that foreground what is at stake for representations of Latina reproductive decisions through Latina theories of embodiment in cultural texts written and produced by Latinas, such as theater and performance, this case study sheds light on how serialized television mediates Latina/x representation of parenthood and pregnancy in the 21st century.

Jane the Virgin (CW 2014–2019) wrapped its series finale August 2019 with 660,000 viewers (Ramos 2019). It is not accidental that the popularity of this show coincides with the successful run of its predecessor ABC's *Ugly Betty* (2006–2010) and the rise of melodramatic television series on television networks such as ABC.[1] *Ugly Betty* was loosely based on a successful Colombian *telenovela,* RCN's *Yo soy Betty, la Fea* (1999–2001). *Ugly Betty*'s success can be attributed to the inclusion of Latina actors such as America Ferrera and Tony Plana, and the inclusion of domestic Latinx situations, relying on common *telenovela* tropes such as the working-class, close-knit Latino family. As media scholar Guillermo Saavedra argues, *Ugly Betty* "brings in another layer of otherness based on ethnicity that is arguably relevant to an important portion of the audience" (135). As another loosely based adaptation, *Jane the Virgin* represents a similar parody of the telenovela because it also relies on traditional *telenovela* plotlines and Latino tropes, such as the unknown/long-lost father, single-parent household, and close-knit family.

Prior to *Jane the Virgin*'s success, ABC/Lifetime's *Devious Maids* (2013–2016) emerged out of the successes of ABC's *Desperate Housewives* (2004–2012), and Eva Longoria's TV stardom.[2] The show focuses on oft-used Latina stereotypes like the maid/domestic worker or the hypersexualized Latina. These stereotypes are easily identifiable in the show as the female characters are hypersexualized through clothing and explicit body movements.[3] In viewing *Devious Maids* and *Ugly Betty* as representative of serialized television based on *telenovela* formulas, these shows represent female characters in binary terms, such as good/ bad and play with the commonly used Cinderella story (rags-to-riches) trope, elements frequently recognized as characterizations prevalent in *telenovelas*.[4] Eva Longoria and Jencarlos Canela starred in ABC's comedy *Telenovela* (2015–2016), a fictional behind-the-scenes look at making a *telenovela*. In this series, recognizable stylistic elements of a telenovela within a telenovela through parodic elements that constructed sexy, bad women and her wealthy and gorgeous, male, counterpart.[5] In this series, much like *Devious Maids* and *Ugly Betty*, *telenovela* stylistic elements are present and implemented, but what makes these shows successful during their run, especially *Ugly Betty*, is that they take into consideration the domestic US Latina/o audiences that may be familiar with *telenovelas* and integrate quotidian Latina experiences, such as being bilingual or monolingual or living through uncertainty because of one's immigration status.

As scholars in media and cultural studies have argued, mass media is effective in recycling Latina (stereotypical) images in popular culture, especially in television and film.[6] Spectators of all ages and across generations are exposed to fossilized, yet nuanced representations of men and women, including stereotypes about mothers and parenthood. Some mediatized representations like *telenovelas* portray women as either good or bad, and more importantly for this chapter, people who choose to or not to become parents are more scrutinized on screen as either good or bad.

Television shows like *Jane the Virgin*, inspired by the soap opera in style and tone offer specific constructions about reproductive decision-making, such as motherhood. Traditional telenovelas focus on certain storytelling techniques such as the "love triangle" or "Cinderella story."[7] Carolina Acosta-Alzuru (2010) identifies traditional telenovelas as "telenovela rosa" ("rosy") where the content of the story implicates a romantic storyline where two heterosexual people fall in love and have to endure multiple obstacles to finally end happily ever after (188). In addition, Acosta-Alzuru notes that there is usually a socioeconomic twist to these stories tell a rags-to-riches narrative, usually a poor, naïve, but beautiful woman falls in love with a wealthy, handsome and perhaps "evil" man (188). Nora Mazziotti (2006) also defines melodrama's purpose in the *telenovela*: "[. . .] provocar la emoción de los espectadores, la risa, la compasión, el temor, el llanto" (to provoke audience emotions, laughter, compassion, fear, weeping) (21). Acosta-Alzuru and Mazzioti's work illustrates that telenovelas' melodramatic aspects resonate across generations, across texts (written and visual), and socio-historical time, while at the same time knowing how to reach a variety of audiences beyond Latin America, especially Latina/x audiences. Media scholars such as Jillian M. Báez (2018) and Isabel Molina-Guzmán (2018), for example, argue that there are stark differences between Latinx generations in terms of reception, specifically between mother-daughter relationships. As Báez argues in her book on Latinas, media, and citizenship, *In Search of Belonging* (2018), age, gender, and sexuality matter as a vector for analysis when considering media reception in Latina audiences (114). While reception is not the focus of this project, an ethnographic study of Latinas viewership of *Jane the Virgin* and other Latina-centered shows like Norman Lear's reboot, *One Day at a Time* (2017–2020) starring Justina Machado and Rita Moreno, is warranted.[8] Petra Guerra, Diana I. Ríos, and D. Milton Stokes analyzed the award-winning Mexican telenovela, *Alborada* (Televisa, 2005–2006) in relation to the constructions of the Latina mother in mass media. In their case study, the authors divided their analysis of "mother" stereotypes found in the telenovela into four types, following in the work of Charles Ramirez Berg and Aída Hurtado. Guerra, Ríos, and Stokes found that the telenovela supports both traditional illusions of domesticity, such as the *marianista* mother, while at the same time creating a space where some mother-like figures do not fall in either the good or the bad mother categories, like the femme-macho (219). It is also important to mention that viewers, unless they are familiar with the telenovela, may not be aware that *Alborada* is a "period piece," therefore, the traditional mother role seems "appropriate" whereas, in a telenovela set in the present, it becomes anachronistic and dated. For these scholars, telenovelas present traditional gender roles as normative and as part of a larger relationship to power in media representation to reinforce heteropatriarchal expectations.

Unlike telenovelas, television series provide the viewer continuity and same characters, themes, and settings during a specific run (seasons and through episodes). As a precursor to *Jane the Virgin, Ugly Betty*, is also a hybrid of the sitcom, television series, and telenovelas. *Ugly Betty* also takes from a Colombian telenovela and draws on the Cinderella plot line to shed light on the story of Betty Suárez and her family. According to Tanya González and Eliza Rodríguez y Gibson's thorough analysis of ABC's series, *Ugly Betty* is sometimes problematic in its reproduction of stereotypes and its celebrations of the American dream, but at the same time, they argue, "by using camp aesthetic sensibilities, the show's humor and campiness offers complex and potentially critical structures of Latinidad" (10). In their analysis, González and Rodríguez y Gibson call attention to the different ways in which *Ugly Betty* draws attention to ambiguities produced by lived experiences reflecting Gloria Anzaldúa's concept of the borderlands. By combining the concept of the borderlands and a media analysis approach to the show, the authors contend that *Ugly Betty* is successful in avoiding cliches through humor and camp sensibilities to manipulate stereotypes (2). For these scholars, taking a "funny looking" approach to *Ugly Betty*, has "the potential of humor and comedy to illuminate the complexities of race and class to critique social inequalities" (7). *Ugly Betty*'s humor and presentation of Latinidad can be powerful in attempting to represent alternative ways of being. As such, *Ugly Betty* does pave the way for shows like *Jane the Virgin* and the reboot of *One Day at a Time* that use stereotypes to draw attention to the experiences of Latinos/as/x communities beyond types and offers viewers a way to see Latinidad without replicating preconceptions of it.

Structurally, *Jane the Virgin* offers viewers continuity in each episode throughout different seasons. Most importantly, each episode can provide viewers with a story, self-contained, but part of a larger, single narrative that moves toward resolution. One of the most interesting elements of the show is the use of a narrator throughout. This male narrator serves as the viewer's guide, adding information to what is already occurring in the episode and giving the audience context about a subject matter. The episodes build on each other and the characters evolve throughout the seasons, unlike telenovelas which have limited number of episodes, and tend to run less than a year. *Jane the Virgin* falls somewhere between a telenovela, a soap opera, and a sitcom. For Juan Piñón, this series manages to create a "soapy" mood that engages various viewing demographics because it reminds viewers this not a *telenovela,* but they can enjoy the over-the-top situations and the comedy just as much (26). Monica Bednarek (2010) in her work on the language of television notes that the most prevalent contemporary TV genre is the dramedy, a hybrid genre that combines elements of comedy and drama (2). The mix of drama and comedy make *Jane the Virgin* a very contemporary television series, making it successful in a variety of ways: commercially (viewership on the CW and now streaming on Netflix) as well as a plethora of websites dedicated to the series, for example on Fandom.com and Pinterest, and several Twitter and Instagram character accounts (@RogelioDeLaVega). While it is true that there are a series of newspaper, magazine articles, and interviews on *Jane the Virgin*, few academic or analytical publications were present before this project, apart from brief mentions in books and journals (Aldama, Piñón, Báez, Molina-Guzman, and Rose).[9] For this case study, I will rely on a close reading of several episodes of the first season of *Jane the Virgin* supported by the work of other media scholars and Latina/Chicana theorists to analyze Latina/x reproductive decisions in the three generations of Latina women in the series.

In this analysis of *Jane the Virgin,* I will rely on Latina media scholars to build a critique of traditional mother stereotypes still prevalent in mass media. At the same time, this case study will argue that through the character of Jane and the women around her, Latina reproductive decisions are reconceptualized to garner a more nuanced understanding of Latina/x reproductive decision-making in the 21st century. Through mass mediums such as television and film, women of color have been misrepresented through ideological and heteropatriarchal values.[10] For scholars like Ramirez Berg, Valdivia and Molina-Guzmán, understanding socio-historical contexts of stereotypes and mainstream media structures and institutions allows for a more complex understanding of the prevailing Latinx stereotypes such as the "good, virginal woman," "Latin lover," and "harlot." Television and film reinforce structures of power in representation and beyond, exposing viewers to limited definitions of the Latina/x community. For example, Latinx and Chicanx scholars build on the work of Black cultural theorists, like Stuart Hall and bell hooks to incisively critique the relationship between representation, ideology, and domination (Hall 1990; hooks 1992). Even though *Jane the Virgin* also plays with some Latinx stereotypes through its narrative structure of the telenovela, it uses that same structure to deconstruct stereotypical Latina/x images of reproductive decision-making. Instead of being totalizing or generalizing about Latinas, *Jane the Virgin*'s nuanced representations become a "site of struggle" (hooks 1992).

In *In Search of Belonging* (2018), Jillian M. Báez illustrates the complex relationships Latinas develop with mediated texts such as advertisements, movies, and television series in the context of their lived experiences. Báez's utilized ethnographic frameworks to access deep and meaningful insight into intersectional experiences from the Latinas she interviewed in Chicago, IL. In her research, Báez discerns that by paying attention to Latina audiences, specifically, and their relationship to media consumption, affects how they interpret mediated images of their community and how these participants "talk back to media through the discourse of belonging" (6). By "talking back," the Latinas interviewed shed light on how their experiences affect perceptions to those texts, critiquing or reinforcing certain stereotypes. Báez argues that Latinas assert a type of "symbolic citizenship" or "feelings of belonging and recognition" rather than material, nation-state citizenship (112). The participants' gaze is multidimensional and hybrid according to Báez's findings, however it is not inherently oppositional because it functions within the logic of consumption and patriarchy. In her analysis, Báez contends that her participants offer contradictions and affirmations about the mediated texts revealing how women evoke cultural and sense of belonging.

Báez's work also interrogates how her participants viewed *Ugly Betty*. The participants' responses highlight how they view other women's bodies and sexuality. Some of the participants connected with Betty's (America Ferrara) "inner beauty," compared to their disagreement with some of the other non-Latino and middle-to-upper class characters. As Báez observes, "these Latina audiences might be using Betty as an icon of moral superiority (in her chase femininity and nonconformist physicality) to assert power in a sphere where limited agency exists for racialized and gendered subjects" (98). It is possible that the same can be said about the characters in *Jane the Virgin*, especially Jane (Gina Rodriguez) versus her mother, Xiomara (Andrea Navedo). According to Báez, some of her participants referenced Betty's sister, Hilda (Ana Ortiz) and expressed frustration with her. For one participant, Hilda represented a hypersexualized mom, reminiscent of the spitfire or the sexy Latina in other shows or film. Báez concluded that Hilda's characterization functions as "a foil for Betty, making her intelligible only through Hilda's" representation of a stereotyped Latina (98). It is important to note that while Hilda's characterization might follow in the traditions of the sexy Latina, she also represents a more nuanced Latina mother, a sister, a daughter, and a budding entrepreneur. Báez was struck by the reception Betty got in relation to Hilda, since most women identified with Betty over Hilda, demonstrating that "sexuality and class are intertwined within Latina audiences' ideal Latina femininity" (100). As such, we can conclude that perceptions of Latina representation are heavily influenced by factors, including past representations and the adoption of some of the same narratives and apply them to themselves and their family.

Ugly Betty does help us understand the treatment of the Latina stereotypes in *Jane the Virgen* as representations that negotiate between those types, like the virginal, chaste character or the sexy Latina and a more nuanced representation of Latina womanhood and sexuality. As such, as Tanya González and Eliza Rodríguez y Gibson also argue, Hilda's hypersexualization in their chapter "Bringing Sexy Back: The Complexities of Latina Sexuality," *Ugly Betty*'s use of humor and camp to challenge representational misgivings about the virgin/whore dichotomy by "cleverly illustrating the sexism and homophobia and realism that exists in television and in the real world" (103). The scholars describe Betty as a feminist but with maternal qualities as she takes care of her father and family sometimes, while at the same time labeled as undesirable because of her looks. Meanwhile, Hilda is representative of the spitfire, but also motherly and a dreamer, searching for her prince charming. As such, in their reading, Hilda does not adhere to the traditional Latina mother as sacrificial and loyal to her family, but she challenges those stereotypes to provide another way of being Latina. Ultimately, the role of representation in the series gives us an evolving sense of Latina/x characters in the 20th century by shifting preconceived notions of stereotypical under-standings of Latina womanhood and sexuality with Betty and Hilda.

Representations of motherhood have ranged and reflected the cultural context of their time and place, as seen in *Ugly Betty*. The Venezuelan tele-novela, *Juana la virgen* (2002), which inspired *Jane the Virgin*, presents the *madre María*, in the form of Juana's (Daniela Alvarado) grandmother (Aura Rivas) who spends her time suffering, and upholding patriarchal values in the home, like attending to her son's every need. In *Ugly Betty*, the mother figure is absent due to her death, but Betty steps in as a surrogate mother and displays the qualities of a "good" mother towards her sister, nephew, and father (Avila-Saavedra 139–140). In *Ugly Betty,* for example, a more nuanced and nontraditional version of the mother, through Betty, becomes a substitute mother of sorts to her sister, nephew and as a caretaker for her widowed father. As Tanya González and Eliza Rodríguez y Gibson argue, Betty refuses to marry or pursue having children unlike Hilda, who dreams of her prince charming, because Betty dreams of having a professional life and working (115). As Betty transforms into a professional working woman in Europe, she "defies binaries used to pigeonhole her, therefore representing a hybrid, mul-tifaceted and shifting subject" (121). Given the importance of *Ugly Betty* and *Juana la virgen* for *Jane the Virgin*, it is no surprise that *Jane* builds off *Ugly Betty's* success and represents a more complex representation of Latina/x identity. Through this analysis of *Jane the Virgin*, the female characters and related story elements serve to can challenge traditional notions of reproduc-tive decision-making, pointing to more inclusive understandings of people's experiences, specifically in relation to reproductive decision-making. For this analysis, I will rely on Alicia Gaspar de Alba's typologies of the "Marias syndrome" like *la madre María* or the mother who suffers; building on Aida Hurtado's the femme-macho; and the hybrid Latina as conceptualized by José Piñón. Furthermore, the work done by Tanya González and Eliza Rodríguez y Gibson and Jillian Báez serve as foundations to further analyze variations of these types that can be found in traditional *telenovelas*, serialized narratives and in Hollywood films.[11] Lastly, this case study presents critical discussions regarding how constructions of Latina/x reproductive decision-making some-times reinforce negative stereotypes and promote traditional roles for Latinas while at the same time providing other ways of being Latina/x.

ABOUT *JANE THE VIRGIN*

Jane the Virgin, based on the Venezuelan telenovela, *Juana la virgen*, pre-miered in 2014 on the CW and ran for five seasons, with the last episode airing on July 31, 2019, and is currently streaming on Netflix.[12] The show's popularity led to several recognitions including a Golden Globe for Best Actress in a Television Series Musical or Comedy for Gina Rodriguez (Jane) at the 72nd awards. During its run, the show also received critical acclaim for its writing. The show has complex and nuanced characters, romantic tension, melodramatic elements, and addresses socio-cultural contexts such as mixed migration statuses in families, language identity, and motherhood. The main protagonist, Jane, navigates her identity as a third-generation Latina who unexpectedly becomes a mother as she is completing her college degree and thinks about pursuing graduate school. Jane's story can resonate with elements of 21st century Latina/x viewers' lives by depicting interpersonal issues such as reproductive decision-making, relationships with family, love life, and professional goals.

Jane the Virgin's outlandish premise is that the 20-something virgin named Jane Villanueva (Gina Rodriguez), is accidentally inseminated during a routine gynecological exam. The series leaned into its *telenovela* roots through its stylistic elements such as a love triangle between Jane, Michael (Brett Dier), and Rafael (Justin Baldoni), and the appearance of Jane's absent father, Rogelio (Jaime Camill). The series portrays this multigenerational Latina female household of Venezuelan origins, living in Miami. Furthermore, important to this case study, is the female representation of reproductive decision-making. For example, Jane's grandmother, Alba (Ivonne Coll) is a Venezuelan immigrant, very religious, and a role model for Jane. Even though Alba reminisces throughout the series about her home country, the family's experience is more reflective of a generic US Latina/x experience. As such, Alba encourages Jane to stay a virgin until marriage, reflected in Alba's religious and traditional upbringing, and criticizes her daughter, Xiomara (Andrea Navedo) for being sexually liberated. Much to Alba's consternation, Xiomara is very open about her sexuality, however Xiomara respects Jane's perspective. Alba's world views early in the series mark the beginning of Jane's journey toward motherhood and questions about Latina reproductive decision-making. As Piñón asserts, Alba's character calls upon patriarchal traditions, particularly the woman remaining chaste and pure before marriage (24). Alba represents the head of household as the values and morals-driven mother typically seen in traditional *telenovelas*. Alba's inherent goodness, her caregiver status and as nurturer are positive qualities, however, she is constructed as the figure that supports more traditional gender roles. Xiomara on the other hand builds on *Ugly Betty*'s Hilda, constructed as the spitfire mother to Jane, challenging conventional notions of mother as it relates to how she dresses and acts. It is at the intersection between Alba and Xiomara's perspectives that we find Jane, a more complex characterization of a young Latina looking to understand what is at stake in her reproductive decision-making once she learns she is inseminated by mistake. Jane is similar to Betty in that both young women navigate their personal and professional environs by shifting or allowing for ambiguity, especially at work. Betty working at Mode negotiates her desire to become a businessperson with the challenges that working in a place driven by looks can bring while Jane also maneuvers in and out of her home space and the Marbella, the resort where she serves mostly white, affluent customers. Both women are considered loyal and pure, but they defy binaries used to pigeonhole them, specifically the good and virginal women. The series' storylines demonstrate the complexities of being Latinx and what that means for different generations of women. Specifically, in *Ugly Betty* the role of the absent mother destabilizes preconceived notions of the traditional family, shifting the maternal responsibilities to Hilda and Betty. By challenging preconceived notions of Latina womanhood, the women in *Ugly Betty* and *Jane the Virgin* also navigate their own reproductive decision-making past and present to make sense of a more nuanced representation of Latinidad by providing viewers a broad understanding of the ins and outs of Latina identity at the intersection of gender and class.

In the current socio-political climate, such as in the US, many women of color are speaking out more about the role of reproductive justice in different spaces as a way to see themselves reflected in representations of reproductive decisions beyond notions of choice. *Jane the Virgin* illustrates some ruptures in our understanding of Latinx reproductive decision-making based on the relationship to constructions of Latina motherhood-maternity. In the end, this series supports more nuanced and intricate constructions of Latinas. The main character, Jane, subordinates the truncated media representations of Latina reproductive decision-making beyond the overjoyed pregnant woman or the suffering mother. Furthermore, the women in her life, like her grandmother and mother also bring complexity to understanding of generational Latina reproductive decision-making in the 21st century.

Overview of Telenovelas and Serial Narratives

For many, the inaccurate representations of Latina women across various television products provide harmful stereotypes about what viewers are to expect from the Latina/o community, such as the domestic worker or the immigrant family. According to media scholars, the Latina/o community and the national imaginary has remained fully entrenched within black-white binaries and as a way to further categorize and understand non-white media cultural products such as television series (Valdivia 2010). Some examples include the oft-used Hollywood stereotype "Mexican spitfire" or the "bandido" (Ramirez-Berg 68–70). These same stereotypes also show up on television. Mary Beltrán's work (2009) on Latinas/os in television has documented the Latino types and the role of casting used and she notices an increase in "ethnic roles," at the onset of the 20th century which could be filled by actors of any ethnicity that have the same "look."[13] This emphasizes the persistent invisibility and erasure of a multifaceted Latinidad on television and in film. As such, as Isabel Molina-Guzmán (2018) argues in her work on colorblind comedy on television, "the hypersexualization of Latina/o characters in film and television remains a dominant narrative convention" (17). It is Latina characters that typically fall on opposite sides of the spectrum, either the *madre virgen* or the sexy Latina.

Nora Mazziotti (2006) discusses telenovelas in her work *La industria de la Telenovela* "as something that tells a love story, overcoming obstacles in love . . . it should overcome distance and time as well as all the tragedies possible" (21–22). Hence, the content of telenovelas invites audiences to immerse themselves in a melodramatic narrative, vicariously following the love life of others by also experiencing the tensions and emotions of the main characters through daily viewing. Other media scholars note that the melodramatic elements of telenovelas, films, or other mediums inscribe melodrama alongside gendered social positioning and highlighting those moments when they erupt on the visual and social sphere (López 149). On the other hand, research indicates that telenovelas are not a homogenous genre that have a love story on one extreme and on the other "telenovela de ruptura" (rupture) (Acosta-Alzuru 3). Acosta-Alzuru indicates that the latter type breaks the mold by creating characters and storylines more complicated and nuanced by combining more complex and socio-cultural issues in their stories that speak to historical or contemporary contexts (3). In this latter sense, *Jane the Virgin* and other television series like *Ugly Betty* can contribute to a more complex and nuanced understanding of Latinx communities and imagery about Latinas. Although the original telenovelas, *Betty la fea* and *Juana la virgen* are not *novelas de ruptura,* the US Latina/x versions further push those narratives along those lines. *Ugly Betty* is more than a *novela de ruptura*, it is more of a parody/farce, while at the same time, *Jane the virgin* serves as a parody, which in a sense, that is what the US adaptations do. By parodying the genre these adaptations are breaking with Latino traditions/representations. Juan Piñón (2017) has argued that despite the *telenovela* elements, *Jane the Virgin* is not a *telenovela* (23). For Piñón, the series' appeal stems from the producer's assumptions about their intended audiences in conjunction with Latina/o audiences across the US The intended audience for the CW show can be 18–34-year-old women, not necessarily identifying as "Latino/a."[14] Most recently, Natalie Rose's (2019) article on *Jane the Virgin* and the modernization of the melodrama highlights the connection between the sentimental novel and *Jane the Virgin*. Rose's work argues that *Jane the virgin* evokes melodrama through common techniques such as improbable plotlines (Jane's virgin pregnancy), coincidental events (Jane's father is a telenovela star) and the use of a narrator. However, Rose's argument negates the work of many creators who have done *novela de ruptura*. Rose's work, building on Piñón's, argues that part of the success of *Jane the Virgin* is the modernization of the plotlines and the fact that the protagonist, along with the plotlines, demystifies social problems, such as the unwed Latina mother, and explores new ideas about being Latinx (1084). For both Piñón and Rose, *Jane the Virgin* does offer its viewers a telenovela-like narrative, especially in terms of storytelling techniques, such as the love triangle and secret identity of the father. In the case of *Jane the Virgin* and the relationship to content and intended audience, the adaptation from a Venezuelan telenovela crossed with a US serial narrative is successful because it adapts to the US Latina/o context of the series. In this case study, however, the hybrid elements of the series, like the bilingual characters, the use of the narrator, along with the characterization of the protagonists emphasize the power of a Latina/x representation as it relates to reproductive decision-making.

There has been little to no specific scholarship on telenovelas and series with special focus on reproductive decision-making, even though serialized television has been created for female viewers. Sisson and Kimport (2017) emphasize that popular culture aims to entertain and not to correct public misperceptions about medical care, such as maternal care or even access to abortion. As such, medical issues in telenovelas are included for dramatic effect and not meant to thoroughly discuss the issue.[15] Television representations of all aspects of life, including different areas of medical care, often depart from reality for the sake of a good story. As previously mentioned, when abortion does show up on TV, portrayals of the procedure are often misleading, and do not show reality, but tend to moralize about the issue. We can think of representations of safe sex in film and television as well as the problematic framing of teen pregnancy. Media plays a role in reflecting and perpetuating currently existing attitudes and agendas, sometimes rooted in stereotypes. As the role of the good/bad mother or the sexy Latina is consistently perpetuated in telenovelas so is the ways in which the media perpetuates certain reproductive decision-making.

Although scholars such as Isabel Molina-Guzmán, Angharad Valdivia, and Jillian M. Báez have analyzed the *marianista* and sexy Latina stereotypes in telenovelas, media, and sitcoms, the specific ways in which reproductive decisions are concerned are portrayed is unexamined. Part of the larger conversation around reproductive decision-making is not just access to reproductive healthcare for women of color and their communities, but more importantly, reproductive justice advocates for full reproductive rights so that women and men have viable alternatives from which to choose and that the best social and political conditions exist that allow women to decide, if, when, and how many children to have and how to care for them (Ross 2008). Framing Latina/x reproductive decisions in the media as a moral dilemma or statement to create shock, or to lure viewers is problematic. This framing conforms to patriarchal notions of motherhood as indicated above and it explicitly forces women to fall into two categories. Those maternal or non-maternal scripts are perpetuated by heteropatriarchy, and as such, those one-dimensional representations distort lived realities, in turn, shaping attitudes and socio-political agendas. More nuanced understandings of representations of reproductive decision-making concerns in the media is garnered.

Davies and Smith (1998) analyzed pregnancy and birth narratives of *I Love Lucy* and *Murphy Brown*. These snapshots provide us with representations of pregnancy that can be read as highlighting femininity, heteronormative whiteness, and the construction of national identity during the 1950s and 1990s (34). Similarly, mainstream shows like *Sex and the City* also portray varying degrees of white female sexuality and reproductive women, but through a more middle- and upper middle-class lens. These women are sexually liberated and able to pursue access to reproductive decision-making because of racial (white) and class privilege. As Rickie Solinger (2001) notes, "According to many Americans, however, when choice was associated with poor women, it became a symbol of illegitimacy. Poor women had not earned the right to choose" (199–200). There are several soap operas, evening television dramas, and sitcoms that have portrayed negative stereotypes and outcomes of teenage pregnancy (*Grey's Anatomy, One Life to Live,* and *Family Guy,* to name a few). The framing of negative, tragic situations of pregnancy and motherhood are problematic in these examples. These limited representations of promiscuous or irresponsible women reinforce the notion that any young, unmarried mother is unfit to be a good mother. As such, understanding traditional media representations of reproductive decision-making reinforces dangerous attitudes and stereotypes about women of color, especially given the preexisting attitudes and policies that undergird our healthcare system, and television and media networks.

Jane the Virgin is one of those series that highlights the ways in which women of color face reproductive oppression within a particular context. Even though the Villanueva women's experiences are fictional and individual, their experiences as women are framed problematically as well: Xiomara as promiscuous and sexy or Alba as a pious and pure mother. By examining the ways reproductive decision-making concerns are framed in *Jane the Virgin* beyond notions of promiscuity or purity, we can shed light on the complexities of reproductive concerns beyond notions of "choice."

Representing Reproductive Decisions

The contemporary representation of reproductive decision-making and Latinidad in *Jane the Virgin* is a call to connect her role and image to other Latinx millennials or Generation Z, especially those living a more middle-class lifestyle. For Piñón, *Jane the Virgin* uses the family as a recognizable trope to present a non-threatening Latinidad (24). The three women in the series, Alba, Xiomara, and Jane, are a strong representation of a Latina/x family without the stereotypical role of the father-figure, especially as we view Jane's father, Rogelio, as very feminized, decentering the machista role. Each category within the traditional family as presented in media include categories can include the aforementioned categories such as the *madre* María (virginal and self-sacrificing), the femme-macho, and in the case of Jane, a hybrid Latina. The series is not only woman-centered, but more importantly, it is Latina-centered. For example, in *Ugly Betty* and *Jane the Virgin,* the storylines do call for a reading of the complex ways of being Latinx from different generations. The former different from the two men in Betty's household, her nephew and father, and the latter through three generations of women. In the case of Alba, her immigration experience also resembles Betty's father Ignacio's, pointing to the oft-used trope of the suffering and sacrificial migrant. However, differing from Ignacio, Alba's story as a female-identified migrant becomes important given of the importance of female narratives surrounding migration on television and in film.[16] For this analysis, the female types, such as the harlot that Ramirez-Berg and Valdivia identified in television and Hollywood and extending that characterization to also include the femme-macho, identified by Hurtado in her analysis of Chicano Theater are represented. Lastly, scholars like Anzaldúa, Moraga, and Gaspar de Alba have identified la madre María as another archetype, however, I extend the use of Norat's categories where she identifies patriarchal and expectant mothers in theatre to apply to *Jane the Virgin*. For Norat, these two categories present in feminist theater can be potentially radical (24). In building on these categories, I further complicate what reproductive decision-making looks like in a television series that sometimes reproduces and upends traditional notions of Latina/x womanhood.

The main characters in the series represent a cross-section of generational differences anchored within Latino/a culture's perpetuation of *marianismo*, the code of conduct expected for females rooted in the Virgin Mary as an ideal mother. In striving for the perfect mother, like the Virgin Mary, the expectant mother should be sacrificing, caregivers, sexless, and accepting of perpetual suffering (Stevens 1994). In selected episodes from Season 1 of *Jane the Virgin*, Alba, Xiomara, or Jane share the bond of negotiating the challenging role of being Latinas within a heteropatriarchal society that values mothers while also devaluing them for being women, complex and full of desires and aspirations.[17] The series' original metaphor of the flower, which is also included in the opening song of the show, "Una flor" (A flower) by Colombian singer, Juanes, symbolizes virginity and it is at the core of marianismo.

In the pilot episode ("Chapter 1" 2014), a young Jane's grandmother teaches her about virginity through the metaphor of a flower. As is typical in the entirety of the show, the male narrator guides the viewers through these two important moments in Jane's life: her grandmother's teaching juxtaposed to adult Jane having an intimate moment with her boyfriend, Michael (Brett Dier) in her bedroom. Her character's upbringing and moral compass is visually emphasized when she glances over at her wall and sees the framed flower and decides to slow things down with Michael. The original flashback to Jane learning about the flower gives us a glimpse of Xiomara, Jane's mother, questioning Alba:

ALBA: Notice how perfect it is. How pristine. Now Mija, crumple it up—

XIOMARA: Really, mom?

ALBA: Sssh—

XIOMARA: But this is so lame—

JANE: Mommy, shhh!

ALBA: Crumple the flower, Jane.

ALBA: Good. Now try to make it look new again. Go on. Try.

YOUNG JANE: I can't.

ALBA: That's right. You can never go back. And that is what happens when you lose your virginity. You can't ever go back. (Episode 1, Season 1)

In this flashback, the framed rose takes on a magical power for Jane and the viewers because it underscores Alba's moral philosophies and the impact that has on Jane. This opening scene illustrates the merging of all three generations of Villanueva women and their perspectives on virginity. It sets up the characters as stereotyped, especially Alba and Xiomara, as marianista or as femme-macho respectively; on the one hand, Alba is focused on maintaining Jane's virginity until marriage, while Xiomara pushes back and criticizes her mom's instructions. As depicted in the dialogue, the initial development of Alba and Xiomara as strictly marianista or more liberated is never fully dependent on the typical Hollywood and telenovela tropes. Instead, Alba and Xiomara represent more nuanced versions of these tropes since Xiomara actually questions and challenges Alba's perspective. Xiomara is counterpoint to

Alba's more traditional perspective, demonstrating the complex ways of being in these three generations. This initial dialogue demonstrates a more restricted discussion about reproductive decision-making between the three women even though there are hints that Xiomara has challenged Alba's perspectives. This opening scene shows us that the writers want to challenge dominant television representations of Latinidad in a conscious manner.

Alba and Xiomara are set up to frame the hybrid nature of Jane's perspective as a 21st century Latina. The look and tone of the show, like *Ugly Betty,* demonstrates a hybrid space, focused on taking on the telenovela structure and dominant stereotypes of the Latina. For example, in a later moment in the pilot, in a scene between Jane and Rafael (Justin Baldoni), where she feels ambivalent about the baby because it was not part of her plan. As such, Jane's approach to living her life frames the show as hybrid, just like her. Not only does she implicitly demonstrates ambivalence in keeping her child but she also challenges what others might expect from her.

This aspect calls upon audiences' familiarity with Latina stereotypes and the juxtaposition between Alba, Xiomara, and Jane. In the scene, Rafael and Jane discuss their first encounter five years ago, Jane responds, redirecting the conversation:

JANE: Look, I don't want to be pregnant. And right now it's just cells, cells that could fit on top of a pinhead—

RAFAEL: So . . . an abortion you're thinking?

JANE: But if I terminate it, I'll become someone my grandmother wouldn't be proud of. And that's pretty much been my whole life's goal, so . . .

RAFAEL: We'd take it—

JANE: And then what? Live the rest of my life knowing that my kid is out there, I don't know if I'm strong enough for that. Look, I know the reasons for wanting to end the pregnancy are so . . . selfish. That I'm not ready. That this wasn't the plan. That I have worked so hard - every second-so that my life would be different from my mother's—I was an accident. And I know my mom loves me, but I also know, in some ways, I derailed her life (Chapter 1, Season 1).

The solemnity in the scene is called for given the complexity of the topic. It calls audiences to acknowledge the difficulties that Jane is experiencing because of her unintended pregnancy. In the dialogue, Jane reflects on her upbringing and Alba's insistence on Jane being a virgin before marriage, sheds light on how complicated reproductive decision-making can be for Latina women. Julee Tate researches Marianist women and women who do not conform to society and who are known as "wild women" in many telenovelas (Tate, 2018). Tate highlights the consistency of representation of good and bad women in telenovelas across Latin American countries that deal with the imagery of the ideal woman (good) and the less ideal (bad) (97). Jane's dilemma in this dialogue contrasts the traditional marianista woman that yearns to keep her child. In questioning whether or not she'll keep her child, Jane plays into tropes that deem expectant mothers who do not want their unborn children as "selfish." Oscillating between identifying with the happy expectant mother to reacting more transgressive and thinking about abortion or adoption, Jane does undermine heteropatriarchal expectations that dictate that she become a good woman, fit for mothering, as self-sacrificing.

The conversation between Jane and Rafael invites viewers to see a non-stereotypical representation of a Latina wrestling with impending motherhood, without drawing attention to oft-used stereotypes of the sacrificial mother or the wild Latina. Marianismo in general can be problematic in its representation and interpretation. Many Latina/Chicana scholars critique traditional representations of the suffering mother, who should accept repression (Trujillo 220). Conversely, marianismo can also be used and reinterpreted to empower women to tap into sources of feminine power (Trujillo 220). The hybrid nature of the conversation and in the presentation of Jane and Alba, for example, very much fits the marianista figure early in the series, by teaching Jane about virginity through the flower. Alba is presented as a good woman, who sacrificed a lot to raise her daughter and granddaughter. Her qualities underscore virtues present in traditional telenovela plotlines, emphasizing supporting mothering, kind, passive and self-sacrificing. For Piñón and Rose, Alba represents and appeals to the long-standing Latin American representations of womanhood, as a good, self-sacrificing mother. Later in the series we learn more about Alba and her life before and after moving to the US from Venezuela, like that she was not a virgin when she married and that she also asked Xiomara to consider abortion. In addressing real-life experiences and taboo subjects through the telenovela framework and building off *Ugly Betty,* the characters deconstruct some the prevalent types of the Latina, offering ways of being without succumbing to reproducing the same stereotypes. The initial representation of the marianista figure in Alba is characterized as a caring widowed mother that raised a daughter and created a better place for her and her granddaughter.

At first glance, marianismo offers positive ideals for girls and women who may want to become mothers. All of the marianista characteristics juxtapose being a good mother with displaying the following characteristics: kindness, charity, and self-sacrificing. In Jane's case, there is a play on marianismo with the fact that it was an "immaculate conception," since both Jane and Mary did not have sex. These representations are presented differently and in a nuanced manner as the first season progressed because Jane makes sure people around her understand what actually happened: it was a medical mistake. Whereas

Alba's character initially fits into the marianista category, we soon learn that she has defined her life to a certain level of self-determination and preservation. The self-sacrificing (grand)mother is a common element in telenovelas and it can take on different guises, such as abuse, betrayal, and infidelity, to name a few.[18] Alba did sacrifice a lot by moving to the US with her husband in order to raise her family in a better place, shifting the trope of the suffering mother to that of the suffering immigrant. While this is not strictly related to the suffering mother type, we can infer that Alba's strong belief in God and her devout Catholicism contributes to her reservations about certain aspects of Xiomara and Jane's life. In a candid moment between grandmother and granddaughter, Alba explains to Jane that she tried to convince her mom, Xiomara, to have an abortion (Season 1, Chapter 1 31:00). Even though the pilot is tinged with a lot of marianista tropes through Alba's character, Jane's grandmother calls upon a patriarchal tradition, present in Latin American telenovelas, in which women remain [. . .] chaste and pure before marriage (Piñón 24). Given the many barriers in Alba's life, like her migration to the US, the death of her husband, and her limited English skills, the road to becoming a role model for Jane is difficult but warranted. Despite her hardships, Alba does not become bitter toward those ups and downs, but she toils at the Marbella resort and demonstrates love, labor, and humbleness as virtues that represent the qualities of a traditional marianista. In Season 2, Alba also reveals to Jane that she had premarital sex, with someone before her late husband. In this exchange, Alba comes clean because she feels like Jane did not want to share her thoughts on deciding to have sex with Michael. She wants to be part of Jane's life and wants to make sure that their relationship does not fray because Alba has not been forthcoming about her own experiences with sex before marriage. Alba realizes she has been punishing her daughter, the way she was shamed by society for her own actions, perpetuating the good and bad notions of womanhood, rigidly grounded in marianista codes of maternity.

Aída Hurtado argues that the virgin or whore binary was available to women artists who were known to be sweet off stage or sexy and rough in real life (387). The femme-macho, falling between the marianista and whore, was also available to women actors. According to Hurtado, femme-machos are often villainous because of their "inherent deviant" nature; and are sexually ambivalent, attractive and exude power and strength (387). Similar to Betty's sister Hilda, Xiomara, Jane's mother, is the femme-macho figure. She represents a stereotypical yet unique kind of Latina/x woman thorough the lack of qualities often associated with the marianista, or her mother, Alba. Xiomara is also what Hurtado calls a "men's challenge" (387), since she has a strong personality, she's sexually active, and can at times be aggressive towards her current or past loves. As Hurtado describes, the femme-macho can "express a wider range of emotions than other women . . . and therefore obtain some sense of freedom . . . " (388). By embracing the femme-macho, characters like Xiomara can escape the narrow representation of women such as the marianista or the whore. Ultimately, by espousing a more liberated type of woman, Xiomara's character is able to present to the audience a more nuanced understanding of the single Latina/x mother and her reproductive decisions. Furthermore, she demonstrates to her daughter that there are alternative ways of being and seeing the world as a Latina beyond the long-suffering virginal mother.

Julee Tate explains that it is a given that the good woman is self-sacrificing, decent, and sexually pure, or at least monogamous. Tate discusses another distinction that telenovelas consistently establish between good and bad women that involves the treatment of maternity (2007). Representing the femme-macho, Xiomara exercises a freedom to say and do as she pleases. As a second-generation Latina, Xiomara represents the in-between territory, that is, she can be the femme-macho with her mother, but she too can be loving, tender, and sacrificing for her daughter. Tate mentions how the good woman (Alba) is often associated with all things maternal; that is, if she has children, she is an exemplary mother who is willing to sacrifice all for the sake of her children. Tate then analyzes the "bad" woman or the woman who is not maternal; that is, if she has children, she is "only interested in them in so far as they can play a role in advancing her own personal agenda," and if she is childless, she wants to stay that way (2007). In the case of Xiomara, she too can fall under the varying degrees of the good mother, but at the same time represent a more nuanced version of Latina reproductive decision-making. Xiomara represents a more nuanced representation of Latina womanhood and reproductive decision-making in that by learning more about their lives in the story line, these women are multidimensional characters, moving beyond stereotypical categories such as the "good mother" or the harlot. In the following exchange between Xiomara and Jane, as she considers what to do with her pregnancy:

XIOMARA: Abuela asked me never to tell you what she said. And I didn't want you to look at her differently, so . . .

JANE: Look at you, being all selfless. . . . But no more secrets, okay?

XIOMARA: I just wanted you to know you had a choice. Because having one— it helps, I think. Whatever you decide. (Chapter 1, Season 1)

The scene illustrates the strong relationship between Xiomara and Jane and how Jane's experience and emotions are placed front and center, which can be considered atypical characteristics used to portray Latina women beyond notions of marianismo, bad women and the hypersexualized Latina. In this scene, the focus is placed on the intergenerational bond between the women, moving beyond telenovela and US television representational legacies about Latinas. For Xiomara, the notion of having a choice to move forward with the pregnancy strays from traditional representations of impending motherhood in traditional telenovelas or television series portraying Latinas. Framing the issue of reproductive choice first as negative and against the values of the Villanueva matriarch, Alba, and then as something negotiated through Alba's subsequent revelation about asking Xiomara to abort highlights the way reproductive oppression can be imposed by external values and mores related to religious or cultural beliefs within a particular context. Furthermore, once we learn about Alba's perspective and Xiomara's decision to keep her child, we can argue that her decision is framed and supported by larger familial and societal structures beyond an individual choice. Furthermore, Alba's initial reaction to discovering the abortion medication can suggest her view on the act being immoral and un-Christian, however upon further reflection, and a shift in tone, learning about Alba's petition to Xiomara underscores the importance of agency and stresses the importance of moving beyond a right or wrong decision when it comes to reproductive decision-making. As Rose argues in her article, *Jane the Virgin* "gives audiences the opportunity to vicariously explore new ideas surrounding Latina identity . . . " (1083). Responding to Rose's observation, the role of a more nuanced representation of a Latina identity becomes the driving force for the show. Furthermore the notion of reproductive decision-making beyond middle-class white women's narratives about choice underscores the importance of the multifaceted Latina/x representations beyond pregnant teenagers or promiscuous women while at the same time viewing reproductive decision-making through the lens of reproductive justice by having access to healthcare and information about abortion. The role of the relationship between the women, their experiences as Latinas, and the minimal stereotyped and racialized characteristics contribute to a more nuanced understanding of Latina/x experiences beyond framing them as hypersexualized or marianista.

As Charles Ramirez-Berg argues, the representation of the stereotypes tend to also cast a shadow on the newness and importance of a different Latinx story, one that does not continually play into Hollywood stereotypes. However, the hot-blooded Latina trope is prevalent in Xiomara while at the same time, the stereotype of the Latina mother is manifest with Alba, further shaped by immigration and the geographic and social spaces, like Miami and their home. Alba mostly moves within the private sphere and Jane and her mom tend to be more public, either at the Marbella resort, Xiomara's dance studio or at school. These two tropes fall on opposite sides of a spectrum. Alternatively, we can also see Xiomara as someone that quickly evolves into a more complex character, much like Alba, and the types dissolve, making them more than just types. Like the over-the-top representations, like Sofia Vergara's character in *Modern Family,* or storylines focused on self-sacrifice, *Jane the Virgin* does present motherly sacrifice associated with Catholicism and female sexuality as noted in the pilot episode. In *Modern Family,* Sofia Vergara's character, Gloria, is constructed as sexy Latina, wearing tight-fitting clothes; furthermore, she also embodies the dramatic Latina, with her rambunctiousness, through physical actions, especially as they relate to religion. These characteristics, although stereotyped and anchored on fictional and imagined constructions of Latina reproductive decision-making, contrast with the development of Jane's process into motherhood. Even though the narrative that drives the series is based on heteronormative and heterosexual relationships, Jane's experience as a hybrid Latina, as theorized by Juan Piñón, drawing attention to a middle-class narrative and storyline, emphasizes positive representations and challenges our understanding of reproductive decision making for Latinas. As seen in the pilot, Xiomara and Jane considered abortion or adoption respectively for their children. While Jane's situation is at present the task at hand for her, Xiomara's experience as a young mother does perpetuate stereotypes about Latina teen pregnancy, however, by learning that Alba suggested terminating the pregnancy, suggests a more nuanced perspective about Latina motherhood in the 21st century.

In the second episode, Jane lives moments of confusion and ambivalence about having a child. In the opening scene, Jane calls a family meeting, which now includes her partner, Michael, to discuss the baby and her future. For Jane, the baby will not impede on her future plans to finish school and get a teaching job, and she tells her family that the baby will now be called a "milk-shake" (3:04). In this episode, Jane navigates the uncertainties that come with accepting the pregnancy to eventually give the baby to Rafael and Petra. In this pivotal episode, Jane struggles with the idea of having a child that is not hers in the midst of wanting to finish school and get her teaching placement. This episode frames Jane's ambivalence in reproductive decision-making as something anchored in making the right choices for herself and the baby.

Jane represents a more nuanced characterization of a young Latina millennial. As scholar Cristina Herrera noted in her book *Contemporary Chicana Literature: (Re)Writing the Maternal Script* (2014), Chicana writers always engage in rewriting motherhood, contesting the static image of the marianista but also engaging in multifaceted representations of Chicana mother-daughter-grandmother relationships (7). Although I do not engage in a discussion of specific Chicana representation in this case study, I would venture to say that there are connections to Herrera's perspective as it relates to Latina media representation. Of course, the difference between some of the literary works and a television show is that the approach to storytelling varies or gets modified. In the case of *Jane*, the showrunner, Jennie Snyder Urman, is not Latina but her group of writers and directors do come from different backgrounds, including several Latinos. While the writers may be diverse and not specific to an essentialized Latino experience, the show does a good job in portraying a complex Latina identity through all three Villanueva women. Furthermore, as Cherríe Moraga explained in her influential essay, "A Long Line of Vendidas," "it is our tradition to conceive of the bond between mother and daughter as paramount. . . . Las hijas who remain faithful a la madre, a la madre de la madre" (*Loving* 129). The mother is a complex figure for Moraga because of strong bonds between the two, but Moraga also contends that the bond can be constraining if left as a heterosexual and patriarchal construction. In the Villanueva household, the bond is strong between the women, but at the same time it is constrained by a heterosexual construction of maternity, in that it is confined to a traditional understanding of motherhood through these women. In a way, the relationship Betty and Hilda have resembled a mother/daughter dynamic given that their mother is not alive. While Betty cannot image becoming a mother, she does take on the motherly role for her sister and as her father's caretaker. Through the construction of matrilineal bonds, Alba and Xiomara raised their children on their own, without the support of father-figures or an extended family, however their stories are constrained by a heterosexual and traditional narrative. As such, their generational and matrilineal alliance lies at the core of their Latinidad and in their maternal connections.

Even though Alba and Xiomara appear, at the outset, to suggest they will be framed as stereotypical Latinas, it is important to note that throughout the series, they are more complex and nuanced characters that demonstrate the strong bonds between them and Jane. Jane is a hybrid Latina, one that speaks perfect English, represents third or fourth generation women, with a middle-class perspective on her dreams, vocation, and future as a writer. In a way, Jane's character falls somewhere in the middle between the immediate stereotypical tropes materialized in Alba and Xiomara, as the marianista and the sexy Latina. This can be visualized at the first sonogram appointment where Jane invites Michael, her family, Petra, and Rafael. In the absurdity of this moment, Jane and her entourage are met with resistance by the technician as she asks that the biological parents be the only people present. The humorous scene harkens back to other telenovelas and television series that place emphasis on the large Latino/x family situations or the importance of the grandmother, mother and daughter relationships in Latina households. In the end, Jane and Rafael are the only ones allowed in the room and through this experience, Jane and Rafael are able to connect over the sonogram. As a strong Latina character, Jane confides in Rafael her reservations about moving along with the pregnancy, while still pursuing her dreams of finishing school and teaching.

Jane's character represents a hybrid Latina. Following in the steps of Betty Suarez in *Ugly Betty*, Jane is a third-generation Latina, who speaks English without an accent, is pursuing her dreams to become a writer through hard work and professional development (Piñón 24). While the role of the family is important to Jane, she is a strong and admirable character beyond notions of stereotypical Latinidad. Jane calls upon notions of hybridity, growing up in a bilingual household, having her education in English, more middle class; perhaps reflective of the majority of the Latino population in the US and the type of audience the show wanted to draw. As viewers, we see the desire to fully enter the middle class through higher education and work, but more importantly for Jane, her child will be that realization. The series, like the description of the hybrid Latina challenges preconceived notions of Latinidad and reproductive decision-making. Beyond bringing to life a Latina story embedded with Latina American and US traditions, *Jane the Virgin* offers viewers a new Latina/x narrative, one anchored on being Latina in the 21st century.

Jane represents a fusion between the marianista and the femme-macho and more. Jane escapes the narrow confines of good or bad woman and embraces a new, modern identity, steeped in both Latin American and US roots. She stands in-between her grandmother and mother in terms of her identity, and as one that resonates with young viewers. Although one could argue that there is an assimilationist discourse there, or at least it is presented as one, since the goal is to enter the middle class and be fully assimilated. Far from being a harlot or a maid, Jane's character, and her drive to become a teacher and writer, represents for Latina/x viewers the value of getting an education, following one's dreams, and being a hard worker. Jane's reproductive decision-making while consistent with a more normative choice to keep her unborn child does break with typical Latina stereotypes, such as the hypersexualized woman, pregnant teenager, or domestic worker. In the case of Jane, her presence underscores the sacrifices that her immigrant grandparents made to come to the US and make a better life for future generations.

In many ways, the first two episodes and beyond use the telenovela paradigm to appeal to young Latinas who have gained access to education and other life experiences, since telenovelas were created as products for and by modernity. Like its predecessor *Ugly Betty*, *Jane the Virgin* uses melodrama and familial sensibility by exploring topics that are imperative to the women in the family, specifically female agency, and family dynamics. As Natalie Rose argues, "*Jane* regularly wrestles with motherhood and all of her plans to become a professional and find a meaningful, and loving partner" (1095). Within the context of telenovela techniques in storytelling, such as over-the-top reactions and situations surrounding her to her pregnancy or her grandmother's fervent religiosity to connect to a wide audience base, like first and second-generation Latinas but also with third or fourth generation Latinas that connect to a Latina/x sensibility of trying to live in the 21st century. Furthermore while neither Xiomara nor Jane explicitly identify as "pro-choice" their actions and solidarity makes evident that the US reproductive rights debate consistently remains between pro-choice and life, positioning the act of termination as an isolated event.

While we cannot say that Jane fits into either virgin or femme-macho categories, she is not defined by her actions or beliefs. As a Latina, she is not being pigeon-holed into certain rigid categories by her family or partners. Jane and her mom speak candidly about her pregnancy, noting Jane's disappointment with the turn in her life. Jane, refusing to talk about the situation is pressured by her mom, and here we witness an exchange between the two realms Hurtado discusses in "The Politics of Sexuality": "the reward for women who save their virginity until marriage is to enter the revered status of wife, and eventually mother and grandmother" (398). Similarly, as seen in *Ugly Betty*'s final season, Betty has a pregnancy scare, though she is not considered to be a virgin. In the episode, "Be-shure" (Season 4, 2009) Betty's pregnancy scare brings forth a series of contemplations surrounding her future and what a child would mean for her career and future with Matt (Daniel Eric Gold). On the one hand, Betty imagines a traditional future with Matt, as a family, but on the other, she is not ready to forego her professional aspirations and breathes a sigh of relief upon learning that she was not pregnant. Betty does not completely disregard a future with a family, but at the moment, Betty declares that she cannot see herself as a mother, maintaining a "reputable" and good woman role. While not traditionally characterized as the virginal woman as Hurtado states, Betty's reward for containing her sexual freedom and connecting it back to her "maternal" qualities as an aunt, sister, and daughter, comes in the representation of a complex subjectivity, no longer bound by binaries, able to maintain her agency while at the same time desire potential maternity and fulfilling her professional and personal goals. Betty's character is not defined by the notions of a stereotypical Latina, instead she engages in "mobile subjectivity" (Sandoval 59). Like Betty, Jane offers an unstable Latina identity through the use of telenovela tropes like the good woman and virginal young woman.

As noted in the exchange between Jane and Xiomara, Jane does not want to talk, and Xiomara iterates that she too knows how she feels since she was 16, pregnant, and scared. By Xiomara further indicating that she can have a choice and decide how she'll proceed with her life, it turns to a more nuanced and complex understanding of Latina/x reproductive decisions. Jane's reaction perpetuates dominant and idealized notions of what Latina behavior should look like or what one should not do. The marianista motif as reflective of patriarchal needs to maintain power over women is demonstrated in Jane's reaction: "you were irresponsible . . . and I've done everything right, my whole life, to do everything right so. . . . " (Season 1, Episode 1 24:31; 24:35). Xiomara interjects and finishes Jane's sentence, "so you wouldn't turn out like me" (Season 1, Episode 1 24:36). By saving herself for marriage and not getting pregnant young, Jane gets placed in the good woman category and differentiates herself from her mother, who is described as irresponsible and depriving Jane of her father. In separating herself from her mother, the women's experiences are not compatible, and Jane reinforces a heteropatriarchal system that betrays her own mother and other women, by policing her mother's actions, further creating a strange dynamic between being a US Latina versus her mother, and immigrant grandmother.

In the series, Jane complicates the classic "virgin" and bad woman telenovela character. She does not represent the traditional, essentialist view of the Latina unwed mother. Through the pregnant virgin plotline, Jane upends the stereotypical role of the unwed mother since she is still a virgin and continues to hold true to her moral ground. Jane defies traditional gender norms by expressing her desires to pursue her career while she is pregnant while at the same time attempting to also have a relationship with Michael or Rafael. By asserting her desire as a woman, sexually attracted to both men, Jane, still a virgin in these first two episodes of Season 1, may resonate with 21st century Latina cultural ideologies, and in doing so, exposes and engages the challenges of Latina/x representations. Jane acts on her desires with the men she loves and also takes on the role of motherhood, while continuing to be a good daughter and granddaughter.

In Season 1, episode 6, Jane is placed in a Catholic High School to do her student teaching. She is aware of the implications of having an unmarried pregnant woman as a teacher in a Catholic school. Even though she is attempting to keep her perspective professional, she eventually lets the school know she is pregnant. Unfortunately, her father's step-step children are also in the school and they let their entire classroom know, including the head nun that she is an unwed mother-to-be. She has to explain to the nuns what the situation is and can negotiate her job by making sure that she remains focused on her job. As the episode progresses, the nuns decide that it would be a great tactic to use Jane's experience as a pregnant virgin to facilitate the entry of new parishioners to the church because they have a pregnant virgin at the school. Rogelio's stepdaughters create a website titled "The Pregnant Virgin" to make Jane's life miserable. Unbeknownst to her, this website gains a ton of views and the nuns find themselves using her likeness, resembling the Virgin Mary, to draw attention to her "immaculate" status.

The telenovela trope of the pregnant virgin frames Jane's characterization as the good girl works to establish expectations about the trajectory of her life, as well as critique the limits of female subjectivity upon which being a good mother depend. Throughout the remainder of this episode, Jane has to negotiate her new popularity as "Jane the Virgin" while she works at the school. During several moments, while at work (at school) Jane is approached by couples wanting to have children, most indicating that they are waiting for a miracle child. The Flannigan couple meets Jane early in the episode and ask her for a hug because they would like to have children one day. They thank her for the hug and depart by saying "God Bless You," and the nun says: "let's hope her fertility rubs off on you." This comedic scenario is critical of the manner in which the nuns, as representative of the Catholic Church, use Jane's situation to draw more parishioners to the church, while at the same time, demanding that Jane act and behave a certain way because she works in a Catholic school. Furthermore, the nuns' hope for fertility in their parishioners is taken to the extreme by mobilizing Jane's experience as fundamental to their plan. The nun believes Jane was brought to them for a purpose, to bring more people into the church, and she orders the other nun to continue distributing the coins with Jane's image as a pregnant virgin Mary. In these exchanges, Jane is visibly distraught because she is unaware of how the school is exploiting her pregnancy, especially when she encounters Nora and Ben. Nora and Ben ask Jane for a hug and show Jane a coin made in her likeness (by the nuns at the school) as a symbol of "hope" and "fertility" for couples. Jane confronts the nuns about the coin, and she is upset that they would sell the coin, to which the nun responds that they are not selling, but "distributing."

For the nun, Jane's situation is a miracle, as a pregnant virgin, regardless of being a "medical mistake or not" (Season 1, episode 6, 23:13). Jane's pregnancy, more importantly, the pregnancy itself, functions as hope for others given her "extraordinary fertility." Jane returns to work dressed in her party outfit-the nun does not approve-looking down on her like she was not "appropriate," and she negotiates with the nun to continue working at the school if she gives out a few more hugs. The nuns accept this and allow her to continue teaching. This comical scene sheds light on how the show parodies Christianity and the belief of "miracles" or people who have a gift to help others. Furthermore the exchanges between the nuns, students, parishioners, and Jane are founded in disidentificatory practices as theorized by José Esteban Muñoz: "These identities-in-difference emerge from a failed interpellation within the dominant public sphere. . . . Comedic disidentification accomplishes important cultural critique while at the same time providing cover from, and enabling the avoidance itself of, scenarios of direct confrontation with phobic and reactionary ideologies" (1999, 7 and 119). Building off the work of Chicana theorists Norma Alarcón and Chela Sandoval, Muñoz's theorization is helpful in understanding the varying degrees of identity negotiation that Jane navigates in her experience at the school. The complex and varied ways of being Latina/x in *Jane the Virgin* offer perspectives through which to understand how disidentificatory practices allow for Jane's character to defy binaries used to restrict her and other women, representing "mobile subjectivity," shaping her narrative in concert with her family and professional life.

Chapters 9, 13, and 15 focus on various moments in Jane's pregnancy that require medical assistance prior to her baby's birth. These episodes are important in representing a hybrid Latina pregnancy and reproductive decision-making without emphasizing the importance of reproductive biology in defining femininity. These episodes present pregnancy by using real-life situations and framing them in the context of Jane's experience, as a hybrid Latina. In these moments, Jane and Rafael consider sonograms and amniocentesis, as real-life experiences of future parents. The show represents these scenarios without completely defining Jane and just a first-time mother, but as a young woman armed with information and willing and able to ask questions and advocate for herself.

Jane enacts agency and represents reproductive decision-making by working through routine appointments and overcoming challenging times in which her faith in the power of knowledge and planning overwhelm and challenge her. In Chapter 9, Jane and Rafael visit the doctor for a routine sonogram. Unfortunately, Jane notices the technician not saying much and starts to worry about the results of the scan. Jane keeps whispering a number and indicates to Rafael that she read it on WebMD while she quickly ran to the bathroom. She was supposed to not read or look anything up online prior to her appointment, but she decided that she needed to double-check the information. Although the moment in the episode where we learn about what the sonogram is looking for is very short, as viewers we are put in a personal situation that seldom occurs on television, let alone in telenovelas. Jane learns that the sonogram at 13 weeks measures the nuchal fold, which can diagnose fetal abnormalities. Jane was looking to get confirmation from the technician, who is not allowed to read the results, but the technician mentions that she should wait for the doctor to interpret the results. Interestingly, Jane demonstrates her active agency in asking questions and advocating for her reproductive health and the health of her unborn child. In contrast to other shows or telenovelas that navigate pregnancy and birth, Jane's experiences at the doctor can be used to discuss the importance of reproduction-related issues, such as birth defects, that can be detected with routine visits and conversations with a doctor. A vital part of the argument for shows like *Jane* and how they remake and upend heteropatriarchal conceptions of Latina/x identity are episodes like these because they demonstrate the importance of television in reframing discussions surrounding reproductive health care beyond contraception and abortion.

In Chapter 13, Jane and Rafael are excited to see the 3D sonogram, which will also confirm the sex of their unborn child. The tension felt between Jane and the technician, who notices that something might be off on the sonogram. Like in the previous episode, Jane and Rafael are very nervous and once the doctor reveals to the couple that the abnormality in the sonogram might reveal heart and intestine defects. Even though this is a challenging time for the couple, they are able to receive the information needed to figure out whether or not what the doctor found is something to worry about. Again, while these appointments are routine during a pregnancy, the representation of the scene with Jane interacting with the technician and the doctor open up spaced for Latina/x feminist readings grounded on Latina reproductive justice. This show serves to underline reproductive justice because it demonstrates and represents issues at stake for women when it comes to their reproductive decision-making. Furthermore, Jane's sonogram identifies potential problems and she now has to decide whether or not she will go through amniocentesis to find out more information about the well-being of her unborn child. Instead of completely jumping to a new scene or bypassing the results to show a happy couple awaiting the next steps in the nine-month gestation period, *Jane* emphasizes the way the media can provide informal information surrounding reproductive decision-making. While quantitative analysis about media consumption and knowledge creation surrounding reproductive health care is beyond the scope of this project, the length at which the show discusses reproductive decisions and shows Jane and her loved ones navigating difficult yet common decisions is helpful in viewing new framings that counter disinformation or silences surrounding those decisions. During the remainder of the episode Jane contemplates having the procedure done, understanding the consequences: miscarriage. During the exchange between her OBGYN and Jane, the doctor explains what will happen during the procedure and gives Jane and the viewers statistics on the outcome of the procedure. This presentation can be substantiated by close attention to the way the issue around finding out if your unborn child may have genetic or chromosomal abnormalities and having amniocentesis done. Once these tests are conducted, the future parent(s) can decide to proceed with a traditional gestation period that can result in a healthy child or a child with disabilities or decide on aborting the fetus. Both of these situations are treated in a nuanced manner, focused on a complex negotiation between using dramatic and over-the-top telenovela tropes and the realities of reproductive decision-making. As such, these episodes speak to larger conversations surrounding reproductive justice as an avenue for disseminating information by reproductive justice advocates and their constituents. Instead of glossing over the process, and the anguish and ambivalence Jane feels, the episode frames the intricacies of the process and the realities of pregnant people in an appropriate and sensitive manner based on the intersections of multiple experiences.

Jane used the time she needed before deciding on having the procedure done to further test her unborn child. She researched the risks and weighed the pros and cons. She consulted with Rafael and had a heartfelt conversation with the women in her life regarding her options if the test results show something is horribly wrong with her unborn child. Xiomara asks if she would consider an abortion, which Alba rejects, but Xiomara sternly notes that considering termination is part of the question and a viable option if the couple chooses it (27:22). Alba considers that too risky and Jane understands both sides of the dilemma and Jane would not consider an abortion if things were not well with her unborn child. Once she combed over the literature and considered the risks, she ultimately decides to have the procedure. Once in the doctor's office, Jane, and her entire family, including Xiomara and Alba are present. Obviously allowing entire groups of people into the examination room would fall under the fictitious and over-the-top category, reminiscent of telenovelas. Rafael and her mom and grandmother are very supportive post-procedure and take care of her while she rests for 48 hours per the doctor's orders. Rather than simply overlooking the risks and unexpected bumps that pregnant women face, *Jane the Virgin* strategically elucidates the different issues at stake as a pregnant woman that go beyond oft-cited rose-colored perspectives. In terms of Latina/x reproductive decision-making, Jane questions her preparedness for the risks and consequences of negative test results. The position of valued maternity, one that positions the future mother as self-sacrificing and nurturing of her future child, that of the good mother, is weighed against the possible loss of her unborn child. In presenting a more nuanced perspective of what it means to go through varying degrees of uncertainty in a seemingly healthy pregnancy speaks volumes to the ways in which television can change awareness and attitudes about reproductive decision-making.

As the first season ends, Jane is getting prepared for the baby's arrival while at the same time dealing with some ups and downs in her relationship with Rafael. In Chapter 17, Jane attends parenting classes with her mother, making it clear that she is prepared to take this on as a single parent with the help of her mother and grandmother. She also gets overwhelmed because she is unsure if she's ready for the end of her pregnancy: does she use a doula? Does she breastfeed? In order to quell her anxiety and feel better prepared for the arrival of her child, she agrees to babysit with her friend from her writing group. After her babysitting experience, fraught with calm, then crying, Jane gets panicked and admits to her mother and grandmother that she may has reservations about taking care of her child. Similar to some of Teatro Luna's characters, Jane feels unprepared and ambivalent about her future now that she is closer to giving birth, Jane reconsiders her options and makes it evident to the viewers that she acknowledges that there are aspects of motherhood that are uncertain and leads to questioning her ability to take care of her child. By focusing on her birth plan, she is able to take into consideration all of her insecurities and rely on her mother and grandmother's support. In these moments of uncertainty and happiness, Jane and the women in her family come together to negotiate the ambivalence Jane feels as she prepares for motherhood.

In the final episode of Season 1, Jane finally gives birth to a healthy baby boy, which she was not expecting. After a whirlwind of a day, feeling some contractions, but still going to her graduate school interview, she has to take the bus to the hospital. Once at the hospital Rafael meets her there and they wait since the baby is not ready to come. During these precious and seemingly calm moments in the maternity room, both Jane and Rafael talk about their fraught relationship and how they will approach impending parenthood. While Jane's labor is stalled until the next day, both her mom (who is traveling for her own audition) and grandmother are able to make it and be present for the birth. In these moments before the birth of her son, Jane connects with the three women in her family and reinforce the maternal connection they share, especially as Jane gives birth. Not only are they present at her birth as a support system, but they also represent three powerful women that have been able to maneuver through their lives negotiating their identities as widowed or single Latina women.

As a reflection of the complexities of identity, the Villanueva women represent a cross-section of generational differences anchored within Latino culture's perpetuation of marianismo and the role of the bad woman as the marianista's opposite. By representing Latina reproductive decision-making, *Jane the Virgin* exposes the complexities of being a Latina in the 21st century. In the series, the Villanueva women place their experiences as reproductive women front and center to reflect on and speak of their experiences, pushing stereotypes about Latina maternity and womanhood, while also addressing reproductive justice concerns, such as pregnancy, maternal care, breast cancer, and menopause on screen. The series explores the complexities of a Latina/x identity while at the same time making use of a fictional narrative to navigate reproductive decision-making concerns for women of color.

In Season 2, Xiomara finds out she is pregnant even though she was not interested in having more children. Xiomara's desire to not have more children mobilized her recent breakup with Rogelio, Jane's father. Previously, Xiomara had made it clear to Rogelio and her family that she did not want more children, echoing the importance of reproductive decision-making and agency surrounding wanting to have more children or not for a woman in her 40s. This example highlights the importance of reproductive decision-making beyond traditional "reproductive years" for people. In the examples from *Juana la Virgen*, *Ugly Betty*, and *Jane*, we encounter women between the ages of 17–26 navigating the ambivalence surrounding pregnancy or mother-hood. While depictions of maternity beyond the age of 26 is not uncommon (*Murphy Brown,* or *Sex and the City*, for example), depictions of abortion on television are. Xiomara finds out she is pregnant from a one-night stand with Rogelio's archenemy at the end of Season 2 and viewers are left wondering how the series might handle her decision, especially after Jane decided to keep her child and given the support Xiomara and Alba gave her following Jane's unplanned pregnancy. In Season 3, she reveals to Rogelio that she is pregnant with Esteban's baby, much to Rogelio's disgust, but Xiomara starts to feel uncomfortable with how Alba reacts to her finding out Xiomara had an abortion. While the show deals with conversations surrounding abortion, with Xiomara, the subject was dealt in a subtle and empathetic way. Alba comes to question Xiomara about a medical bill and Xiomara starts to feel anxious about keeping her abortion from Alba and the narrator reveals to viewers that she had a medicated abortion that caused cramps, but she told Alba she had the stomach flu. Xiomara then discusses with Jane and Michael whether or not Alba is suspicious or knows that she did (14:50–52). Xiomara reveals to her that she did have an abortion and Alba does not agree with Xiomara's decision, emphasizing Alba's perspective on the matter. Xiomara highlights the importance of her making this decision given where she is in life at the moment and recalling why then did Alba suggest an abortion back when she was a teen (23:50). Xiomara's experience is relevant and critical because it reflects decisions and conversations that women have regarding a taboo subject. In light of what we do not see on screen, it is still critical to see an abortion positive narrative surrounding Xiomara's reproductive decisions. For Xiomara, the decision has been made and Alba struggles with Xiomara's choice, as she reveals to Rogelio: "She's making me feel guilty. N-not for the abortion. She's making me feel guilty about not feeling guilty" (27:22). Rogelio is very supportive and reminds her that if she was sure about her choice, that that is all that matters. This reveals the importance of reproductive decision-making as a more nuanced lens we should consider decisions like abortion since for everyone that goes through with it or not is different and we cannot view it with broad brush strokes. While Alba views Xiomara's decision through her religious identity, feeling guilty about asking Xiomara to abort Jane, Alba cannot cope with Xiomara's current decision, opting to ignore having a conversation with Xiomara or Jane. Alba alludes to religious contexts, such as Xiomara going to hell or burning and after hav-ing a brief conversation with Jane, Alba decides that everyone should move forward even if she does not agree with Xiomara's decision and agrees that it was Xiomara's decision to make. In going against her mother's views on abortion, Xiomara questions and acts upon traditional gender roles, those traditionally represented by good/virginal women/mothers, reminiscent of the Virgen de Guadalupe. Instead of showing sacrifice and values of love and devotion for her unborn child as a heteropatriarchal system desires, Xiomara acts on her desire to remain childfree. Her fallen sexuality as a teenager when she became pregnant with Jane has now turned into a second fall from grace through a form of a Malinche. In seeing how Alba reacts, it is evident that there is still a strong sense of viewing female sexuality and reproductive decision-making by defining them in terms of La Malinche or La Virgen. As Yvonne Yarbro-Bejarano argues in her seminal article on Chicana representation in Chicana/o theater, "The prevalence of cultural nationalism (in the Chicano Movement) also led to the reinscription of the heterosexual hierarchization of female/male relationships" (390). In this example, Yarbro-Bejarano addresses the traditional family structure and values that were not criticized in early Chicano teatro. By looking at the way Xiomara's actions are represented, it is clear that there is a possibility of seeing and being in the world beyond constrained notions of sexuality. Instead of playing the passive, self-sacrificing role of the mother, Xiomara exposes Alba's contradictory stance during her first pregnancy and rejects the passive female role of accepting to keep a child when she knows it would not be what she desires.

Pregnancy and maternity are experiences rarely talked about openly on television let alone on a series meant for young viewers. In telenovelas, the role of the expectant mother tends to fall into the good/bad as Julee Tate argues. By establishing the differences between the good and the bad woman in telenovelas through the treatment of reproductive decision-making, the characters either embody or do not the principles of marianismo. In many telenovelas, as Tate and Acosta-Alzuru have argued, the role of the good woman par excellence is to give her husband the gift of a baby. In the US, as early as 1950, Lucille Ball's actual pregnancy was written into her portrayal of Lucy Ricardo in *I Love Lucy*. Since the 1990s and throughout the last two decades, there is a growing interest in pregnancy and pregnant bodies. Media influence and changes in technology have garnered more interest in celebrity and non-celebrity pregnant bodies (Tropp 2013). A wide range of examples of pregnancy and maternity on television from *Murphy Brown*, *Gilmore Girls*, *Supernanny* to *Keeping up with the Kardashians* appear on television today. Niche reality shows also present a huge interest in pregnant bodies, such as *16 and Pregnant*. It is worth noting that the absence of non-white bodies and narratives in some of these shows plays an important function in emphasizing racial and class privileges. Part of the importance of *Jane the Virgin* is to also shed light on Latina/x reproductive decision-making narratives that seldomly make it to the television screen. Consequently, in some of the episodes in seasons 1, 3, and 5 (final season), the Villanueva women are a perfect example of the varying degrees of Latina/x reproductive decision-making who may or may not reject the good and the bad mother/woman codes. The representations of more nuanced and complex Latina/x identities in *Jane the Virgin* build on the representations spearheaded by *Ugly Betty*. All three Villanueva women navigate normative assumptions and representations of about Latinidad. On the one hand Alba represents the marianista mother, the sacrificial woman, devoted to her family and the matriarch, while on the other extreme Xiomara seemingly represents the femme-macho or Malinche figure because of her openness to sex and by becoming pregnant at an early age and most recently, having an abortion. For Jane, while she became pregnant by an accident at the gynecologist's office, she still represents the good girl, a virgin, and a family-oriented daughter. However, after a closer examination, these characters complicate understandings of reproductive decision-making within Latina/x representation. While Alba and Xiomara represent more stereotypical Latinx roles it becomes evident that they move beyond the marianista and femme-macho figure. Furthermore, Jane's character is a hybrid one, like Betty, examining her place in the world and not bound by traditional representation of Latina identity. By examining the ways this show represents a more nuanced Latina womanhood and its relationship to reproductive decision-making as they are framed in this dramedy to consider the framing of Latina/x maternity more critically in the 21st century.

NOTES

1. Riding on the initial success of *Ugly Betty*, US remakes/adaptations of telenovelas there were other attempts by networks, but they failed. MyNetworkTV *telenovelas* were Fox Television's attempt to create a successful low-cost programming franchise by adapting Spanish-language telenovelas for US audiences. While the creators and writers implemented the *telenovela* format, they were unsuccessful because they negated references to the Latinx experience or communities in the US MyNetworkTV's attempt to successfully run shows like *Wicked Games* (adapted from a 1998 Venezuelan series, *Aunque me cueste la vida* [Though It Might Cost Me My Life]), whitewashes something that is linked to the Latinx experience (generations of Latinxs or newly arrived immigrants).

2. Longoria served as one of the producers of *Devious Maids*. The show focused on a close-knit group of maids working in affluent Beverly Hills homes. The protagonists, all Latina-identified actors, such as Roselyn Sánchez and Ana Ortiz (*Ugly Betty*), interpret maids and women with dreams and aspirations.

3. See the work of Charles Ramirez Berg (2002), Chon Noriega, and Alma López (1996), Isabel Molina-Guzman (2018), Angharad Valdivia (2010), and Jillian Báez (2018).

4. See Nora Mazziotti (2006) and Carolina Acosta-Alzuru (2013).

5. See Nora Mazziotti (2006).

6. See Charles Ramirez Berg (2002), Chon Noriega and Alma López (1996), Isabel Molina-Guzman (2018), Angharad Valdivia (2010), and Jillian Báez (2018).

7. Nora Mazziotti (2006) and Carolina Acosta-Alzuru (2013) argue that telenovelas serve as a televisual medium that uses melodramatic tone, with excess of sentiment and hyperbole while at the same time allowing for a daily yet limited broadcast schedule which distinguish itself from US soap operas and other serials.

8. Questions surrounding reception for these newer shows may be difficult to answer within the scope of this project. How do we measure perceptions surrounding reproductive decision-making for shows like *Jane the Virgin*? Building on Báez's work, a comprehensive ethnographic approach would garner more information about perception and influence in Latina/x viewership.

9. See the work of Darien Perez Ryan and Patrick E. Jamieson (2019) on how media portrayals of health and habits can impact adolescent viewers. The authors analyzed *Juana la virgen* and *Jane the Virgin* to compare and contrast risky habits found in the two and concluded that the US version tends to have more unhealthy and risky behaviors portrayed than the Venezuelan version.

10. See Charles Ramirez Berg (2002), Chon Noriega and Alma López (1996), Isabel Molina-Guzman (2018), Angharad Valdivia (2010), and Jillian Báez (2018).

11. See Charles Ramirez Berg (2002), Chon Noriega and Alma López (1996), Isabel Molina-Guzman (2018), Angharad Valdivia (2010), and Jillian Báez (2018).

12. *Juana la virgen* (Venezuela, 2002) was written by Perla Farías and produced by RCTV (Radio Caracas Televisión). *Jane the Virgin* (USA, 2014) was developed by Jennie Snyder Urman and produced by Warner Brothers and CBS.

13. These characters could be Latino, but they could also be "Filipino, Samoan, half-African American, or Asian, or simply light-skinned 'ethnic' types," which, as the term suggest, creates this ambiguity surrounding these characters (Beltrán, *Latina/o* 159).

14. A 2018 Nielsen study found that 24% of Jane viewers identified as Latino while the vast majority were non-Hispanic white (https://www.nielsen.com/us/en/insights/article/2018/mass-appeal-a-look-at-the-cross-cultural-impact-of-on-screen-diversity/).

15. Alirio Aguilera (1995) argues that the dramatization of illness is generally exaggerated for dramatic effect, while placing the love conflict front and center, emphasizing a "miraculous recovery" (11).

16. See films like *El Norte* (1983), *Paraíso Travel* (2008), *Under the Same Moon* (2007), for example, and on television, Sofia Vergara's character on *Modern Family* or Rita Moreno's on *One Day at a Time*.

17. See Anzaldúa (2007), Castillo (1995).

18. See Guerra, Ríos, and Stokes (2011).

Chapter 3

Navigating Reproductive Decisions and Transgressions in *Vida* and *Quinceañera*

Issues related to women of color and reproduction, particularly with pregnancy and abortion, have historically been controversial or absent in the US, and at times have led to a perpetuation of Latinx stereotypes like hyperfertility, coming from and wanting large families, or promiscuity.[1] In the current social and political climate, attempts to undermine and strip women's access to reproductive healthcare, including reproductive health care and abortion, are increasing. Like in previous chapters, this one analyzes two cultural texts, one television series and one film, both centered on Latinx worlds. The Starz series *Vida* (2018–2020) and the film *Quinceañera* (2006) challenge representations of Latina/x reproductive decision-making on the small screen. These two cultural texts build on and contrast with the varying degrees of reproductive decision-making in *Jane the Virgin* and in Teatro Luna's work, all exploring boundaries and challenging historical, political, and social limitations of Latinidad. This chapter links Chicana/Latina theories and the cultural texts as a way to understand and emphasize different ways of being Latina/x. Mediatized representations of Latina/x women are a burgeoning site of analysis within cultural studies and media studies.[2] Although these two texts differ in genre, distribution, and production, they explore representations of Latina/x reproductive decision-making, where the main characters that are faced with pregnancy regulate and transgress heteropatriarchal and cultural norms that underpin the characters' social and cultural positions.

This chapter is divided into two sections. After briefly summarizing other mediatized texts emphasizing Latina/x worlds, specifically reproductive decision-making, on television and in film, I will summarize *Vida* and *Quinceañera* and the reasons for choosing these texts as the subjects of this chapter. Then I closely analyze several episodes from *Vida*, focusing on

Season 4, episodes 4 and 5, highlighting one of the main characters' experiences with pregnancy and abortion. Followed by my analysis of three scenes from the film *Quinceañera* that reflect another pregnancy experience, that of a young Latina protagonist. I then turn my analysis to trace the ways the two characters comply with and resist various stereotypical norms that underpin Latina/x representations, such as the marianista or bad woman as seen in *Jane the Virgin*, a more nuanced understanding of Latina reproductive decision-making. As mentioned before, in no way is this analysis an authoritative reading of these two cultural texts nor do I claim that all viewers are uncritical consumers of popular culture. Finally, I discuss the implications of viewing these cultural texts through the lens of feminist theories in relation to agency and resistance. These two texts reflect and transform social contexts, expectations, and norms for pregnant characters and they also show characters struggling with unwanted or unplanned pregnancies. Both *Vida* and *Quinceañera* explore how social and cultural contexts complicate reproductive decision-making while at the same time showing Latinas do and do not choose to pursue motherhood. These two examples take on the rhetoric of choice over bodily autonomy but also negotiate unplanned pregnancies, both representations manifesting ambiguities surrounding pregnancy.

VIDA (2018–2020)

Based on driving questions and themes of the current project, Starz' *Vida* (2018–2020) navigates the lives of two Mexican American sisters reunited by the untimely death of their mother. *Vida*'s showrunner is Tanya Saracho, one of Teatro Luna's co-founders. After working on HBO's *Looking, Girls,* ABC's *Devious Maids,* and *How to Get Away with Murder*, Saracho signed a deal to work on content creation for Starz. Most recently, she signed a deal with UPC (Universal Content Productions) to develop original television projects and establish an incubator for Latinx voices. Much like her work in Teatro Luna, Saracho curated an inclusive writer's room for *Vida* made up primarily of voices of color and LGBTQ writers, including Richard Villegas Jr., who wrote the short story "Pour Vida," that inspired the series. Saracho's approach and influence over who helped write speaks to her commitment to representing Latinx stories.

In the drama series, series, Lyn (Melissa Barrera) and Emma Hernández (Mishel Prada) navigate complex issues such as identity, gentrification, and immigration as they negotiate their identities. Emma has a career in Chicago as a corporate executive and has been estranged from her family in California. She returns to Boyle Heights, LA, to deal with the death of her mother, Vidalia (Vida). Lyn, also estranged from Emma comes to Boyle Heights from life in San Francisco, to deal with the untimely death of her mother, and to figure out what's next after breaking up with her wealthy white boyfriend who supported her. This series offers a refreshing and complex take on what it means to be Latinx. Even though the series centers on a Mexican-dominant neighborhood in Los Angeles, the writers, and creators craft nuanced queer and nonbinary Latinx characters and many queer and nonbinary actors embody those characters. While the focus on a Mexican American family is well-known and oft-used, Saracho and her writer's room worked to craft and create a series made up of tiny brush strokes not broad ones, to understand Latinx experiences in the 21st century.[3] Emma and Lyn, along with Eddy (Ser Anzoategui), and the spirit of Vida navigate the ins and outs of dealing with the consequences of Vida's death, her "secret" relationship and marriage to Eddy, the absence of their father, the onslaught of problems by taking over their mother's bar and building in a gentrifying Boyle Heights (LA), while challenging viewer expectations of what it means to be Latinx in the 21st century.

The show challenges Latinx stereotypes including and upending the role of motherhood, mothering, and family. First and foremost, though not the focus of this chapter, Emma and Lyn's mother, is absent from the story, aside from flashbacks of a young mother with two girls or as seen in her relationship to Eddy. Vida challenges conventional motherhood to offer a queer approach to theorizing her maternal experience. The portrayal of motherhood in *Vida* through Vida's character and those around her such as Eddy, Lyn, and Emma, focus on giving voice to her history, specifically one focused on the role of mother and lover. In light of the show's focus throughout the series on the settlement of Vida's estate, her daughters learn the secrets she has kept from them: she's taken a loan against the building she left them; the bar on the building's ground floor is now a lesbian bar; and Vida had a wife, Eddy. Considering Vidalia kept her relationship secret from her daughters and she also kept their father's whereabouts a secret, Vida's commitment to her queer family, in absentia, exemplified by Emma and Lyn's fraught relationship is redefined according to specific social, political, and generic circumstances. Vida is a second-generation Mexican American, born to two-working class parents in Boyle Heights, and she married young, raising her children alone. She had to tend to the bar her father left her while also caring for her two girls. The imaginary constructs of mothering and the ideal family are filtered through what Ann E. Kaplan calls "motherhood ideology" (121). Within this framework, the mother provides for the children and the family, psychologically, domestically, and economically in order to perform the mother role. However, the representation of Vida and her experience as a single parent leads viewers to assume she betrays her responsibilities by sending Emma off to her grandmother and raising Lyn while working at bar. Vida is the counter to the sacrificial mother and modest and honorable woman, ministering to the needs of a partner or her children. As we come to find out in the final season, Vida sends Emma to her grandmother to protect her from her father's wrath after Emma is caught kissing a girl.

From the onset, the mother-daughter relationship is fraught and at the same time the premise of the show revolves around Emma and Lyn coming to terms with their relationship and their mother's history. Even though the relationship is strained, all of the women favor closeness primarily with each other through the need to figure out what to do with the building/bar and to understand how to navigate the world they live in. While the focus of this chapter is not Vida or her coming into motherhood, her specter in the building/bar, her relationship to Eddy, more importantly, it is the different relationships she had with her daughters that sets the tone for the narrative surrounding Emma and Lyn's decisions to perhaps remain childfree. Specifically, for the scope of this section, the range of reproductive decision-making and the role of bodily autonomy in the characters' lives, specifically for Lyn and Emma, center the analysis on the characters and how the show mines complex constructions of Latinx identity and center narratives around ways of being Latinx in the 21st century.[4]

Emma and Lyn's mother, Vida, and her specter set the tone for the reproductive decision-making story arcs where Emma chooses to remain childfree and have a medicated abortion. Before addressing the specific scenes of her decision, it is important to take a detour to talk about the sound and tone of the show, specifically a song about bodily autonomy, that further resonates with the importance of moving beyond stereotypical notions of Latinidad, including and not separate from sonic spaces. Moreover, it is important to note that the soundtrack was carefully curated by Saracho and her producers to set the tone for the series and the topics and themes it would address, including reproductive decision-making. One of the songs as it relates to the tone and theme of the show, also foreshadows Emma and Lyn's experiences with reproductive decision-making is "Dueña de mí" ("Boss of myself") by La Misa Negra. Season 2 opens with the song by La Misa Negra, a band from Oakland, California, known for their unique blend of cumbia and high-energy, Afro-Latin music.[5] The song captures the type of lifestyle that both Emma and Lyn abide by free to make decisions about how to live, love and be as Latinx women, as the female vocalists in the group sing: "yo no quiero hijos, reclamo [. . .] quiero estudiar [. . .] eres dueña de todo tu cuerpo y no te diran cuando procrear [. . .]."[6] While the soundtrack and this song are not the focus of this analysis, the song does drive much of the scenes and episodes surrounding what are and are not priorities for the two sisters. The images and sounds of a woman, particularly one that takes matters into her own hands, especially as they relate to bodily autonomy and reproductive decision-making, disturbs the unavailable and impossible gender and sexuality subject positions that underlie and structure the space of the traditional home and family structure, as well as larger expectations of what Latina/x reproductive decision-making looks or sounds like.[7] The main vocalist of La Misa Negra, Diana Trujillo penned the cumbia and song for *Vida*'s episode right after the 2017 Women's March on Washington, DC.[8] In it, she asserts her right to make her own decisions, including when to have children: "I am the owner of my destiny and I want to live it with freedom," Trujillo sings in Spanish over the sound of an accordion. The video for the song showcases images from the 2017 march immediately following former President Donald J. Trump's inauguration. Music plays a large role in the show, which is made evident as Season 2 gets underway with La Misa Negra's song about female agency, propelling the audience to think differently about Latinx reproductive decision-making. Furthermore, this song disrupts the construction of the notion of what it means to be Latinx and women in the 21st century as the Trump administration and GOP-led legislatures and politicians undertook attacks against women's reproductive rights.

Emma's Choice

Emma's pregnancy and abortion surfaces in the third season (episodes 4 and 5). While the episodes and season do not solely revolve around the pregnancy and her decision to have an abortion, the unfolding of Emma's situation is tied to larger conversations surrounding representation of reproductive decision-making and can be seen as a strategy for negotiating and resisting stereotypical understandings of Latinx and reproductive decision-making. While Emma does not have an ongoing or serious relationship when she returns to LA, she does fall for Nico (Roberta Calindrez) in Season 2. During that time, she also becomes sexually involved with Baco (Raúl Castillo), the local contractor hired to help fix the bar. Shame does not shape the love triangle that Emma is in, but secrecy and privacy does. While she is torn between becoming too involved with Nico, she is drawn to Baco in a way that she cannot explain nor does she want to. On the other hand, Lyn is more open about her sexual experiences. As the seasons progress, Emma and Nico become more romantically involved but Emma maintains a physical relationship with Baco. After several encounters and conversations about what they were doing (from Baco), Emma decides not to continue and apologizes to Baco for treating him like garbage. Emma is attracted to Baco, but she confesses to Nico that she is in love with her, despite Emma's refusal to become romantically involved with anyone. As episode four opens, Lyn, and Marcos (Tonatiuh) prepare for his queer quinceañera event at the bar. As guests arrive, Marcos, Lyn, his friends, and Emma huddle around Marcos, who thanks them for being there to support him on his journey and his 30th birthday celebration.[9] To celebrate, Marcos shares hallucinogenic mushrooms with the group, including Lyn and Emma. They consume copious amounts of mushrooms, especially Emma, who is distraught about her rocky relationship with Nico, who lied to her about her past partner and current situation. To relieve her anxiety or stress, she consumed more than ever, and acted loving and carefree to which Lynn (sober) was utterly confused. Towards the end of the party, Emma reveals to Lyn that she is pregnant. Emma calls them "a collection of cells" inside of her; she covers herself in blue tule; reminiscent of the Virgin of Guadalupe as she meanders throughout the party still high on mushrooms.[10]

Dawn Heinecken contends that "a guiding principle in Hollywood films is that women and their bodies are consistently disempowered and contained" (3). *Vida*, although not a film, does resist this logic, and instead Emma's control represents the liberal feminism, aimed at taking control of her body and destiny by choosing to terminate her pregnancy. Enacting the tenets of liberal feminism, by being a career queer woman, taking ownership of the bar, choosing her partners, Emma is placed in contrast to femininity and womanhood and embodies what is considered a femme-macho or considered more masculine (i.e., sexually liberated, tough, not overly emotional). She is placed in opposition to her sister, although Lyn also recognizes the power in her choices, like having different lovers or, as she reveals to Emma, having an abortion. Furthermore, there is a radical queer feminist expression in Emma and Lyn. While some of their neighbors are fighting and criticizing Emma and Lyn for fixing the bar (i.e., seeing it as gentrifying) and calling them "sellouts," the sisters fight back and reclaim their space by asserting their family's history there but also as a safe space for queer folk of color in the neighborhood. In addition, despite living in a working-class, yet vastly gentrifying area of Los Angeles, Emma and Lyn are not your stereotypical Latinas: subdued, virginal, or the stereotypical spitfire. In this way, neither woman, especially Emma, discipline their bodies in heteronormative codes of Latino or Anglo behavior. Emma remains childfree throughout the rest of the series and does not demonstrate any guilt or grief.

Similar to Xiomara's experience in *Jane the Virgin*, Emma gets a medicated abortion, and in episode 5, Season 3, Emma at a pharmacy, receiving instructions on how to take the pills. She pays with her credit card and consumes the first round of pills that will trigger an abortion.[11] In this scene it is evident that access to the medication is not an issue for Emma. Emma has access to an income that does not prevent her from purchasing the pills even though she is no longer working for her firm in Chicago. Throughout the remainder of the episode, viewers take in how the medication makes Emma feel nauseated and in pain. It also represents how she contends with the physical reaction of the medicated abortion different from Xiomara's experience, as viewers do see how Emma physically reacts to the medication. Early in the episode Lyn and Emma talk about the abortion experience and Lyn laments not being with her at the clinic to support her since Lyn also had a medicated abortion. Emma goes through the abortion process alone while trying to help Lyn manage an event at the bar.[12] Given Emma's strong-willed attitude, she refuses to ask for help or tell others what she is going through. Even though Emma's abortion is not explicitly mentioned, her experience is visualized. By not explicitly stating that something is wrong, Emma does get help from Nico (Roberta Calindrez) even though she at first refused her help due to their fall out.

Ultimately, Emma represents an abortion-positive representation helping in break stigma surrounding abortion, moving beyond the politicized expectations of pro/against discourse.[13] Similarly, as Carruthers (2021) argues in her work on pregnancy in film, some film may include well-recognized tropes, like the pregnancy test, the scans, or pregnant bodies, however, in the case of *Vida*, the show is designed to allow an abortion-positive message about the importance of abortion and reproductive decisions. There is no tension between Emma or Lyn about their respective experiences and while Emma does not reveal to others what she is experiencing, they take care of her. The show's depiction of Latinx reproductive decision-making as an individual yet collective decision exemplifies that there is a public and a private understanding of abortion, specifically as something that is both liberatory, devastating yet empowering (Thomsen 2013). For Lyn, she recounts her experience with medicated abortion as something she chose freely and without reservation, but at the same time she found it difficult to endure alone.[14] Similar to the Xiomara in *Jane the Virgin*, Emma's experience is notable and subdued given that the medicated abortion is experienced by characters embodying seldom represented identities: racialized, financially secure, older, and queer-identified (Emma). These representations suggest a positive relationship between abortion discourses and call for reproductive justice. According to reproductive justice proponents, reproductive justice understands and emphasizes the inextricable link between a person and their reproductive life (Ross 2006). While these examples offer positive representations of medicated abortion, they also demand viewers see them differently. These texts can give viewers different meanings about abortion and reproductive decision-making. The critical visual elements surrounding pregnancy when it appears in fiction, like television or film, can be deployed as a narrative device, at times, conflating womanhood with pregnancy and maternity, as we see in the example of *Jane the Virgin* or in more traditional telenovelas. In contrast, the narrative device in *Jane* then, can be turned on its head to create an abortion-positive narrative in the case of Xiomara. Furthermore with Emma in *Vida*, the theme of pregnancy and abortion is as critical to a sociopolitical understanding of abortion as it is to represent it in fiction. As such, shows like *Vida* aid in presenting nuanced representations of Latinx people and their reproductive decision-making. In this fictive world, everyday life, sibling relationships, queer bodies, and experiences reflect distinct neighborhoods and cultures.

NOT YOUR TRADITIONAL QUINCEAÑERA

Quinceañera (2006) is an independent film, directed by Richard Glatzer and Wash Westmoreland that earned two awards at the Sundance Film Festival in 2006, including the Dramatic Grand Jury Price and the Audience Award, and it received positive reviews from critics.[15] The film centers around the life of Magdalena (Emily Ríos) and her family as they prepare to celebrate her quinceañera, or her 15th birthday celebration, an important coming-of-age celebration for many Latin American families The young protagonist Magdalena is a Mexican American from Echo Park, California, coming of age in her parents' very traditional home: her father is a pastor and a cop and her mother stays home to take care of the house. In the opening scenes of the film, Magdalena, and her extended family, including aunts, uncles, and cousins celebrate Magdalena's cousin Eileen's quinceañera. At the party, Eileen's brother Carlos (Jesse García) is not welcome because his parents and extended family do not agree with his queer identity. Magdalena and her family are excited because her celebration is coming up soon and she is looking forward to having a celebration just as big as Eileen's. Her parents want Magdalena to share her cousin's quinceañera dress because of their limited means. Unfortunately, Magdalena's plans are up in the air when her borrowed quince dress from Eileen no longer fits leading to speculations about Magdalena's status: Is she pregnant?

A particular scene relevant to this analysis unfolds within the first 40 minutes. In this scene we learn that Magdalena is dating Hernán and that they fooled around (we later learn that he ejaculated on her thigh and that is how she got pregnant). Once her celebration dress does not fit, Magdalena's mother, María (Araceli Guzman-Rico) confronts her and forces Magdalena to go to the pharmacy to get a test. Her mom tells her father, Ernesto (Jesús Castaños-Chima), about the pregnancy and this three-minute scene demonstrates Ernesto's anger and fury, indicating Magdalena's transgression and affront to the family and the church.[16] Magdalena defends herself and makes sure that her parents understand that she did not have intercourse, but her father does not believe her and she quietly leaves her home in the middle of the night. The next morning we learn that she is now with her great-great uncle Tomás (Chalo Gonzalez) and her cousin Carlos.

In this film, Magdalena's unintended pregnancy becomes the focus of discussion and her pregnancy brings shame to the family, as well as an act that is inappropriate for someone her age. While the pregnancy is an accident and Magdalena maintains her innocence stating that she and Hernan did not have intercourse, her family, friends, and Hernan turn their back on her. As scholar Evelyn Stevens (1973) has argued in relation to marianismo that the male/female binary behavior discussions revolve around the perceived moral and spiritual qualities of the (virgin/good) woman capable of reproduction. The complexity of gender roles and the concept of marianismo in a traditional working-class home bears heavily on the conversations surrounding Magadalena's transgression. Magdalena's pregnancy represents the total opposite of the quinceañera celebration: a young, pure, virginal woman preparing to come of age and celebrate her entrance into society. However, she maintains her innocence and sees the reality of a baby as something that gives new meaning in her life, despite having to leave her parents' home or the onslaught of criticism from her family. For Anne Carruthers (2021), in the film, pregnancy has an effect on the wider community, and this is shown through the narrative of Magdalena's controversial pregnancy: as a teenager and a virgin. For the remainder of the film Magdalena's family and friends have conversations about what is and what is not appropriate behavior for a 15-year-old. In the eyes of her family and friends, she no longer represents a virginal young woman or *marianista* figure. As such, she no longer emulates the values of her home culture and faith.

Despite Magdalena's innocence, and the inherent contradictions in the criticism she faces, Magdalena's great-uncle visits her father Ernesto to talk to him, to assure him that Magdalena is a good girl.[17] The conversation surrounding whether or not she is good or bad continues to be the standard for Magdalena and in turn, the representation of how Latina feminine virtue is judged, both in film and in real life. Unfortunately, Ernesto does not feel the same way and rejects Tomás' view. The scene cuts to Tomás holding a Virgen of Guadalupe charm as he talks about Magdalena signaling a direct link to Magdalena's pregnancy, one that was virginal, but at the same time within the context of a Marianist motif, as a virtuous woman, fairly untreated, suffering from an injustice, awaiting a favorable outcome.[18] The image of the Virgen de Guadalupe and Tomás' other religious iconography in his garden provide a level of comfort or perspective regarding the expectations since the main protagonist, a "good" young woman, leads the viewers through her experience as an unwed pregnant teen. In her uncle's house along with her cousin Carlos, Magdalena does not feel shame nor does she get negative comments like from her father and her school peers. Her father declares her a liar because how could she be pregnant if she claims she did not have intercourse.[19] Magdalena's transgression and her expulsion from her home and her circle of friends "propels us to think differently about the home as the ontological bedrock of essential and inviolable Latino communal identity" (Bondy 90). For Bondy then, Magdalena's traditional home space is hostile and no longer welcoming of a young woman who violated patriarchal and heteronormative understandings of Latinidad, one facet being that she stay a virgin until marriage. As such, Bondy argues that Magdalena's "home" space is with her uncle and Carlos, giving viewers a sense of a more welcoming space despite Tomás' displays of saintly imagery, family keepsakes, and religious iconographies like the Virgen de Guadalupe (90). As we saw in *Jane the Virgin*, Jane's virginal pregnancy was not linked to her having intimate relationships and as such, her family does not reject her, yet they support her decision to keep the child. In both instances, the narratives surrounding family and kinship do surround the presence of a pregnant body, adding to the importance of space and presence in meaning making. I agree with Bondy's analysis because Magdalena's traditional home space has rejected and shamed her for her transgression despite her innocence, while at the same time, Tomás' home offers Magdalena and Carlos a safe space where they can negotiate their identities without the shame and stigma.

Even though Magdalena pleads her innocence, her mother, father and even Hernán do not believe it. Magdalena's transgression and her insistence disrupts the ways in which we understand the all-too-common figure of the asexual or sexually pure Latina. The film also sends the message that she is hyperfertile given her intimate encounter with Hernán, despite no intercourse, resulted in her pregnancy. Furthermore it is important to note that Magdalena while still critical of Carlos, demonstrates a sibling-like bond when she confronts him and says that she will have her baby and continue her life as planned, and he tries to further connect with her by saying that no one in their extended family believes them. In this space, both Magdalena and Carlos are considering the "demands of a particular patriarchal and heteronormative representation of girls' [and male] roles" (Bondy 91, 2012). Magdalena also asserts her innocence to Hernán, but he is in disbelief because they did not have intercourse; plus he's not willing to take care of the child because he is bound for college and his mother disapproves of anything that would derail his future.[20] In this example, the double-standard and burden emerge whereas Hernán refuses to take responsibility and even rejects the possibility that it is his child since they did not have intercourse. Magdalena can be viewed as the suffering mother, being noble, having silent penitence, while everyone is criticizing or judging her for becoming pregnant. She has the double burden of demonstrating her innocence while at the same time navigating the unrealistic and patriarchal expectations about her role as a young Latina woman.

More importantly, Magdalena's transgression and subsequent move to her great uncle's house forces the viewers to question heteropatriarchal discourses on notions of what it means to be Latina in the 21st century. Furthermore, her mother, while not explicitly on her side, is sympathetic to her plight, going with Magdalena to the gynecologist, who confirms to her mother that it is possible for Magdalena to be pregnant without penetration. Her mother does protect her from her father's rage while at the same time helping Magdalena navigate her pregnancy. Even though as viewers we only see Magdalena navigate the whispers and gossip about her pregnancy, as well as her growing belly, her pregnancy and her subsequent plans become the space where we can come to understand her emotional and physical needs are best met in her uncle's home, along with Carlos' support.

As Magdalena's body begins to visibly change, she is confronted with the unexpected death of her uncle, knowing she does not rely on Hernán for support, and she realizes she cannot afford to live alone, let alone with a child. As viewers we never directly see her body in close-up scenes but we see her growing belly through several long shots.[21] At the same time, she adopts to the changes and impending shifts by accepting Carlos' help, and even though the onset the film can seem to take on the stereotypical Latina teen pregnancy drama, it provides more than the young "mujer sufrida" (*suffering woman*). Instead of offering the oft-presented patriarchal gaze or the expected gaze with regard to societal attitudes regarding teen pregnancy, Magdalena's story offers a different view of a young woman navigating her identity and her future child while at the same time rejecting others' opinions about her innocence. Even though her uncle's home space and her family's religious identity are juxtaposed to Magdalena's visible transgression, the iconography present throughout the film envelope her stand in contrast to her family's beliefs. Similarly, by not reinforcing the stereotypes of Latina "bad" woman, irresponsible and deviant, the film represents Magdalena in a new light, giving her agency and refusing to represent an essentialized pregnant teen. Not only does she transgress the expectation of being a virgin quinceañera, but she is also accepted as representative of an immaculate conception, as a miracle. She is no longer burdened by trying to plead her case about her pregnancy and she feels liberated once she realizes that she will have quinceañera. In the final scene the camera pans to Magdalena gleefully entering her father's church and making her way to the front where she sits down in a chair, now the center of attention, and the camera shot does not focus in on her growing belly, but it establishes the importance of her experience as a quinceañera, getting her own dress and limousine.[22] By completely upending the ways in which Latina womanhood and subjectivity are presented, the film navigates the challenges of heteronormative and patriarchal understandings of virginity and agency.

Magdalena's parents and her extended family save Tomás and Carlos, fear and do not understand what is happening nor do they want to believe her at the onset of the film. These men challenge and upend the discourses of Latino patriarchal notions of family and purity that maintain the representation of the virgin Latina and pure young woman within the space of the family and the larger notion of Latina/Chicanx *familia*. Magdalena refuses to give in to the demands of her family and stands firm in viewing her actions and experiences as a "virgin" mother as something that she will take on and does not deem them going against norms. She disrupts and transgresses patriarchal and heteronormative conceptualizations of the virginal Latina mother by disrupting physical space, home space, and the space of the traditional notion of a quinceañera. The ambivalence shown in Magdalena suggests that there is no right or wrong way to understand and represent Latina experiences. In essence, she was exploring her sexuality and she became pregnant in a less conventional way. It is a way to celebrate her decisions and not place judgment or stigma upon her choices or actions based on antiquated forms of representation and understanding a young woman's role.

CONCLUSION

It is possible that in experiencing these two visual texts some viewers may view *Vida* and *Quinceañera* as perhaps perpetuating racialized, patriarchal, and heteronormative representations of Latinx identity and reproductive decision-making. These representations of Latina/x women and their decisions to continue or not with their pregnancies offer a critical tool for another way of being and seeing Latina/x reproductive decision-making. To discerning viewers distorted representations of Latina/x identity and reproductive decision-making offered in traditional telenovelas or some films, for example, are not a fictitious reality that they must accept or reject. Furthermore, the images present in both *Vida*, navigating a medicated abortion, and in *Quinceañera*, Madgalena navigating her pregnancy as a teen, are perceived by the viewers as a crucial element in the narrative. For example, in the case of *Quinceañera* Magdalena is expected to conform to staying a virgin and without any sexual desires or experiences as a young woman coming up in a traditional, religious home. Even though she has not had intercourse with Hernán she becomes pregnant. She is kicked out of her house and shamed and criticized by her family and friends but finds a home in her great-uncle Tomás' place. Magdalena is expected not to transgress certain norms like having a sexual encounter before marriage, let alone her 15th birthday. Despite the inherent contradictions in the marianist ideology and representation, *Quinceañera* works to upend such characteristics such as the sacrificial woman, or the inherently bad, transgressive woman and complicates our understanding of transgression as a young woman that did not lose her virginity but did end up pregnant. In this example, Magdalena is positioned as a transgressor but she maintains her innocence throughout her representation as a young, teen, Latina and pregnant sends the signal that she is another hyperfertile Latina, however, she also comes to emulate the Virgin de Guadalupe, combining virginity and impending motherhood. In a way, the film gives teen pregnancy a positive spin since the character is able to have her quinceañera and her parents, especially her father forgives her after learning she is still a virgin. Her great-uncle, cousin, and mother are sympathetic to Magdalena's plight while at the same time others such as her father and school friends censure her. As the film progresses, Magdalena finds solace and a safe home in her great-uncle's home and eventually, after his death, she gets to celebrate her party with a new dress and her cousin Carlos by her side. Magdalena and her family seem to accept her pregnancy and as such it problematizes the inherent dissonance in the parameters for womanhood within the context of the familial relationships. Thus, Magdalena's transgression within the space of a traditional and religious home maps out a different way of being for her and disorganizes the viewing space for spectators because it represents a more nuanced way to represent a difficult situation.

Vida demonstrates an "abortion-positive" representation to reproductive decision-making in Season 3. Emma's decision to get an abortion, within a hegemonic and heteronormative context, may read as careless, shameful, and tragic given her various encounters with Baco. Her pregnancy and abortion may read as the stereotypical hyperfertile and promiscuous Latina, acknowledging that all aspects of her queer identity perpetuates risky behavior, the complete opposite of the marianista figure. Emma goes through a medicated abortion while trying to navigate her daily tasks at her deceased mother's bar, contending with her broken relationship with Nico and trying to find a connection with her sister, Lyn. By narrowly and reductively focusing on the show's single representation of reproductive decision-making, *Vida* demonstrates and exceeds standard and heteronormative representations and resonates with a more nuanced presentation of her decision to have an abortion. This representation also resonates with reproductive justice because it does not demand that the audience consider the right or wrong of abortion nor does it perpetuate the stigma surrounding reproductive decisions. As such, Emma's experience in *Vida* suggests that ambivalence characterizes the abortion experience and that people who seek abortions do not view their decision on pro or against life but rather, this text demonstrates that abortion-positive representations honor the complex and varied experiences of reproductive decisions in people's lives.

NOTES

1. See Elena R. Gutierrez (2008), Patricia Zavella (2020), and Lorena García (2012).
2. See the work of Gónzalez, Rodriguez y Gibson (2015), Jillian Báez (2018), Valdivia (2020), and Beltrán (2022).
3. Most recently, Tanya Saracho, along with actor/producer Selena Gomez, have been working on a Latinx rendition of the John Hughes movie, *Sixteen Candles.*
4. See the Saracho interview with Felix Contreras from Alt. Latino (2018).
5. Lipsky (2017).
6. "I do not want children, I demand . . . I want to study . . . you are boss of your body and nobody will tell you when to procreate" (my translation). "Dueña de mí" by La Misa Negra (2018). YouTube video. Dir. Marco Polo Santiago. youtu. be/5ssVCoyPaC4.
7. Ibid.
8. Orozco, Gisela. 2018. "La Misa Negra: Cumbia contracorriente." *Chicago Tribune.* June 28, 2018. www.chicagotribune.com/hoy/entretenimiento/ct-hoy -entretenimiento-la-misa-negra-cumbia-contracorrientesi-20180628-story.html. Accessed March 9, 2022.
9. *Vida.* Season 3, episode 4. *Starz.* Dir. Tanya Saracho, written by Esti Giordani. May 17, 2020. Accessed May 30, 2021. Cable.
10. Ibid.
11. *Vida.* Season 3, episode 5. *Starz.* Dir. Tanya Saracho, written by Jenniffer Gómez. May 24, 2020. Accessed May 30, 2021. Cable.
12. Ibid.
13. Ludlow 2021.
14. *Vida.* Season 3, episode 5. *Starz.* Dir. Tanya Saracho, written by Jenniffer Gómez. May 24, 2020. Accessed May 30, 2021. Cable.
15. Holden, Stephen. 2006. "'Quinceañera': Turning Sweet 15 in Los Angeles's Immigrant Stew." *New York Times.* Review. August 4, 2006. www.nytimes.com/2006 /08/04/movies/04quin.html?smid=url-share. Accessed October 20, 2021.
16. *Quinceañera* (2006), dir. Glatzer and Westmoreland.
17. Ibid.
18. Ibid.
19. Ibid.
20. Ibid.
21. Ibid.
22. Ibid.

Chapter 4

"Mi cuerpo. Yo decido"

Reproductive Decision-Making and Social Justice

Reproductive decision-making is politically significant in creative work by and about Latinas/x, specifically in theater and performance as well as in media. Teatro Luna's characters Miranda, Coya, Chelly, and Tanya defy heteropatriarchal notions of Latina/x reproductive decision-making by resisting traditional representations and expectations of pregnancy and motherhood. When the strong female women in *Jane the Virgin* share with the viewers their struggles with reproductive decision-making, these struggles are common experiences lived by other women, especially when considering abortion or adoption. In a 2020 interview, Latinx artist Favianna Rodriguez argues that "Art helps us imagine the world in a different way, and it can also illuminate what is not [so easily] seen. . . . In doing so, art can help us imagine solutions to move forward" (Day 2020). As Rodriguez's quote exemplifies, the power of art in representing reproductive decision-making for Latinas not only makes evident the veil of shame often associated with difficult conversations such as miscarriage or abortion, but rather, artist representation provides an avenue to imagine better possibilities. This chapter turns to representations of reproductive decision-making in social justice posters that seek to upend the shame and silence surrounding reproductive decisions.

Art historian Jennifer A. González (2019) argues that "embodiment emerges as a key site for the exploration of subjectivity, cultural heritage, and aesthetic invention in Chicano/a art" (177). For González and other scholars, the recurring trope of the mestizo/a is a site of exploration for Chicano/a and other Latino/a artists.[1] González also argues that for many, male and female bodies were heavily policed, especially in the early years of the Chicano Movement, emphasizing significant male images such as César Chávez and the pachuco figure in artwork and social justice posters.

As the movement opened up to more inclusive notions of Chicanidad (shared sense of Chicano/a identity), including women, queer bodies were becoming more prevalent in enunciating repression and calling for real socio-political change.[2] Despite these changes and calls to include and recognize Chicana and LGBTQ folk in the movement, "the male archetypes and tropes remained patriarchal and heteronormative" (González 177). These male dominated tropes within the movement as represented by posters, art, handouts, etc., permeated the movement and influenced artwork and other sources of social justice work beyond the movement. The onset of the Chicano Movement witnessed a radical transformation for the variety of approaches to Chicano/a and Latino/a art, especially social justice artwork. Out of this movement and the various struggles within and beyond the movement came changes and new approaches to representing Chicana and Latina bodies, especially in response to heteropatriarchal representations such as the hypersexualized Latina or virginal icons such as the Virgin Mary. Clara Román-Odio (2013) argues in her monograph on Chicana/Latina iconographies that *mestizaje* has had an impact on contemporary Chicana/Latina theories and practice, especially in literature and art. Román-Odio analyzes the artwork of Ester Hernández and Liliana Wilson, for example, to trace how these artists enact the mestiza body as it is articulated by Chicana theorists such as Anzaldúa and Moraga.

Representations of the Latina/x body by mainstream media frequently define it as deviant or dangerous or hypersexualized.[3] So much of these mediatized representations have been framed around discourses that pit good versus bad models of Latina/x embodiment as noted by Gaspar de Alba, Latorre and Román-Odio. The Virgin of Guadalupe was used as a powerful symbol during the Chicano Movement and it continues to be a dominant icon in US Latino/x lives. Artists across mediums have tried to rewrite these limited representations by directly critiquing these binaries and images. Artists Amalia Mesa-Bains, Ester Hernández, Yolanda López, and Alma López have addressed female representation in the Latina/o community through muralism, painting, and print work. More than just representing these iconic figures, these artists transform the icon, by emphasizing the queer and racialized potential of such figures and disentangle the body from the binaries of shame/*vergüenza*. Alma López's case, for example is well known for causing a controversy with her images of women in the likeness of the Virgin of Guadalupe, such as "Our Lady" (1999), an image of a woman, López herself, donning roses covering her naked body in her breasts and pelvic area while posing on top of a bare breasted angel as a woman. This imagery caused controversy because of her appropriation of the image and symbolism of the Virgin. As Chicana scholar Alicia Gaspar de Alba (2011) notes in her edited volume with Alma López on the 2001 controversy, the image garnered debate and disrupted the expectations of a cultural icon, the Mother of God (234).

López did not reproduce the image of the Virgin, but she did appropriate dominant signs such as the gown that covers her, the crescent moon where she stands and the aura around her body, and López challenged the viewer by showing us her defiant gaze, her confrontational stance and her bare feet and legs (235). Guísela Latorre (1999, 2008) analyzes how López and other Chicana artists in the 21st century rethink not just religious icons, but popular symbols like the images on Lotería (Mexican-style bingo). In Latorre's work in analyzing López and other artists like Yreina Cervántez's murals and Latorre (1999) argues that these women employ Latina/Chicana theories through their practice by depicting experiences: "Cervántez's mural presents us with representations of both the grounded affirmations of Latina identity posited by the Chicana writers and activists as well as with the still fluctuating identities present with in the Latino community, identities that have not yet been processed and packaged by academicians" (108). By representing brown bodies through art, these visual artists resist the patriarchal ideology that promotes female passivity and obedience, but they also insist on representing unstable and fluctuating Latina identities. Favianna Rodriguez is an artist that imagines and demands a better world for women of color.

Favianna Rodriguez is an interdisciplinary artist, cultural organizer, and social justice activist. Born and raised in Oakland, CA as the daughter of Peruvian immigrants, she became socially conscious of the anti-immigrant and anti-Latino rhetoric imbued in California with Proposition 187 and across the nation with NAFTA and Operation Gatekeeper (Interview, *Journal of Visual Culture* 152). Her work explores the intersections of art and practice in addressing issues of migration, gender justice, racial equity, sexual freedom, and climate change. Her work includes visual art, public art, writing, cultural organizing, and coalition building, in particular with pro-immigrant and reproductive justice movements. Her work circulates widely, such as her butterfly piece, "Migration is Beautiful," which launched in 2012.[4] In her online artist statement, Rodriguez believes the "artist must fight for justice and peace." As such, her artwork critically engages the viewer to visualize women of color embracing their identity beyond notions of the virginal or hypersexualized Latina. She has collaborated with reproductive justice organizations across the country, including NLIRH's campaign, "Soy poderosa and My Voice Matters." In this campaign, Rodriguez allowed NLIRH to use her images with their own messaging as well. At the local and global levels, Rodriguez's work connects women of color, reproductive justice, and politics to mobilize viewers against injustices that disproportionately affect women of color.

Rodriguez's social justice posters tell us a story about the experiences of women of color by reshaping stories, myths, and practices in order to force the spectator to take inventory of the present and past injustices. In this case study, I explore how Rodriguez explicitly addresses reproductive decision-making through her posters, and how it highlights the damaging discourses around promiscuity and body-shaming. How is shame and vergüenza deployed to imagine reproductive decisions differently? When examining Rodriguez's posters, specifically the "Slut Series" and "Pussy Power" posters, I am reminded of Anzaldúa's notion that images are bridges between evoked emotion and conscious knowing. In *This Bridge Called by Back*, Anzaldúa prefaces the collection of essays and creative work by saying that "To bridge means loosening our borders, not closing off to others. . . . To bridge is to attempt community . . . " (3). Not only does the woman of color build bridges and serve as a bridge, but as an artist she can also bridge art and social justice. Anzaldúa's understanding of women of color's "creative acts" is relevant, especially when considering Rodriguez's work. Anzaldúa declares that for women of color, "writing, painting, performing and filming are acts of deliberate and desperate determination to subvert the status quo. "Creative acts," she says, "are forms of political activism employing definite aesthetic strategies for resisting dominant cultural norms and are not merely aesthetic exercises" (xxiv, 1990). For Anzaldúa and other Chicana/Latina theorists the constant dialogue between identities can be a fruitful space to create and build coalitions between women of color. Rodriguez's "Slut" and "Pussy Power" posters call Latinas/xs and women of color to unite around reproductive rights restrictions, such as limited or no access to abortions.

Rodriguez's work employs visual strategies similar to those used by Chicana/Latina feminists and other women of color artivists. In Anzaldúa's essay, "La prieta," the author highlights what her mother kept telling her when she was a teenager: "Keep your legs shut, prieta" (*This Bridge* 205). This sentiment stems from the expected traditional role of Latina/Chicana women when it comes to virginity until marriage. For writers like Anzaldúa, shame and ambivalence pervaded their upbringing, especially as young women. Anzaldúa further illustrates the role of her family in perpetuating the virgin/whore binary: "My mother and brothers calling me puta when I told them I had lost my virginity and that I'd done it on purpose" (227). In Anzaldúa's essay, the role of a Chicana/Latina woman is limited by obedience and alignment with the traditional role of a woman as a passive and obedient virginal subject. As such, Rodriguez's posters extend beyond the personal, they signal the political, and they undo shame by reclaiming bodies and words that tend to carry stigma, like abortion and uterus. By using a means of art widely seen and accessible to a larger audience, Rodriguez calls into question the oppressive nature of how we understand and view women's reproductive decision-making beyond notions of choice.

Women's bodies, specifically brown bodies presuppose a violent history of colonization and (forced) transculturation beginning in the 16th century.[5] As

Guísela Latorre (2010) has argued, the visual becomes a particularly powerful tool for politicization in the hands of Chicana/o artists (113). She goes on to say that "One recurring strategy that many Chicana/o artists have deployed to illicit or promote political awareness is the use of familiar imagery to the assumed audience of their work, imagery which they in turn reformulate with new meaning. Many of these images had previously circulated via the mass media or community settings and were thus collectively recognizable" (113). The imagery Rodriguez uses places brown bodies front and center and gives these voices agency to speak out about the dangers of restrictive reproductive health ideologies and policies. Furthermore, by naming the spaces that bring about shame and *vergüenza*, Favianna Rodriguez's work upends heteropatriarchal images of Latina/xs by documenting reproductive rights and reshaping how women of color experience reproductive decision-making.

The posters Rodriguez produces in her "Slut Series," illustrate the conversational process and elements of her work. These posters focus on women's bodies, specifically targeting heteropatriarchal politics of control over women's bodies. In the description for the poster *"Mi cuerpo. Yo decido,"* Rodriguez described why she began this series in 2012: "This poster is part of a series of feminist reactions in 2012, as politicians and conservatives were waging an all out war on womxn's bodies, our access to health, our right to birth control, and our right to free, accessible and safe abortion. The attacks on abortion continue today, and 2012 was a special year for me because it's when I came out about my abortion" (Favianna.com). The artist's description of the poster speaks of a feminist positioning, aligned to the oft-used adage, the personal is political. Representing women of color in her images along with language such as "pussy" and "poontang" would appear derogatory, but in her work, these words are appropriated to take on a powerful meaning for the spectators. In these posters, Rodríguez uses women of color images/faces to represent an expression of their Latina/x identity. Two of her "Slut Series" posters are informed by the stigma surrounding abortions. The poster, "Come out. Share your story . . . ," showcases one body and three heads. The central female figures are images of women of color and places their likeness front and center. Along with the image, the message also highlights the call to action to break the silence around reproductive trauma. A recurrent strategy of social justice posters and feminist work on abortion representation is the deliberate emphasis on naming the process and removing the shame surrounding reproductive decisions. As Rodriguez (2014) has indicated in her blog, this poster "[. . .] is a call to speak out against the shame, the isolation, and the secrecy surrounding abortion. By not telling our stories about abortion, and by endorsing a code of secrecy, we are giving into the right wing machine that shames women who have abortions" (favianna.typepad.com). In that very sense, the poster series points to the power of shared experiences since these posters, along with her collaborative work with NLIRH, look to dismantle and rearticulate gendered dynamics that attribute shame and stigma around reproductive decision-making.

The posters question shame associated with women talking about or even considering sharing their experiences with abortion. These posters represent what Anzaldúa called "taking inventory" (82). The first step in "the Mestiza way" is taking inventory of we that have been constructed by traceless historical processes. Then, we must put history "through a sieve, winnow out the lies, looks at the forces that we as a race, as women, have been part of" (104). Through this process, the power is in the "we," and therefore, Rodríguez's call to action substantiates Anzaldúa's notion of. . . . These posters would not have been possible without a conversation between and among women. As noted in her description of one of the series' posters, Rodriguez uses her experience as a Latina to "alter the walks and make them a framework for new windows and doors" (Anzaldúa xxv). By taking inventory, Rodriguez addresses issues that are pressing within the Latina/x community and female community nationwide. The women in the posters are not depicted with any visible signs of pregnancy, as such, this shifts the viewers focus on the woman and the message. This context serves to inform and empower women who may still feel stigma in sharing their experiences with reproductive decision-making. This inventory process causes "conscious ruptures with all oppressive traditions of all cultures and religions. She [then] communicates that rupture, documents the struggle, and reinterprets history, and using new symbols, she shapes new myths" (104). Rodriguez's work on reproductive justice and mobilization around women's access to abortion speaks to a need to reframe and challenge how Latina/x identity and the community have been imagined, explored, constructed, or defined by heteropatriarchal ideologies grounded in purity, virginity, and shame surrounding our bodies.

In Rodriguez's "Pussy Power" series, she deconstructs the trope of the bad/loose woman. Part of Anzaldúa's methodology in constructing her mestiza identity relies on taking inventory, as mentioned before, critically sorting it and transforming herself in order to continue on her path to *conocimiento*. Rodriguez's poster titled, "It's My Pussy. It's My Body" also represents women of color, in the use of a darker skin-toned image. This visual storytelling juxtaposes brown color on the partial face with her red lips and sections of yellow/gold on her neck and head. This image and colors send resounding positive imagery to the viewer and place the woman's image front and center. The colors can represent the strength and optimism of the woman, by emphasizing yellow and red. Unlike linking red and gold to passion or wealth, these colors frame a powerful message below the image: "It's my body. It's my pussy. Get over it you patriarchal fuck head woman hater." This image claims space for the brown woman reclaiming her right to bodily autonomy, resisting heteropatriarchal discourses that push reproductive rights restrictions. The prominence of the words along with the image of the woman desilences reproductive decisions like abortion, locating the woman at the center of the discourse surrounding access to abortions. By taking inventory about how patriarchal ideologies embedded in institutions such as the family or religion, Rodriguez's posters frame and construct the female reproductive system, specifically the vagina, Rodriguez calls our attention to imagery and words that have been used to construct the female body as passive, devoid of desires.[6] Instead of disciplining and controlling sexuality and desires, this image and message signals to the spectator the importance of calling out the misogynistic views and policies present in our institutions, specifically in health care and government. As Moraga has discussed, "if the simple act of sex . . . implies female debasement and non-humanness, it is no wonder Chicanas often divorce ourselves from conscious recognition of our own sexuality" (*Loving* 111). The title of Rodriguez's poster attests to the power of embracing one's body and recognizing the importance of socio-cultural discourses that removes desire and sexuality from women's bodies. The representation of the women in the posters is that of resolute and proud women and it is significant in multiple ways. On the one hand, the resolute expressions may indicate power in their choices and in understanding their agency and on the other, by representing a woman of color, generalized perceptions about women undercuts the stigmatization and shame that is prevalent in mainstream cultural representations surrounding abortions.

In her poster titled, "Politicians off my Pootang!" Rodriguez further explores the connections between socio-cultural attitudes toward women and wanting to control their bodies. As Aída Hurtado argues in her work on Chicanas in theater, "Many Chicanas, struggling to escape the narrow confines of the whore/virgin dichotomy, embrace the femme-macho characteristics as a form of liberation" (388). The femme-macho element is reconstructed in Rodriguez's work, especially in the poster's sub-statement: "My uterus is mine." She challenges and rejects the patriarchy that continues to undermine women's rights to have autonomy over reproductive decisions. In "Politicians off my Poontang!" Rodriguez presents a woman's face, facing the spectator. She is a mestiza, with dark hair, dark eyes, and a resolute look, one that speaks to those who try to impose restrictions on women's bodies or mobilize policies that affect women's right to do what she pleases with her body. In the artist's words: "The right to control your own reproduction is the most fundamental right we have as human beings."[7] An important component of Rodriguez's work as well as other Latina/x artists is the inclusion of sexuality and gender in her subject matter because these identity categories play a role in further oppressing women of color. By also integrating the word "poontang" in her message, Rodriguez gives the derogatory word power in the voice of a woman. This image juxtaposes the multiple histories and cultures (pre-Hispanic, Mexican, American and Latina) that insist upon the good/bad woman and suppress the right of bodily autonomy. In reclaiming bodily autonomy and agency surrounding reproductive decisions, Rodriguez records a politicized and mobilized Latina/x figure to enact change in her world, and like other artists before her generation, like Alma López, Rodriguez utilizes digital tools to create these posters. Art historian Guísela Latorre categorized López's digital work "cyberwomanist activism" as contributing to a growing group of Chicana artists that utilized new technologies as a way to counter and upend traditional forms of producing artwork ("Icons of Love" 149). Latorre borrows the term from digital media scholar Anna Everett (2004) focused on women of color using digital tools for organizing and activism. Rodriguez's utilizes YouTube and her website to teach others how to make social justice posters. For the viewer and the artists, the power to represent your community and help imagine what is possible is inspired by Black, Chicano, and Latin American social justice movements and posters. These digital tools, be it those used to create posters and inspire others to follow suit, compel the viewer to reflect on the importance of art and social justice. In her work, the mestiza is consistently placed front and center because she is represented as speaking directly to him/her. In removing the stigma and vergüenza from defending a person's right to bodily autonomy, the poster desilences and destigmatizes the sexual body. This poster represents Latina/x women beyond stereotypical notions of white-Latinidad and womanhood.

Similarly, in her poster "Mi cuerpo. Yo decido" (My body. I decide) the same mestiza image appears. The mestiza woman is facing the viewers directly and underneath her image the following text in Spanish and English: My body. I decide. I vote. The bold, primary color palette, such as yellow and red are juxtaposed to the text sends a strong message to viewers about the power to speak up and use the ballot box to mobilize change. The simplicity in the phrase in Spanish also signals Rodriguez's approach to making posters, keeping it short so you can have a bigger impact. Rodriguez's own words sum up the importance and imperative of reproductive justice and its connection to art: "I developed four posters demanding safe and accessible abortion for all. I decided it was time for some slut positivity and confronting woman-hating men" (Favianna.com). Through the use of limited but powerful words along with a female image that she has already used beforehand, Rodriguez's poster makes it easy and simple to understand, regardless of the location of the poster. By taking inventory of how Latinas are read and represented, Rodriguez's poster draws on that history of Latina representation and critically addresses what's been inherited or imposed: men's control over women's bodies, especially brown women. In this respect, Rodriguez's image imagines and creates a strong and politicized Latina. The mestiza symbol along with the words in Spanish and English, ending with "Yo voto" (I vote) asserts the woman's right to bodily autonomy which can begin and end at the ballot box as an informed voter. In "There is No Place like Aztlán: Embodied Aesthetics in Chicana Art," Alicia Gaspar de Alba (2004) identifies place-based aesthetics of Aztlán in the work of Chicana artists and associates it with home and place. One of those typologies is "Feminist aesthetics (women artists subscribing to a 'feminist' agenda)" (108). In this category, the notion of place cannot be tied down to a nation or location, but for feminist artists, this aesthetic uses and emphasizes the female body, "Rather than expressing their attachment to place as either dispossessed of or exiled from their native land, Chicana artists have a more intimate and embodied connection to place. . . . Transmuted into art, this politics of the body produces an embodied aesthetic, one that frees the Chicana artist from the shackles of a relational identity as someone's wife, mother, daughter, or mistress" (127). This embodied aesthetic present in Rodriguez's work stems from her politicization that extends into her artwork and it is not specifically tied to a Chicana aesthetic, but rather a woman of color aesthetic, building coalitions with other women of color. She engages in the task of taking inventory and imagining an empowered mestiza in control of her reproductive decision-making. These images suggest that the way to upend restrictive policies that restrict access to reproductive rights is through the woman's power at the ballot box.[8]

In another poster from her "Slut series," titled "I am a Slut. I vote!" also calls into question the restrictive and misogynistic policies that focus on reproductive health care, specifically those regulating women's reproductive decision-making like using contraception or getting access to a safe abortion. The poster also presents a similar mestiza woman facing the viewer on the upper right-hand corner. The combination of primary colors, such as red, and blue, along with what looks like a hoop earring on one ear. The presence of the mestiza image is placed next to the message reading: "I'm a slut. I vote. So does everyone I sleep with" places emphasis on appropriating the word "slut" and empowering the viewer to call out hypocritical aspects of certain heteropatriarchal discourses that continue to stereotype and police her gender and sexuality. Rather than a frail and passive mestiza figure, Rodriguez represents an empowered woman no longer willing to sit back and allow assaults on women's reproductive rights. Furthermore, it also brings into focus the importance of exercising one's right to vote, especially as a woman of color. In this respect, as an embodiment of sexuality, Rodriguez's "Slut Series" posters give women agency to reclaim words like "slut" and use it as a way to mobilize against sexist words and meanings behind certain expectations about women. In that very sense, Rodriguez's work resonates not just with Latinas, but with other women of color.

The series, "Slut Series" and "Pussy Power" fall into representational strategies that are more nuanced and addresses micro and macro issues. By not using an oft-used symbol like the Virgin of Guadalupe or La Malinche, Rodriguez's work emerges from the experiences of women of color as reclaimed by Moraga and Anzaldúa's theory in the flesh. "A theory in the flesh means where the physical realities of our lives-our skin color, the land or concrete we grew up on, our sexual longing-all fuse to create a politics born out of necessity . . . " (*This Bridge* 23). Moraga and Anzaldúa emphasize the materiality of the brown body and make a case for the particular site of painful experiences that the body holds. Similarly, building on Gaspar de Alba's typology of embodied aesthetics in feminist Chicana art, Rodriguez's work grounds bodily experiences as reproductive women in lived realities by locating political agency at the intersection of language and body. Not only does Rodriguez's work in this series disrupt traditional images of Latina/xs that present the women as virginal or pure, but rather, these images are sites of hybridity, and dialogue meant to demystify and challenge preconceived notions of Latinidad and reproductive decision-making. Like her counterparts in this project, Rodriguez's work demonstrates that nuanced representation matters and brings to the fore important issues like reproductive decision-making.

Specifically, in her "Pussy Series" posters and prints, Rodriguez draws on Moraga and Anzaldúa's theory in the flesh to represent women's sexual empowerment as an aesthetics of sexuality. In "Pussy Power," a poster released in 2012, juxtaposes an image of a woman of color with the initials 'p.p.' on her neck, seemingly representing the woman as a superhero. A very vibrant color palette, along with primary colors, is used in this poster, including pink and teal. The mestiza woman reproduced in the poster is located below the message and her likeness is multiplied behind her, showcasing her hair in blue, pink, and yellow. Underneath the woman's shoulders the message reads: "The war on women is a war on everyone." She is part of a larger movement here to fight for women's right to have bodily autonomy. By focusing on female body parts, Rodriguez's poster recontextualizes the visual metaphor that identifies people by their reproductive organs, as a commentary about how women are always essentialized to remain in their reproductive/sexual roles in heteropatriarchal societies. The absence of the vagina as part of the poster then centralizes the woman's entire body and her voice, implying a certain agency in the power of making the personal, political.

Her posters and prints in this series speak to Moraga, Anzaldúa, and Gaspar de Alba's notion emphasizing the materiality of woman's body, specifically one that exists within social structures that deem her body unwanted, abhorrent, or unworthy. To be fully present and represented, Rodriguez embodies the feminist aesthetics beyond representing images. Through her social justice posters and activist work, Rodríguez makes it her focus to create work that reaches many as a way to promote social justice in reproductive decision-making for all women of color. Rodriguez describes this perfectly in one of her prints, "Deliberate Orgasm AP 1": "I realized that I was not talking about the systemic conditions around my abortion, that is, the way that our society scrutinizes, shames, and represses all expressions of sexuality" (Favianna. com). By revisiting fear-based and stigmatizing messages surrounding Latina/x sexuality and pleasure, Favianna Rodriguez's work illuminates the importance of what it means to move toward reproductive justice. Latinos construct their sexualities within what sociologist Marysol Asencio (2002) calls the "sex-gender systems," which are shaped by dynamics such as ethnic-cultural heritage and socioeconomic status, to name a few. Rodriguez utilizes the image of the woman's vagina in several of her posters and prints in this series as a source of strength and agency. The Latina body has been hypersexualized in the media and at the same time contradicting notions of femininity and womanhood permeate Latinx culture. Similarly, Rodriguez's work brings these competing perspectives together in her prints and posters to upend stereotypical notions of Latinaness, specifically in regard to pleasure. As Chicana scholar, Alicia Arrizón has argued, "sexuality and sensuality are different, and yet overlapping, concepts that shape, influence, and inspire one another. While sexuality may be expressed in ones' sensuality, a subject's sensuality stimulates her/his sexuality" (193).

In her series with Soypoderosa.com, "Yo te apoyo," also shows women of color from different generations inspiring viewers to reflect on how women's voices and opinions about reproductive decision-making have always fallen to the wayside, instead of asking the women themselves to make those decisions. Rodriguez's images are highlighted on the foreground by images of other women at a rally or march illuminating the overall importance of the legacy of the women's right movement and those Chicana and Latina women also mobilizing in the 1970s. Rodriguez's work aims to serve as a bridge from the early work of Chicana/Latina artists and activists to the work being done now by younger generations of women of color. The two images juxtaposed demonstrate the legacy of women mobilizing for the right over their bodies, especially over brown bodies. Patricia Zavella's work, *The Movement for Reproductive Justice*, addresses the work of artists like Rodriguez and her collaboration with NLIRH. Zavella argues that organizations like NLIRH work to empower and promote reproductive justice through community-based advocacy. For Zavella, the collaboration between Rodriguez and NLIRH is powerful because these collaborations help amplify and widen the scope of the movement by including social posters to frame women's rights. In an interview with Zavella, Rodriguez notes that with "Slut series," she is "'trying to frame our power and give people a stake they can attach themselves to, in order for them to continue their work'" (43). As such, Rodriguez makes a case for art helping women find ways to critique those in power.

Rodriguez's collaboration with NLIRH and other organizations brings a spotlight on representation and the power of the image. In doing so, her work along with other reproductive justice organizations focused on Latinas destabilize ideologies of racial and cultural suppression and demand justice from the local and the global. Rodriguez's artwork and the work done by NLIRH and other similar organizations, exemplifies "theory in the flesh" that moves beyond just alliances across Latinas but to build alliances with other women of color in the US.

NOTES

1. See Alicia Gaspar de Alba (2004, 2014), Clara Román-Odio (2013).

2. Scholar Rita Gonzalez (2019) argues that Latina/o artworks range from the didactic to the diffuse, with some employing the use of clear and succinct iconography to celebrate cultural knowledge, and others questioning the very framework of nationality, belonging and authenticity (12).

3. See the work of media scholars Isabel Molina-Guzmán (2018), Angharad Valdivia (2010), and Jillian Báez (2018).

4. This social justice campaign was launched at the Democratic National Convention in collaboration with the UndocuBus, mobilizing against the deportation of migrants, and since then it has remained a symbol for world immigrant rights. favianna.com/artworks/migration-is-beautiful-2018.

5. See Clara Román-Odio (2013), Guísela Latorre (2010), and Alicia Gaspar de Alba (2014).

6. See Gloria Anzaldúa (2007), Ana Castillo (1995), and Cherríe Moraga (2000).

7. Rodriguez, Favianna. 2012. "Politicians off my Pootang." favianna.com/artworks/politicians-off-my-poontang. Accessed February 19, 2022.

8. As of 2019, according to the Pew Research Center non-Hispanic White Americans make up the largest share of registered voters in the US, at 69% of the total and Hispanic and Black voters each account for 11% of the total, while those from other racial or ethnic backgrounds account for the remainder (8%) (Gramlich 2020). In terms of gender breakdown, "In 2018 and 2019, the Democratic Party held a wide advantage with women: 56% of female registered voters identified as Democrats or leaned toward the Democratic Party, while 38% identified as Republicans or leaned toward the GOP" (Igielnik, 2020).

Conclusion

Representing Reproductive Decisions in the 21st Century

The central focus of this project has been to analyze several case studies in theater, television, film, and art produced in the last twenty-plus years amid changes in demographics and politics that attempt to challenge heteropatriarchal notions of Latina/x womanhood connected to reproductive decision-making. Cultural representation and the role of language and image is imperative in shaping meaning through interpretation. These varied cultural texts also provide the reader and audience ways to visualize and hear a more nuanced understanding of Latina/x reproductive decision-making. Beyond notions of representing Latina/x bodies from the virginal woman to the overjoyed expectant mother or the loose woman, these case studies provide alternative ways to understand Latina/x reproductive decision-making. The women represented in Teatro Luna's dramatic texts, in the CW's *Jane the Virgin,* Starz's *Vida, Quinceañera,* and in Favianna Rodriguez's social justice posters, upend and rewrite sacrificial and passive women. This book elucidates the ways reproductive decision-making representation in cultural texts can serve as liberating and new ways of understanding Latina/x representation. Furthermore, these cultural texts can challenge traditional notions of reproductive decision-making, pointing to more inclusive understandings of people's experiences.

Latina and Chicana theorists and artists have also sought to mobilize their resistance to the heteropatriarchal approaches to Latina/Chicana representations to focus on figures like the Virgen de Guadalupe/Virgin Mary, both in creative and critical production. Gloria Anzaldúa and Cherríe Moraga authored and contributed to rethinking the representation of women as either pious or treacherous. These Chicana theorists, among others, contest heteropatriarchal assumptions that women need to be virginal upon marriage, get pregnant, and be overjoyed and sacrificial for her children and family. These theorists and artists reconceptualize what it means to be Latina/Chicana through images that reclaim the voices and the bodies of figures

127

such as the Virgen de Guadalupe and La Malinche, for example, to give back agency, refuting portrayals as passive or submissive. These figures have been instrumental in conceptualizing the ideological underpinnings of the heteropatriarchal vilification of feminine sexuality, consequently connected to reproductive decision-making. Chicana/Latina theorists have reconceptualized the Latina/Chicana woman as no longer submissive or fixated on joyous motherhood, but rather an empowered woman with agency in her reproductive decision-making.

For Chicana/Latina artists and theorists like Anzaldúa, Moraga, and Alicia Gaspar de Alba, the Virgin Mary motifs are common in popular culture like telenovelas. These motifs connected to the Lady of Guadalupe are easily identifiable, culturally rooted in Catholicism, and are juxtaposed to the figure of La Malinche. The good woman based on these characteristics is above-all fit for mothering, she is maternal and exemplary, virginal and self-sacrificing. Gaspar de Alba theorizes about the "Three Marías Syndrome," "the patriarchal social discourse of Chicano/Mexicano culture that constructs women's gender and sexuality according to three Biblical archetypes-virgins, mothers, and whores" (159). Anzaldúa also gives voice and agency to these archetypes in her work in *Borderlands/La frontera* by reconfiguring the myth of La Malinche through her own story growing up Chicana on the border. As she says, "Malini Tenepat or Malintzin, has become known as la Chingada - the fucked one. . . . Because of the color of skin they betrayed me. The dark skinned woman has been silenced, gagged, caged, bound into servitude with marriage [. . .]" (44). For Anzaldúa, the figure of the La Malinche has come to represent all women who betray or go against heteropatriarchal norms such as virginal marriage or heterosexual relationships. For Anzaldúa and other theorists, this figure along with the Virgin of Guadalupe has come to symbolize the power that heteropatriarchal culture has in controlling the female body and expected behavior.

One of the theoretical frameworks that has been instrumental in navigating through these case studies is "theory in the flesh," produced by Chicana theorists Gloria Anzaldúa and Cherríe Moraga. "Theory in the flesh" provides a lens to understand the everyday Chicanx/Latinx experiences and the effects of oppression and resistance. In these case studies, "theory in the flesh" allows us to understand for example, Teatro Luna's work as crucial to envisioning Latina womanhood in reproductive decision-making through characters, based on the ensemble's own stories, that navigate difficult decisions such as getting pregnant or choosing an abortion. Teatro Luna's characters represent more nuanced representations of contemporary Latinx lives without ever suggesting that these experiences are in some way essential or universal. On the contrary, they insist on the plurality of the Latinx experience. Anzaldúa and Moraga's work, along with the work of other writers such as Audre Lorde and Migdalia Cruz, have used their cultural productions to link women of color lived experiences to art's potential for social justice. The work of Teatro Luna and generations of women of color theater-makers contribute to the de-stigmatization of reproductive decisions like remaining childfree, choosing abortion, or pregnancy, adoption.

Representing Latinx Reproductive Decision-Making argues that Latina/x cultural products offer more nuanced representations of reproductive decision-making. These texts make use of the oft-used figure of the sacrificial mother, such as the Virgin Mary, and complicate representations of mother-hood and womanhood. Recognizing that certain figures, such as the *madre marianista,* represent traditional notions of womanhood, these case studies shed light on the deep ambivalence surrounding Latina/x reproductive deci-sion-making. To honor and represent reproductive decision-making as part of a person's everyday lived reality resists and upends limited representations of Latina/x womanhood. Popular culture can correct misinformation and misun-derstanding about Latina/x stories surrounding reproductive decisions, but at the same time it can perpetuate stereotypes.

Teatro Luna's work in the selected vignettes from *Déjame contarte, S-e-x-oh!* and *Sólo tú* honor the Latina/x experience and represent the com-plexities of reproductive decision-making. Through scenes of ambivalence in four selected vignettes, Teatro Luna's work seeks to reclaim the physical realities of their lives by destabilizing traditional representations of Latina/x women as expectant mothers. Interrupting limited representations of Latina/x decisions like choice, Teatro Luna calls for a redefinition of what it means to be Latina/x in the 21st century. Not all characters reject pregnancy or choose abortion; however, the different vignettes can offer more nuanced representa-tions of the ambivalence surrounding reproductive decisions. Beyond choos-ing abortion, some of the characters like Chelly and Miranda, for example, experience their pregnancies in different ways, representing ambivalence, "they experience progressive awareness of changes in their bodies, eventu-ally become conscious of some 'other' within them, and await delivery in much the same sense as the expectant mother."[1] For Coya, her experience demonstrates the challenges same-sex couples face trying to have a fam-ily. For the unnamed character and Tanya, choosing abortion unsettles the viewers in that they each provide compelling accounts about abortion, not devoid of challenges. For as Parker has argued in relation to ambivalence and pregnancy, "contemporary pregnancy discourse bears witness to our culture's overpowering fear of ambivalence."[2] The different representations of reproductive decisions in Teatro Luna's early work challenges heteropatri-archal cultural attitudes toward ambivalence and reproductive decisions and encourage openness to express feelings about varying degrees of reproductive decisions. Teatro Luna's storytelling enables ensemble members to embody other Latinas/xs, as partners, friends, mothers, sisters, and women to better understand who these women are and explore how their identity is tethered to other women of color. Inhabiting others' stories or reimagining their experiences in the script and on stage enables a (re)discovery for audiences and readers alike, while we think we know what Latina/x reproductive decision-making looks and sounds like, examining these experiences through theater give actors and spectators a more intimate look at Latina/x lives.

Centering on narratives of abortion, in the selected vignettes from *Déjame contarte* and *S-e-x-oh!*, "Trapped" and "Cama-Camaleon," respectively, Teatro Luna connects female characters to the challenges faced by one character navigating through hardship after learning she was pregnant as a result of rape, and the other character taking us through her emotional and physical experience while at an abortion clinic. Teatro Luna argues for rescripting of traditional Latina/x reproductive decision-making narratives, especially those represented as bad or loose women. Undoubtedly, Teatro Luna argues for a political approach since they are a feminist theater collective, where the female characters offer an active voice and represent Latinas/xs struggling to navigate reproductive decision-making while living in two or more cultures. By writing and staging Latina/x reproductive decision making in a way that defies traditional images, the spectators and readers are confronted with the "realities" of women's reproductive decision making beyond notions of pro-life or pro-choice. In these abortion narratives, the ideological debate surrounding abortion does not factor into their reproductive decision-making. In Teatro Luna's vignettes, the characters provide concrete expressions of their experiences as women and make visible and audible reproductive decision-making on stage, revealing in public experiences seldomly talked about out in the open.

In "What I want to tell" from *S-e-x-oh!* and "It's never the right time" in *Sólo tú*, the Latina characters navigate through differing experiences as expectant mothers or in desiring motherhood. The characters in these vignettes offer multifaceted versions of Latina motherhood or desiring motherhood. In both vignettes, the characters expose the vicissitudes of pregnancy and their staged realities that defy a heteropatriarchal vision of the overjoyed expectant mother. By bringing attention to physical, medical (ultrasound), emotional, and social (abusive partner) issues, Teatro Luna's vignettes shed light on the social realities of (non) expectant people. The characters and stories exposed on stage by Teatro Luna explore a myriad of experiences like ambivalence toward being pregnant, navigating (in)fertility and in choosing abortion, opting to upend hidden or distorted realities and represent very personal, physical, or emotional experiences that relate to a person's reproductive decision-making. More broadly speaking, as articulated by the work of Moraga, Vilar and other memoirists, the notion of reproductive choices, like carrying an unintended pregnancy to term is socially conditioned, however that does not imply lack of agency because it can be a morally significant choice. However to assume that everyone has the agency to choose certain things ignores larger socio-cultural forces that condition such choices.

Like Teatro Luna's work, the Villanueva women in the CW's *Jane the Virgin* draw attention to representations of Latina reproductive decision-making on television. The series draws from its cultural predecessor, the telenovela, and reimagines oft-used female tropes used in other telenovelas and in media. These tropes, such as the sacrificial mother or the sexy Latina, are often seen as normative and part of a lineage of stereotypes used in mediatized settings. Even though traditional telenovelas can often contribute to stereotyped imagery of Latina womanhood, *Jane the Virgin* uses those stereotypes to turn them on their head and bring in the viewer. By using telenovela tropes and styles, *Jane the Virgin* resonates with viewers who are familiar with telenovelas and also with second or third generation Latinas. In the first season, Jane (Gina Rodriguez) and her mother and grandmother navigate the ins and outs of their daily lives as Latina women in Miami. Jane's widowed grandmother, Alba (Ivonne Coll) is an immigrant from Venezuela, and has helped her daughter, Xiomara (Andrea Navedo) raise Jane. Alba identifies with her cultural upbringing, steeped in Catholicism, and rooted in traditional social order. Alba represents the traditional mother rooted in heteropatriarchal traditions such as virginity and marriage, while her daughter, Xiomara represents a more sexually liberated second generation Latina, steeped in the sexy Latina trope. Alba and Xiomara personify opposite ends of the virgin/whore binary, while Jane, a third generation Latina represents a contemporary, hybrid representation of a 21st century young woman. In the first season of the show, Jane is mistakenly impregnated during a routine gynecological exam by a distracted doctor. The series starts with a typical mix-up seen in telenovelas, Jane's pregnancy, but viewers encounter complex Latina characters that challenge preconceived notions of Latina identity and womanhood. The changing definition of family and motherhood presented in *Jane the Virgin* is reflective of changing Latina/x representations.[3] Alba, Xiomara, and Jane navigate difficult conversations surrounding Latina reproductive decision-making beyond ways to mother. By displacing the patriarchal voice and centering the action on three generations of women, *Jane the Virgin*'s protagonists discuss difficult subjects like abortion, loss and their insecurities surrounding motherhood. As the first season sets up, the complexities surrounding pregnancy and motherhood in the three generations of Villanueva women challenge antiquated notions of Latina womanhood anchored in compulsory motherhood and silence. By including frank conversations between generations, discussing physical and emotional aspects of pregnancy and motherhood, beyond accepting gleefully an unplanned pregnancy, the series captures the importance of the transformative power of reproductive decision-making conversations focused on giving voice and agency to Latinas.

Given the important status that mothers hold in the Latina/o imaginary, *Jane the Virgin* uses telenovela tropes and narrative devices throughout the series to navigate the complexities of Latina identity and womanhood. While the scope of this project was limited to the first season, as a whole, the series centralizes and brings to life nuanced Latina representations. This is not to suggest that the series does not play with oft-used stereotypes; however, it is within those stereotypes that the series challenges and resists a Latinidad based on heteropatriarchal notions of reproductive decision-making. By skewing the glorification of motherhood common in traditional telenovelas, *Jane the Virgin* offers a challenge to television writers and producers to change the way Latinas/os are represented. As a woman-centered show, *Jane the Virgin* focuses on advocating for alternative ways of seeing and hearing Latina reproductive decision-making. While *Jane the Virgin* was not stemming from a 100% Latinx writers' room, there is much to be said about how viewers can shape meaning about Latina reproductive decisions through the interpretation of images and language used in the show. One of my initial questions about the show takes audience responses into consideration: What impact do cultural texts have on everyday Latina/x people and their reproductive decision making? How does one even measure this? In opening up a research avenue into *Jane the Virgin* viewership and reception would shed light on the impact certain episodes had on Latina/x viewers. Furthermore, this line of research could influence public policy as it pertains to reproductive rights and access to healthcare.

The abortion-positive representations in *Vida* challenge preconceived notions of what it means to have a medicated abortion beyond the heteronormative and traditional contexts of shame, stigma, and fear. By challenging the stigma and invisibility that informs abortion narratives, Emma's (Mishel Prada) experience counters the absence of information and knowledge on abortion. While part of the storyline, Emma's abortion in the series draws attention to access as well as a tension understood within the context of unequal access to abortion services given Emma's middle-class environment. By representing a medicated abortion in a nonsensationalist manner, devoid of political arguments for or against abortion, *Vida* represents scenes of reproductive decision-making as commonplace and do not feature rape or stigma. The cultural stories told in *Vida* may resonate with Latinx and non-Latinx viewers alike, and as such, help us understand and hear abortion-positive stories in cultural texts. On the other hand, unlike *Vida*, the film *Quinceañera* (2006) represents a young woman's story about her coming of age and how her unintended pregnancy leads to controversy, rejection, and shame from members of her extended family and friends despite her claims of not having intercourse. Magdalena (Emily Ríos) does transgress her family and friends' expectations of what a young woman should and should not do. The film, while showing a hyper fertile Latina teen pregnancy, rather than showing a negative portrayal of her situation, the film shows the ways she navigates her family and friends' rejection of her innocence since she is still a virgin and did not have intercourse. The film does present the challenges Magdalena will face as a young mother, like finding a place to live after her uncle passes or in the absence of a strong support system. Unbelievably, in the film, reproductive decision-making is not presented as topic, however, the representation of Latina subjectivity as a mother or as a pregnant person is discussed and placed into conversation with the ways in which women, especially young people, are expected to be nonsexual and concerned with notions of honor and virginity. Magdalena's family, except for her great-uncle Tomás (Chalo Gonzalez) and her queer cousin Carlos (Jesse García), reject her innocence and judge and shame her for getting pregnant at such a young age. Certainly as a teenage mother, Magdalena is imagined by others as out of control however, the film does not loathe or emphasize Magdalena's "irresponsibility" or "disgruntled" feelings because of her pregnancy. Like the abortion-positive representation in *Vida*, *Quinceañera* offers images of teenage pregnancy beyond preconceived notions of criminal, promiscuous or shameful. These two representations are sometimes at odds with other film and media representations featuring Latina/x reproductive decisions as stereotypical, fitting into binaries that deem Latinas as either virgins or whores. Furthermore, these two representations of Latina contradict some dominant (white) representations of teen pregnancy as cool or glamorous or an abortion narrative as negative, shameful, or immoral. In sum, while recent Hollywood representations may hint at some of the complexities and nuances surrounding reproductive decisions, representations such as Starz's *Vida* and the independent film, *Quinceañera* do provide more positive and ambivalent representations of abortion and pregnancy, respectively.[4] While *Quinceañera* may embrace more patriarchal and conservative values that endorse Magdalena's right to have her child and celebrate an "immaculate conception," it still provides an ambivalent representation toward reproductive decision-making, devoid of political or ideological categorizations about people and reproduction.

Representations of Latina/x reproductive decision-making in art, specifically social justice posters, blend the personal with the political to try to mobilize people to act. Whether it captures women calling out politicians who challenge reproductive rights or mobilizing women to share their abortion stories, Favianna Rodriguez's social justice posters ultimately challenge and resist presumed notions of Latina reproductive decision-making based on heteropatriarchal notions of Latina identity. Rodriguez's two series studied in this project, "Slut Series" and "Pussy Power" utilizes mestiza imagery and direct and brief words to convey her messages regarding reproductive rights and to speak out about the shame and isolation surrounding abortion. Rodriguez incorporates mestiza-like figures with dominant gazes, a primary color palette, and messages in Spanish and English to challenge heteropatriarchal ideologies that shape reproductive rights for women of color. In blending the personal with the political in her social justice posters, Rodriguez reminds viewers of the social perception of women's bodies. She seeks to reclaim women's sexuality and bodily autonomy by referencing words like "uterus," "my body" and "poontang," for example, and juxtaposing them with fearless women of color, expressing resistance to heteropatriarchal notions of womanhood tied to reproductive decision-making. Through her social justice prints and collaborations with reproductive justice organizations like the National Latina Institute for Reproductive Health (NLIRH), Favianna Rodriguez visualizes and represents empowered Latinas fighting for their reproductive rights as part of a larger movement toward reproductive justice. By creating empowered Latina images, Rodriguez's work challenges Latina communities to come out and share their reproductive decision-making stories to bring about more awareness to the lack of access to reproductive care for Latinas/xs and other women of color.

In response to silence and shame felt around reproductive decision-making, Teatro Luna's work, the characters in *Jane the Virgin*, *Vida*, *Quinceañera*, and Favianna Rodriguez's posters bring an increased awareness to Latina/x reproductive realities, including pregnancy and abortion. Teatro Luna's work links embodied storytelling in their vignettes that theatricalize expectant women by suggesting a reconceptualization of what it means to be Latina/x beyond traditional notions of motherhood. The language and imagery deployed in the selected case studies confront their reproductive decision-making by imbuing their narratives inclusive of physical, emotional, and social challenges in reproductive decisions. Teatro Luna's stories, the Villanueva women in *Jane the Virgin*, Emma in *Vida,* and Magdalena in *Quinceañera* reimagine what it means to be a person confronted with reproductive decisions on television by exposing the oft-used types of the sacrificial mother or the hypersexualized woman. These cultural texts utilize visual tropes that initially play on stereotypes such as the Virgin Mary, hyper fertile Latina/x, or overjoyed pregnant woman, and they are deployed to also critique preconceived notions of Latina/x reproductive decision-making. Favianna Rodriguez's work situates Latina/x reproductive decision-making front and center by calling out restrictions on reproductive health care, especially access to safe and legal abortions. Rodriguez utilizes posters to express a direct political message: Latinas/xs and women of color demand the right to bodily autonomy. Her posters include mestiza women and messaging that refuse to silence and shame women for wanting access to reproductive care. In centering Latina/x reproductive decision-making experiences in these cultural products, these products shift and upend heteropatriarchal notions of womanhood tied to traditional representations of reproductive images, such as the virginal woman ready to have children or the hypersexualized Latina. In visualizing Latina/x representations of reproductive decision-making as destigmatized, Teatro Luna, *Jane the Virgin* and Favianna Rodriguez envision alternative ways of expressing Latina/x bodily autonomy by sharing images that portray the complexities of the 21st century Latina/x community.

NOTES

1. Lundquist, Caroline. "Being Torn: Toward a Phenomenology of Unwanted Pregnancy." *Hypatia.* vol. 23, no. 3. July-September 2008, 145.

2. Parker, Rozika. 1995. *Torn in two: The experience of maternal ambivalence.* London: Virago Press. Quoted in Lundquist 2008.

3. In the last few years, we have seen an uptick in Latinas/xs on the small screen, see Norman Lear's reboot of *One Day at a Time* with Justina Machado and Rita Moreno, Netflix's *Gentefied, On my Block*, Amazon Prime's *With Love,* and ABC's *Promised Land.*

4. In *With Love* (Amazon Prime) there is mention of having an abortion as something that is known but unknown to the matriarch of the family (Season 1, Episode 1); HBO's *Insecure*, Condola shares she had a past abortion as she finds out she is currently pregnant (Season 4, Episode 10); Hulu's movie, *Plan B* (2021), two teenagers in South Dakota (one Latina) look for the morning after pill three-hours away after a pharmacist refuses to provide them with it because of his beliefs.

Bibliography

Abbey, Sharon and Andrea O' Reilly, ed. 1999. *Redefining Motherhood*. Women's Issues Publishing Program. Toronto, Ontario Canada: Second Story Press.

Acosta, LizaAnn and Alexandra Meda. (2015). Teatro Luna Manifesto: Ensemble Collective Work and Our Place in 21st Century Latin @ Theater. *Gestos (Irvine, Calif.), 30*(60), 151–161. Retrieved from Bibliografía de la Literatura Española database. Retrieved from search-proquest-com.denison.idm.oclc.org/docview/1790311393.

Acosta-Alzuru, Carolina. 2010. "Beauty Queens, Machistas and Street Children." *International Journal of Cultural Studies* 13 (2): 185–203. doi:10.1177/1367877909356719.

———. 2013. "Tackling the Issues: Meaning Making in Telenovelas." *Journal of Popular Communication* 1 (4): 193–215.

———. 2017. "Unsettling a Sacred Relationship: The Mother-Daughter-Man Romantic Love Triangle in Telenovelas." *Popular Communication* 15 (1): 1–18. doi:10.1080/15405702.2016.1261141. www-tandfonline-com.denison.idm.oclc. org/doi/abs/10.1080/15405702.2016.1261141.

Aguilera, Alirio. 1995. "La telenovela: mitos y realidades." *Revista Comunicación* 91: Fundación Centro Gunilla, Caracas, 10–14.

Allen, Robert C. 1985. *Speaking of Soap Operas*. Chapel Hill u.a: University of North Carolina Press.

Alvarado, Leticia. 2020b. "Of Betties Decorous and Abject: Ugly Betty's America La Fea and Nao Bustamante's America La Bella." In *Abject Performances*, 89-130. New York, NY: Duke University Press. doi:10.1515/9780822371939-005. www. degruyter.com/doi/10.1515/9780822371939-005.

Anderson, Lisa M. 2008. *Black Feminism in Contemporary Drama*. Urbana [u.a.]: Univ. of Illinois Press.

Anzaldúa, Gloria. 2007. *Borderlands/La Frontera*. Third ed. San Francisco, CA: Aunt Lute Books.

———. 1990. *Making Face, Making Soul*. 1. ed. ed. San Francisco: Aunt Lute Books.

Anzaldúa, Gloria and Cherríe Moraga, Eds. 2002. *This Bridge Called My Back: Writings by Radical Women of Color*. 3rd ed. Berkeley, CA: Third Woman Press.

Anzaldúa, Gloria E. and AnaLouise Keating. 2002. *This Bridge we Call Home: Radical Visions for Transformation.* 1st ed. New York, NY: Routledge.

Aparicio, Frances R. 2017. "Latinidad/es." Chap. 31, In *Keywords in Latina/o Studies.* New York, NY: NYU Press. denison.idm.oclc.org/login?url= search-credoreference-com.denison.idm.oclc.org/content/entry/nyupresskls/latinidad_es/0 ?institutionId=5015.

Arrizón, Alicia. 1999. *Latina Performance: Traversing the Stage.* Bloomington: Indiana University Press.

Arrizón, Alicia and Lillian Manzor, eds. 2000. *Latinas on Stage.* Berkeley: Third Woman Press.

Asencio, Marysol, ed. 2009. *Latina/o Sexualities: Probing Powers, Passions, Practices, and Policies,* edited by Marysol Asencio. New Brunswick: Rutgers University Press.

Avila-Saavedra, Guillermo. 2010. "A Fish Out of Water: New Articulations of U.S.-Latino Identity on Ugly Betty." *Communication Quarterly* 58 (2): 133–147. doi:10.1080/01463371003773416. www-tandfonline-com.denison.idm.oclc.org/ doi/abs/10.1080/01463371003773416.

Babineu, Mary Lou. 2011. "Counternarratives in the Literary Works of Mexican Author Angeles Mastretta and Chilean Author Pía Barros." In *Latina/Chicana Mothering,* edited by Dorsía Smith Silva, 177-193. Ontario, Canada: Demeter Press.

Báez, Jillian M. 2007. "Towards a Latinidad Feminista: The Multiplicities of Latinidad and Feminism in Contemporary Cinema." *Popular Communication 5 (2):* 109–128.

———. 2018. *In Search of Belonging.* Urbana, IL: University of Illinois Press.

Barrera, Vivian and Denise D. Bielby. 2001. "Places, Faces, and Other Familiar Things: The Cultural Experience of Telenovela Viewing among Latinos in the United States." *Journal of Popular Culture* 34 (4): 1–18. doi:10.1111/ j.0022-3840.2001.3404_1.x. onlinelibrary-wiley-com.denison.idm.oclc.org/doi/ abs/10.1111/j.0022-3840.2001.3404_1.x.

Bednarek, Monika. 2010. *The Language of Fictional Television: Drama and Identity.* New York: Continuum. gateway.proquest.com.denison.idm. oclc.org/openurl?ctx_ver=Z39.88-2003&xri:pqil: res_ver=0.2&res_id=xri:ilcs-us&rft_id=xri:ilcs:rec:abell:R05223964.

Behar, Ruth. 1995. *Women Writing Culture.* Berkeley [u.a.]: University of California Press.

Beltrán, Mary C. 2009. *Latina/o Stars in U.S. Eyes: The Making and Meanings of Film and TV Stardom.* Urbana: University of Illinois Press.

Berg, Charles Ramírez. 2002. *Latino Images in Film.* Texas Film and Media Studies Series. Austin: University of Texas Press. muse-jhu-edu.denison.idm.oclc.org/book/2960.

Bielby, Denise D. and C. Lee Harrington. 2005. "Opening America?" *Television & New Media* 6 (4): 383–399. doi:10.1177/1527476405279861. journals-sagepub-com.denison.idm.oclc.org/doi/full/10.1177/1527476405279861.

Blake, Debra J. 2008. *Chicana Sexuality and Gender.* Durham [u.a.]: Duke University Press.

Bloom, Davida. 2016. *Rape, Rage and Feminism in Contemporary American Drama*. Jefferson, NC: McFarland & Company, Inc., Publishers.

Boffone, Trevor, Teresa Marrero, and Chantal Rodriguez, eds. 2019. *Encuentro : Latinx Performance for the New American Theater*. Evanston, IL: Northwestern University Press.

Bondy, Jennifer M. 2012. "Latinas, Heterotopia, and Home: Pedagogies of Gender and Sexuality in *Quinceañera*." *Journal of Curriculum and Pedagogy* 9 (1) (Jan): 81–98. doi:10.1080/15505170.2012.684835.

Bost, Suzanne. 2010. *Encarnación: Illness and Body Politics in Chicana Feminist Literature*.1st ed. ed. New York: Fordham University Press.

Broyles-González, Yolanda. 1999. *El Teatro Campesino*. 1st ed. Austin: University of Texas Press.

Caballero, Cecilia, Yvette Martínez-Vu, Judith Pérez-Torres, Michelle Téllez, Christine Vega, and Ana Castillo. 2019. *The Chicana Motherwork Anthology*. Tucson: University of Arizona Press.

Caminero-Santangelo, Marta. 2007. *On Latinidad*. Gainesville: University Press of Florida. muse-jhu-edu.denison.idm.oclc.org/book/17512.

Canning, Charlotte. 1996. *Feminist Theaters in the U.S.A.* 1. publ. ed. London [u.a.]: Routledge.

Carruthers, Anne. 2021. *Fertile Visions: The Uterus as a Narrative Space in Cinema from the Americas.* New York: Bloomsbury Academic. 2021.

Castillo, Ana. 1995. *Massacre of the Dreamers*. 1. Plume print. ed. New York u.a: Plume.

———. 1993. "Since the Creation of My Son and My First Book." *Frontiers: A Journal of Women Studies* 13 (2): 91–92. www-jstor-org.denison.idm.oclc.org/stable/3346726.

Castro, Desiree T. and Teatro Luna. 2008. "It's Never the Right Time." In *Sólo tú.* Chicago, IL. Unpublished Script.

"Chapter Fifteen." *Jane the Virgin*, season 1, episode 15, The CW, 9 Mar. 2015. Netflix, www.netflix.com/watch/80060558. Accessed 09 Aug. 2020.

"Chapter Nine." *Jane the Virgin*, season 1, episode 9, The CW, 15 Nov. 2014. Netflix, www.netflix.com/watch/80060558. Accessed 09 Aug. 2020.

"Chapter One: Pilot." *Jane the Virgin*, season 1, episode 1, The CW, 13 Oct. 2014. Netflix, www.netflix.com/watch/80060553. Accessed 09 Aug. 2020.

"Chapter Seven." *Jane the Virgin*, season 1, episode 7, The CW, 24 Nov. 2014. Netflix, www.netflix.com/watch/80060558. Accessed 09 Aug. 2020.

"Chapter Seventeen." *Jane the Virgin*, season 1, episode 17, The CW, 6 Apr. 2015. Netflix, www.netflix.com/watch/80060573. Accessed 09 Aug. 2020.

"Chapter Six." *Jane the Virgin*, season 1, episode 6, The CW, 17 Nov. 2014. Netflix, www.netflix.com/watch/80060558. Accessed 09 Aug. 2020.

"Chapter Thirteen." *Jane the Virgin*, season 1, episode 13, The CW, 9 Feb. 2015. Netflix, www.netflix.com/watch/80060558. Accessed 09 Aug. 2020.

"Chapter Three." *Jane the Virgin*, season 1, episode 3, The CW, 27 Oct. 2014. Netflix, www.netflix.com/watch/80060555. Accessed 09 Aug. 2020.

"Chapter Twenty-Two." *Jane the Virgin*, season 1, episode 22, The CW, 11 May 2015. Netflix, www.netflix.com/watch/80060573. Accessed 09 Aug. 2020.

"Chapter Two." *Jane the Virgin*, season 1, episode 2, The CW, 20 Oct. 2014. Netflix, www.netflix.com/watch/80060553. Accessed 09 Aug. 2020.

Chávez, Denise, and Linda Feyder. 1992. *Shattering the Myth: Plays by Hispanic Women*. Houston, TX: Arte Público Press. https://search-ebscohost-com.denison.idm.oclc.org/login.aspx?direct=true&db=e000xna&AN=1511079&site=ehost-live.

Contreras, Felix. 2018. "'Vida,' The Groundbreaking Cable Show That Gets Latinx Narratives Right." Interview. June 12, 2018. www.npr.org/sections/altlatino/2018/06/12/618230479/vida-the-groundbreaking-cable-drama-that-gets-latinx-narratives-right. Accessed March 2, 2022.

Cooper, Cindy and Stacey Linnartz, eds. 2019. *Short Plays on Reproductive Freedom*. New York: Words of Choice, Inc.

Corthron, Kia. 1996. "Come Down Burning." In *Contemporary Plays by Women of Color: An Anthology*, edited by Perkins, Kathy A., and Roberta Uno, 90–105. New York: Routledge.

Corrigan, Lisa M. 2014. "Visual Rhetoric and Oppositional Consciousness: Poster Art in Cuba and the United States." *Intertexts (Lubbock, Tex.)* 18 (1): 71–91. doi:10.1353/itx.2014.0006. muse-jhu-edu.denison.idm.oclc.org/article/554323.

Cruz, Migdalia. 1996. "The Have-Little." In *Contemporary Plays by Women of Color: An Anthology*, edited by Perkins, Kathy A. and Roberta Uno, 106-126. New York: Routledge.

Cruz, Teddy and Favianna Rodriguez. 2016. "In Conversation with Dominic Willsdon." *Journal of Visual Culture* 15 (1): 146–161. doi:10.1177/1470412915619408. journals-sagepub-com.denison.idm.oclc.org/doi/full/10.1177/1470412915619408.

Davies, Jude and Carol R. Smith. 1998. "Race, Gender, and the American Mother: Political Speech and the Maternity Episodes of *I Love Lucy* and *Murphy Brown*." *American Studies (Lawrence)* 39 (2): 33–63. www-jstor-org.denison.idm.oclc.org/stable/40642967.

Day, Adrienne. 2020. "Favianna Rodriguez on Why Art Matters in a Time of Crisis." *The Grist*, July 7. grist.org/fix/favianna-rodriguez-on-why-art-matters-in-a-time-of-crisis/.

Deboeck, Lynn Marie. 2015. "Ultra-Sounding Maternal Subjectivity: A Feminist Reclamation of Pregnancy and Childbirth on Stage." ProQuest Dissertations Publishing.

"Dueña de mí." 2018. La Misa Negra. YouTube video. Dir. Marco Polo Santiago. youtu.be/5ssVCoyPaC4. Accessed March 2, 2022.

Enriquez, Maria Soyla. 2019. "Learning how to do it: Local, Regional, and National Latinx Theatre Alliance Building in the 21st Century." Dissertation. University of Pittsburgh.

"Episode 3." *Vida*, Season 3. Starz. 10 May 2020. Starz, YouTubeTV. Dir. Tanya Saracho, written by Esti Giordani. Accessed 12 June 2021.

"Episode 4." *Vida*, Season 3. Starz. 17 May 2020. Starz, YouTubeTV. Dir. Tanya Saracho, written by Jenniffer Gómez Accessed 12 June 2021.

Espinoza, Dionne, María Eugenia Cotera, and Maylei Blackwell. 2018. *Chicana Movidas*. Austin: University of Texas Press.

Firestone, Shulamith. 1997. "The Dialectic of Sex" Chap. 2, In *The Second Wave: A Reader in Feminist Theory*, edited by Linda J. Nicholson, 11-26. New York: Routledge.

García, Laura E., Sandra M. Gutiérrez, Felicitas Nuñez, and Yolanda Broyles-González. 2008. *Teatro Chicana*. Chicana Matters. Austin: University of Texas Press.

García, Lorena. 2012. *Respect Yourself, Protect Yourself*. New York: NYU Press. www.jstor.org/stable/j.ctt9qfhq7.

García-Romero, Anne. 2008. *Anne García-Romero: Collected Plays*. Dreaming the Americas Series. New York: No Passport Press.

———. 2016. *The Fornes Frame*. Tucson: University of Arizona Press.

Gaspar de Alba, Alicia. 2004. "There's no Place Like Aztlán: Embodied Aesthetics in Chicana Art." *CR (East Lansing, Mich.)* 4 (2): 103–140. doi:10.1353/ncr.2005.0007. www-jstor-org.denison.idm.oclc.org/stable/41949438.

———. 2014. *[Un]Framing the Bad Woman*. Austin: University of Texas Press.

Gaspar de Alba, Alicia, Alma López, and Alma Lopez. 2011. *Our Lady of Controversy*. Chicana Matters. Austin: University of Texas Press.

Gil, Rosa Maria and Carmen Inoa Vazquez. 1996. *The Maria Paradox: How Latinas can Merge Old World Traditions with New World Self-Esteem*. New York: G.P. Putnam's Sons.

Glatzer, Richard and Wash Westmoreland, directors. *Quinceañera*. Sony Pictures Classics, 2006. 91 minutes. DVD.

Glenn, Evelyn Nakano, Grace Chang, and Linda Rennie Forcey, eds. 1994. *Mothering*. 1st ed. London: Routledge.

Gómez, Isabel. 2017. "Interview with the Chicana Motherwork Collective." *Mester (Los Angeles)* 45 (1). doi:10.5070/M3451035851. search.proquest.com/docview/2258143000.

González, Jennifer A. 2019. "Introduction." In *Chicano and Chicana Art: A Critical Anthology*, edited by González, Jennifer A., C. Ondine Chavoya, Chon Noriega, Terezita Romo, 177-181. Durham: Duke University Press.

Gonzalez, Rita. 2017. "Art." Chap. 3, In *Keywords in Latina/o Studies*, eds. Vargas, Deborah R., Lawrence La Fountain-Stokes, and Nancy Raquel Mirabal. New York: NYU Press. denison.idm.oclc.org/login?url= search-credoreference-com.denison.idm.oclc.org/content/entry/nyupresskls/art/0?institutionId=5015.

Gónzalez, Tanya and Eliza Rodriguez y Gibson. 2015. *Humor and Latina/o Camp in Ugly Betty*. Lexington Books: Lanham, MD.

Gramlich, John. 2020. "What the 2020 electorate looks like by party, race and ethnicity, age, education and religion." *Pew Research Center*. October 26, 2020. pewrsr.ch/2TpQBnx. Accessed February 19, 2022.

Grise, Virginia, Irma Mayorga, and Tiffany Ana López. 2014. *The Panza Monologues*. Austin: University of Texas Press. ebookcentral.proquest.com/lib/[SITE_ID]/detail.action?docID=3443704.

Guerra, Petra, Diana I. Rios, and D. Milton Stokes. 2011. "The Telenovela *Alborada*: Constructions of the Latina Mother in an Internationally Successful Soap Opera." In *Latina/Chicana Mothering*, ed. Dorsía Smith SIlva, 209–223. Ontario, Canada: Demeter Press.

Gumbs, Alexis Pauline, China Martens, and Mai'a Williams. 2016. *Revolutionary Mothering*. Oakland, CA: PM Press.

Gutiérrez, Elena R. 2008. *Fertile Matters*. Chicana Matters. Austin: University of Texas Press. muse-jhu-edu.denison.idm.oclc.org/book/13913.

Guttmacher Institute. "Requirements for Ultrasound," last modified 12/1/20, accessed 12/1/2020, www.guttmacher.org/state-policy/explore/requirements-ultrasound#.

Halperin, Laura. 2015. *Intersections of Harm*. American Literatures Initiative. New Brunswick, NJ: Rutgers University Press. www.jstor.org/stable/j.ctt16nzfq3.

Herrera, Brian Eugenio. 2015. *Latin Numbers*. Ann Arbor: University of Michigan Press.

Herrera, Cristina. 2014a. *Contemporary Chicana Literature: (Re)Writing the Maternal Script*. Amherst, NY: Cambria Press.

Holden, Stephen. 2006. "'Quinceañera': Turning Sweet 15 in Los Angeles's Immigrant Stew." *New York Times*. Movie Review. August 4, 2006. www.nytimes.com/2006/08/04/movies/04quin.html?smid=url-share. Accessed October 20, 2021.

hooks, bell, 1952. *Black Looks: Race and Representation*. Boston, MA: South End Press, 1992.

———. 2000. *Feminist Theory from Margin to Center*. South End Press Classics. 2. ed. ed. Vol. 5. Cambridge, MA: South End Press.

Huerta, Jorge A. 2000. *Chicano Drama*. Cambridge Studies in American Theatre and Drama. 1. publ. ed. Vol. 12. Cambridge [u.a.]: Cambridge University Press.

Huerta, Melissa. 2020. "This is how I was Born on the Operating Table of an Abortion Clinic." Chap. 16, In *Representing Abortion*, edited by Rachel Alpha Johnston Hurst, 221–232. London, UK: Routledge.

———. 2014. "We Need the Whole Latina Package: Negotiating the Meanings of Latina in Teatro Luna's Plays (2001-2008)." ProQuest Dissertations Publishing.

Hurst, Rachel Alpha Johnston, ed. 2020. *Representing Abortion*. Interdisciplinary Research in Gender. London, UK: Routledge.

Hurtado, Aída. 1998. "The Politics of Sexuality in the Gender Subordination of Chicanas." In *Living Chicana Theory*, edited by Carla Trujillo, 383-428. Berkeley, CA: Third Woman Press.

Igielnik, Ruth. 2020. "Men and women in the U.S. continue to differ in voter turnout rate, party identification." *Pew Research Center*. August 18, 2020. pewrsr.ch/3kUITya. Accessed February 19, 2022.

Jackson, Carlos Francisco. 2017. "The Chicanx Poster Workshop: A Space Where Subjectivity is Produced." *Aztlán* 42 (1): 257.

———. 2014. "Seriagrafia: Constructing the Chicano/a Imaginary." *Boom: A Journal of California* 4 (1): 78–85.

Jane the Virgin: Seasons 1-3, Created by Jennie Snyder Urman and Perla Farías. Starring Gina Rodríguez, Andrea Navedo, Yvonne Coll, Justin Baldoni, Jaime Camil and Brett Dier. (2014-2019, CW). DVD.

Jaworski, Beth K. 2009. "Reproductive Justice and Media Framing: A Case-Study Analysis of Problematic Frames in the Popular Media." *Sex Education* 9 (1): 105–121. doi:10.1080/14681810802639830. www-tandfonline-com.denison.idm. oclc.org/doi/abs/10.1080/14681810802639830.

Johnston, Chloe and Coya Paz Brownrigg. 2019. *Ensemble-made Chicago: A Guide to Devised Theater*. Vol. 2019. Evanston, IL: Northwestern University.

Kaplan, Elizabeth Ann. 1992. *Motherhood and Representation*. 1. publ. ed. London [u.a.]: Routledge.

Kelleter, Frank. 2017. *Media of Serial Narrative*. Theory and Interpretation of Narrative. Columbus: Ohio State University Press.

Kissling, Elizabeth Arveda. 2017. "All Postfeminist Women do: Women's Sexual and Reproductive Health in Television Comedy." Chap. 15, In *Reading Lena Dunham's Girls*, edited by Nash, M and I. Whelehan, 209-223. Cham: Springer International Publishing. doi:10.1007/978-3-319-52971-4_15. link.springer.com.denison.idm.o clc.org/10.1007/978-3-319-52971-4_15.

Kjeldgaard, Dannie and Kaj Storgaard Nielsen. 2010. "Glocal Gender Identities in Market Places of Transition: MARIANISMO and the Consumption of the Telenovela Rebelde." *Marketing Theory* 10 (1): 29–44. doi:10.1177/1470593109355249. journals-sagepub-com.denison.idm.oclc.org/doi/full/10.1177/1470593109355249.

Klein, Emily. 2011. "Spectacular Citizenships: Staging Latina Resistance through Urban Performances of Pain." *Frontiers (Boulder)* 32 (1): 102–124. doi:10.5250/ fronjwomestud.32.1.0102. www-jstor-org.denison.idm.oclc.org/stable/10.5250/ fronjwomestud.32.1.0102.

Latimer, Heather. 2015. "Pregnant Possibilities: Cosmopolitanism, Kinship and Reproductive Futurism in Maria Full of Grace and in America." In *Whose Cosmopolitanism?*, edited by Glick Schiller, Nina and Andrew Irving, 175-186: Berghahn Books.

———. 2013. *Reproductive Acts: Sexual Politics in North American Fiction and Film*. Montreal: McGill-Queen's University Press. ebookcentral.proquest.com.den ison.idm.oclc.org/lib/denison-ebooks/detail.action?docID=3332606.

Latorre, Guísela. 2008. "Icons of Love and Devotion: Alma López's Art." *Feminist Studies* 34 (1/2): 131–150. www-jstor-org.denison.idm.oclc.org/stable/20459185.

———. 1999. "Latina Feminism and Visual Discourse: Yreina Cervántez's 'La Ofrenda.'" *Discourse* 21 (3): 95–110. www-jstor-org.denison.idm.oclc.org/ stable/41389547.

———. 2010. "New Approaches to Chicana/O Art: The Visual and the Political as Cognitive Process." *Image & Narrative* 11 (2): 111–122. doaj.org/article/40d5043 4624b4494b1ea5c446e276291.

Latorre, Sobeira and Joanna L. Mitchell. 2006. "Performing the 'Generic Latina.'" *Meridians (Middletown, Conn.)* 7 (1): 19–37. doi:10.2979/ MER.2006.7.1.19. dx.doi.org.denison.idm.oclc.org/10.2979/MER.2006.7.1.19.

Lipsky, Jessica. 2018. "La Misa Negra's Second Album Serves Cumbia With a Punk Attitude." KQED. September 21, 2017. www.kqed.org/arts/13809210/la-misa-negras-second-album-serves-cumbia-with-a-punk-attitude. Accessed March 2, 2022.

Loomer, Lisa. 2005. *Expecting Isabel.* New York: Dramatists Play Service, Inc.

———. 2019. *Roe.* New York: Dramatists Play Service.

López, Ana M. 1993. "Tears and Desire: Women and Melodrama in the 'Old' Mexican Cinema." In *Mediating Two Worlds: Cinematic Encounters in the Americas*, eds. John King and Ana M. López and Manuel Alvarado, 147-163. London, UK: British Film Institute.

López, Tiffany Ana. 2009. "Reading Trauma and Violence in U.S. Latina/O Children's Literature." Chap. 17, In *Ethnic Literary Traditions in American Children's Literature*, 205-226. New York: Palgrave Macmillan US.

Lorde, Audre. 1997. *The Collected Poems of Audre Lorde.* 1. ed. New York [u.a.]: Norton.

Lowe, Pam. 2016a. "Conceiving Motherhood." In *Reproductive Health and Maternal Sacrifice*, 79-107. London: Palgrave Macmillan UK. doi:10.1057/978-1-137-47293-9_4. link.springer.com/10.1057/978-1-137-47293-9_4.

———. 2016b. "Introduction." In *Reproductive Health and Maternal Sacrifice*, 1-15. London: Palgrave Macmillan UK. doi:10.1057/978-1-137-47293-9_1. link.springe r.com/10.1057/978-1-137-47293-9_1.

Lowinsky, Naomi R. 1992. *Stories from the Motherline: Reclaiming the Mother-Daughter Bond, Finding our Feminine Souls.* New York: J.P. Tarcher, St. Martin's Press.

Lundquist, Caroline. 2008. "Being Torn: Toward a Phenomenology of Unwanted Pregnancy." Hypatia. 23 (3): 135–55. http://www.jstor.org/stable/25483201.

Major, Laura. 2007. "Audre Lorde-'the Woman Thing.'" *Journal of the Association for Research on Mothering* 9 (2): 208. gateway.proquest.com.denison.idm.oclc.org/openurl?ctx_ver=Z39.88-2003&xri:p qil:res_ver=0.2&res_id=xri:ilcs-us&rft_id=xri:ilcs:rec:abell:R04101007.

Malaver, Laura. 2019. "Vida by Tanya Saracho (Review)." *Chiricú* 4 (1): 199–202. muse.jhu.edu/article/744218.

Manrique, Linnete. 2019. "Starz' 'Vida' Complicates and Humanizes Latinx People." *PopMatters*, Jul 26, 2019.

Mazziotti, Norma. 2006. *Telenovela Industria y Practicas Sociales.* Bogotá, Colombia: Grupo Editorial Norma.

McDaniel, L. Bailey. 2013. *(Re)Constructing Maternal Performance in Twentieth-Century American Drama.* What is Theatre?, edited by Ann C. Hall. 1. publ. ed. New York: Palgrave MacMillan.

McMahon, Marci R. 2013. "Redirecting Chicana/Latina Representation." In *Domestic Negotiations*, 156-180. New Brunswick, N.J. [u.a.]: Rutgers Univ. Press.

Meier, Joyce. 2000. "The Refusal of Motherhood in African American Women's Theater." *Melus* 25 (3/4): 117–139. doi:10.2307/468239. www-jstor-org.denison. idm.oclc.org/stable/468239.

Mezey, Nancy J. 2008. *New Choices, New Families.* Baltimore: Johns Hopkins University Press. muse-jhu-edu.denison.idm.oclc.org/book/3350.

Miller, Lynn C., Jacqueline Taylor, and Carver. M. Heather. 2003. *Voices made Flesh: Performing Women's Autobiography.* Madison: University of Wisconsin Press.

Mitchell, Joanna L. 2011. "Teatro Luna: Bodies that Matter on the Chicago Stage." *Gestos (Irvine, Calif.)* 26 (51): 115–119. search-proquest-com.denison.idm.oclc.org/docview/873729402.

Molina-Guzmán, Isabel. 2018. *Latinas and Latinos on TV: Colorblind Comedy in the Post-Racial Network Era.* Latinx Pop Culture. Tucson: University of Arizona Press.

Moraga, Cherríe. 2000. *Loving in the War Years.* South End Press: Cambridge.

———. 1997. *Waiting in the Wings: Portrait of a Queer Motherhood.* Ithaca: Firebrand Books. search-proquest-com.denison.idm.oclc.org/docview/2138594766.

———. 2011. *A Xicana Codex of Changing Consciousness.* Durham: Duke University Press. muse-jhu-edu.denison.idm.oclc.org/book/69384.

Morales, Iris, ed. 2018. *Latinas: An Anthology of Struggles and Protests in 21st Century USA.* New York: Red Sugarcane Press, Inc.

Muñoz, José Esteban. 1999. *Disidentifications.* Cultural Studies of the Americas. Vol. 2. Minneapolis; London: University of Minnesota Press.

Nielsen Media. "Mass Appeal: A Look at the Cross-Cultural Impact of on-Screen Diversity." Last modified June 28, accessed 08/30/2020, www.nielsen.com/us/en/insights/article/2018/mass-appeal-a-look-at-the-cross-cultural-impact-of-on-screen-diversity/.

Norat, Gisela. 2010. "Hispanic Mothers on Stage: Women Playwrights Undermining Masculinist Values." In *Essays and Scripts on how Mothers are Portrayed in the Theater: A Neglected Frontier of Feminist Scholarship*, 23: Mellen. gateway.proquest.com.denison.idm.oclc.org/openurl?ctx_ver=Z39.88-2003&xri:pqil:res_ver=0.2&res_id=xri:ilcs-us&rft_id=xri:ilcs:rec:abell:R04720249.

———. 2009. "Subverting the Gag Order: Pregnancy in Contemporary Hispanic Women's Literature." *Thirdspace* 8 (2): 1. gateway.proquest.com.denison.idm.oclc.org/openurl?ctx_ver=Z39.88-2003&xri:pqil:res_ver=0.2&res_id=xri:ilcs-us&rft_id=xri:ilcs:rec:abell:R04706759.

———. 2008. "Women Staging Coups through Mothering: Depictions in Hispanic Contemporary Literature." In *Feminist Mothering*, 219: State U of New York P. gateway.proquest.com.denison.idm.oclc.org/openurl?ctx_ver=Z39.88-2003&xri:pqil:res_ver=0.2&res_id=xri:ilcs-us&rft_id=xri:ilcs:rec:abell:R04368879.

Noriega, Chon. 2019. "Introduction." In *Chicano and Chicana Art: A Critical Anthology*, edited by González, Jennifer, C. Ondine Chavoya and Chon Noriega, 13-17. Durham: Duke University Press. doi:10.1215/9781478003403.

Noriega, Chon and Ana López. 1996. *The Ethnic Eye.* NED - New edition ed. Minneapolis: University of Minnesota Press. doi:10.5749/j.ctttt23g. www.jstor.org.denison.idm.oclc.org/stable/10.5749/j.ctttt23g.

Oboler, Suzanne. 1995. *Ethnic Labels, Latino Lives.* 3. print. ed. Minneapolis [u.a.]: University of Minnesota Press.

Oliver, Kelly. 2012. "Accident and Excess." In *Knock Me Up, Knock Me Down*, 81: Columbia University Press. doi:10.7312/oliv16108.7. _www.jstor.org/stable/10.7312/oliv16108.7.

Orozco, Gisela. 2018. "La Misa Negra: Cumbia contracorriente." *Chicago Tribune.* June 28, 2018. www.chicagotribune.com/hoy/entretenimiento/ct-hoy-entretenimiento-la-misa-negra-cumbia-contracorrientesi-20180628-story.html. Accessed March 9, 2022.

Parrish, Erin. 2012. *Lebrón, Lolita.* Vol. 2.

Piñón, Juan. 2017. "Jane the Virgin." *ReVista: Harvard Review of Latin America.* 17 (1). December 3, 2017. revista.drclas.harvard.edu/jane-the-virgin/. Accessed June 15, 2020.

Price, Kimala. 2010. "What is Reproductive Justice? How Women of Color Activists are Redefining the Pro-Choice Paradigm." *Meridians (Middletown, Conn.)* 10 (2): 42–65. doi:10.2979/meridians.2010.10.2.42. search.datacite.org/works/10.2979/meridians.2010.10.2.42.

Ramos, Dino-Ray. 2019. "'Jane the Virgin' Finale Ratings Steady, 'Big Brother' Wins Wednesday again, 'MasterChef' Heats Up." *Deadline.Com*, Aug. 1. deadline.com/2019/08/jane-the-virgin-finale-tv-ratings-big-brother-masterchef-1202658692/.

Redshaw, Maggie and Colin R. Martin. 2011. "Reproductive Decision-Making, Prenatal Attachment and Early Parenting." *Journal of Reproductive & Infant Psychology* 29 (3): 195–196. doi:10.1080/02646838.2011.614106. search.ebscohost.com.denison.idm.oclc.org/login.aspx?direct=true&db=rzh&AN=104673339&site=ehost-live.

Rodriguez, Favianna. "Biography," accessed 09/20/, 2020, favianna.com/about/biography.

———. "Come Out about Your Abortion," favianna.com/artworks/come-out-about-your-abortion.

———. "Deliberate Orgasm AP 1," favianna.com/artworks/deliberate-orgasm-ap-1.

———. "I Am a Slut," favianna.com/artworks/im-a-slut.

———. "It's My Body. it's My Pussy," favianna.com/artworks/its-my-body-its-my-pussy.

———. "Mi Cuerpo. Yo Decido," favianna.com/artworks/mi-cuerpo-yo-decido.

———. 2018. "Migration if Beautiful 2018," favianna.com/artworks/migration-is-beautiful-2018.

———. "My Abortion Story," last modified Oct 10, accessed 10/15/2020, favianna.typepad.com/.

———. "Politicians Off My Poontang," favianna.com/artworks/politicians-off-my-poontang.

———. "Pussy Power," favianna.com/artworks/pussy-power.

———. *Social Justice Poster Making Workshop.* Oakland, CA. favianna.com/resources/guides.

———. "Yo Te Apoyo," favianna.com/artworks/yo-te-apoyo.

Román-Odio, Clara. 2013. *Sacred Iconographies in Chicana Cultural Productions.* Comparative Feminist Studies., ed. Chandra Talpade Mohanty. New York: Palgrave Macmillan.

Rose, Natalie. 2019. "Modern Melodrama: How the American Telenovela Jane the Virgin Updates the Sentimental Novel." *Journal of Popular Culture* 52

(5): 1081–1100. doi:10.1111/jpcu.12849. onlinelibrary-wiley-com.denison.idm. oclc.org/doi/abs/10.1111/jpcu.12849.

Ross, Loretta, Elena Gutiérrez, Marlene Gerber, and Jael Silliman. 2016. *Undivided Rights*. Chicago: Haymarket Books.

Ross, Loretta, Lynn Roberts, Erika Derkas, Whitney Peoples, Pamela Bridgewater Toure, and Dorothy Roberts. 2017. *Radical Reproductive Justice*. First Feminist Press edition ed. New York: Feminist Press.

Ryan, Darien Perez and Patrick E. Jamieson. 2019. "Risk and Culture of Health Portrayal in a U.S. Cross-Cultural TV Adaptation, a Pilot Study." *Media and Communication (Lisboa)* 7 (1): 32–42. doi:10.17645/mac.v7i1.1489. search-proquest-com.denison.idm.oclc.org/docview/2300626337.

Saborío, Linda. 2012. *Embodying Difference*. Madison, NJ [u.a.]: Fairleigh Dickinson Univ. Press.

Sisson, Gretchen and Katrina Kimport. 2017. "Depicting Abortion Access on American Television, 2005–2015." *Feminism & Psychology* 27 (1): 56–71. doi:10.1177/0959353516681245. search.datacite.org/works/10.1177/0959353516 681245.

Solinger, Rickie. 2001. *Beggars and Choosers: How the Politics of Choice Shapes Adoption, Abortion, and Welfare in the United States*. New York: Hill and Wang.

Stern, Alexandra Minna. 2005. *Eugenic Nation*. 1st ed. Berkeley: University of California Press. doi:10.1525/j.ctt1pn5jp. www.jstor.org/stable/10.1525/j. ctt1pn5jp.

———. 2015. *Eugenic Nation*. American Crossroads. 2nd ed. Vol. 17. Berkeley: University of California Press. doi:10.1525/j.ctt19631sw. www-jstor-org.denison. idm.oclc.org/stable/10.1525/j.ctt19631sw.

———. 2017 "Sterilization" *Keywords for Latino/a Studies*, eds. Deborah R. Vargas, Nancy Raquel Mirabal, and Lawrence La Fountain-Stokes. New York University Press.

Stevens, Evelyn P. and Ann Pescatello. 1973. *Marianismo: The Other Face of Machismo in Latin America*. Pittsburgh, PA: University of Pittsburgh Press.

Tate, Julee. 2007. "The Good and Bad Women of Telenovelas: How to Tell them Apart using a Simple Maternity Test." *Studies in Latin American Popular Culture* 26: 97. gateway.proquest.com.denison.idm.oclc.org/openurl?ctx_ver=Z39.88-20 03&xri:pqil:res_ver=0.2&res_id=xri:ilcs-us&rft_id=xri:ilcs:rec:abell:R05572928.

———. 2018. "Taming the Wild Woman in Twenty-First-Century Mexican Telenovelas." *Studies in Latin American Popular Culture* 36: 161–177. doi:10.7560/ SLAPC3610. muse-jhu-edu.denison.idm.oclc.org/article/696191.

Teatro Luna. 2001. "Déjame Contarte." Unpublished Script. Chicago, IL.

———. "History," last modified Jun., accessed Dec., 2019, www.teatroluna.org.

———. 2006. "S-E-X-Oh!" Unpublished Script. Chicago, IL.

———. 2009. *S-E-X-Oh! (the Remix)*. DVD. Directed by Tanya Saracho. 16th St. Theater (Berwyn, IL).

———. 2008. "Sólo Tú" Unpublished Script. Chicago, IL.

———. 2019. *Talking while Female and Other Dangerous Acts*. Teatro Luna. Audible Amazon. (Audio).

Trigo, Benigno. 1900/2006. *Remembering Maternal Bodies: Melancholy in Latina and Latin American Women's Writing.* New York: Palgrave Macmillan US. ebookcentral.proquest.com.denison.idm.oclc.org/lib/denison-ebooks/detail.action ?docID=308100.

Tropp, Laura. 2013. *A Womb with a View: America's Growing Public Interest in Pregnancy.* Santa Barbara, CA: Praeger, an imprint of ABC-CLIO, LLC.

Tumanov, Vladimir. 2011. "Mary Versus Eve: Paternal Uncertainty and the Christian View of Women." *Neophilologus* 95 (4): 507–521. doi:10.1007/s11061-011-9253-5. gateway.proquest.com.denison.idm.oclc.org/openurl?ctx_ver=Z39.88-2003&xr i:pqil:res_ver=0.2&res_id=xri:ilcs-us&rft_id=xri:ilcs:rec:abell:R04714488.

Ulibarri, Kristy L. 2017. "Speculating Latina Radicalism: Labour and Motherhood in Lunar Braceros 2125-2148." *Feminist Review* 116 (1): 85–100. doi:10.1057/s41305-017-0069-4. journals-sagepub-com.denison.idm.oclc.org/doi/full/10.1057/s41305-017-0069-4.

Uno, Roberta, Perkins, and A. Kathy, eds. 1996. *Contemporary Plays by Women of Color.* 1st ed. New York: Routledge.

Valdez, Luis. 1990. *Early Works.* University of Texas: Arte Publico Press.

Valdivia, Angharad N. 2010. *Latina/os and the Media.* 1. publ. ed. Cambridge [u.a.]: Polity Press.

Vega, Maria and Teatro Luna. 2001. "Trapped." In *Déjame contarte.* Chicago, IL. Unpublished Script.

Vida: Season 3, created by Tanya Saracho. Starring Mishel Prada, Melissa Barrera, Ser Anzoategui. (2018-2020, Starz). Cable.

Vilar, Irene. 2009. *Impossible Motherhood.* New York: Other Press.

Yarbro-Bejarano, Yvonne. 1985. "Chicanas' Experience in Collective Theatre: Ideology and Form." *Women & Performance* 2 (2): 45–58. doi:10.1080/07407708508571085. www-tandfonline-com.denison.idm.oclc.org/doi/abs/10.1080/07407708508571085.

———. 1983. "Teatropoesía by Chicanas in the Bay Area: Tongues of Fire." *Revista Chicano-Riqueña* 11 (1): 74. search-proquest-com.denison.idm.oclc.org/docview/1297953323.

Zavella, Patricia. 2020. *The Movement for Reproductive Justice.* New York: University Press.

Index

abortion: ambivalence about, 48–52, 113; anthology of views on, 47–48; clinics influencing decisions, 46–47; in "El vientre," 59–61; in *Jane the Virgin,* 95–97; laws and court decisions, 1, 30n3; personal narratives, 15–16, 17–18, 135n4; positive narratives, 5, 47–48, 95–97, 107, 113, 132; power of storytelling and, 23–25; in *Roe* play, 58; in *S-e-x-oh!,* 130; in "So Ruff, So Tuff," 45; in "Trapped," 48–52, 130; in *Vida,* 105–8; visceral imagery of, 62–63
"The Abortion Diary" (Madera), 23–25
Acosta, LizaAnn, 35, 36–37
Acosta-Alzuru, Carolina, 68–69, 76, 97
adoption, 21, 57–58
Alarcón, Norma, 92
Alborada, 69
Aldama, Frederick, 2
ambivalence: about abortion, 48–52, 113; about pregnancy and motherhood, 39–44; *The Have-Little,* 44–45
Anzaldúa, Gloria: borderlands concept, 70; on Chicana culture, 11, 127; *Coatlicue* theory, 48; experiences as woman of color, 3–4, 14–15; *Making Face, Making Soul,* 19; *marianista*

cult of virginity, 49; "taking inventory," 120; theory in the flesh, 12, 124, 128–29; *This Bridge Called My Back,* 5, 7, 12, 19, 118, 124
Aparicio, Frances R., 3
Arrizón, Alicia, 33, 125
Asencio, Marysol, 125
autobiographical voices, 3–4, 59–60

Babineu, Mary Lou, 48
"Bad Girls" (Kondo), 59
Báez, Jillian M., 2, 69, 71–72, 77
Bednarek, Monica, 70
Beltrán, Mary, 75–76
Berg, Ramirez, 71
Biblical archetypes, 11
"Birthing Healing Justice" (Chavez-Diaz), 22
"Bloodbirth" (Lorde), 13
Boffone, Trevor, 61
Bondy, Jennifer M., 110
Borderlands (Anzaldúa), 12, 128
Bost, Suzanne, 7, 8, 12, 14–15, 16, 27
Brownrigg, Coya Paz, 36, 37. *See also* Paz, Coya
Broyles-Gonzalez, Yolanda, 42–43

Caballero, Cecilia, 20
"Cama-Camaleon," 38, 50–52, 130

in, 3–7; challenging stereotypes, 103–4; importance of, 132, 134–35; soundtrack, 104–5

Vilar, Irene, 15, 16, 17–18, 23, 130–31

Villegas, Richard, Jr., 102

Virgen de Guadalupe, 106, 109–10, 113, 116, 124, 127–28

Virgin Mary, 26

virgin/whore dichotomy, 46, 48–49, 118. *See also Jane the Virgin; marianista* women

Voices Made Flesh (Miller, Taylor, and Carver), 59–60

voters, 126n8

Waiting in the Wings (Moraga), 14–15, 16–17, 23–24, 39, 42

Westmoreland, Wash, 108

"What I want to tell" vignette, 39–44, 130–31

Williams, Emilio, 36

Williams, Mai'a, 19–20

Wilson, Liliana, 116

women, Chicana culture and, 11. *See also* motherhood; virgin/whore dichotomy

Yarbro-Bejarano, Yvonne, 16, 36, 97

"Yo te apoyo" (Rodriguez), 125

Young, Iris, 15

Zavella, Patricia, 9, 37, 125–26

About the Author

Melissa Huerta is associate professor of Spanish at Denison University, where she teaches Spanish language and courses in Latin American and Latinx literature, culture, and history. Her research focuses on Latinx representation, specifically in theater and performance. She has published in *Modern Drama* and *Chicana/Latina Studies*: *The Journal of MALCS*. Huerta's current research focuses on the representation of Latinx reproductive decision-making in popular culture, such as theater and television.

www.ingramcontent.com/pod-product-compliance
Lightning Source LLC
Chambersburg PA
CBHW022321280326
41932CB00010B/1185